Thirteenth Edition

HANDBOOK
FOR
GEORGIA
LEGISLATORS

Edwin L. Jackson, Mary E. Stakes, and Paul T. Hardy

Carl Vinson Institute of Government, The University of Georgia
Athens

Carl Vinson Institute of Government
The University of Georgia
© 2007 Carl Vinson Institute of Government
All rights reserved
Printed in the United States of America
11 10 09 08 07 06   1 2 3 4 5

ISSN 0438-5047
ISBN 0-89854-226-X

FOREWORD

In 1958, the Carl Vinson Institute of Government published the first edition of the *Handbook for Georgia Legislators* for use at the inaugural Biennial Institute for Georgia Legislators. The Biennial Institute is held at the University of Georgia's Georgia Center for Continuing Education following the November general election in order to educate newly elected and veteran representatives and senators about the legislative process and current issues and challenges. The book also has been useful for attorneys, teachers, students, and other citizens interested in the legislative process in Georgia. The first handbook (as well as subsequent editions in the 1960s) was prepared by R. Perry Sentell Jr., who would go on to achieve a distinguished career of 46 years of teaching and service at the University of Georgia Law School.

Edwin L. Jackson has been senior author of the handbook since 1972. Mary E. Stakes became coauthor in 1984, and Paul Hardy, in 2001. The authors are all senior faculty at the Carl Vinson Institute of Government. Wes Clarke, associate director of the Institute's Research and Policy Analysis Division, updated for this edition the explanation of the General Assembly's role in the state budget process.

This 13th edition of the *Handbook for Georgia Legislators* incorporates extensive changes in the law that have occurred since the previous edition, including House and Senate rules changes passed in January 2007. It also contains current information on legislative enactments, House and Senate rules changes, court decisions, agency policies, and other actions affecting the General Assembly and its membership. The changes reflected have occurred during a period of dramatic transformation in the legislature's composition, organization, and rules of procedure.

Over the years, numerous legislative officials and staff members have answered questions, supplied information, and otherwise provided assistance useful in the production of this publication. In particular, the authors would like to thank Clerk of the House Robert Rivers, Secretary of the Senate Bob Ewing, and Legislative Fiscal Officer Robyn Underwood.

January 2007

Steve Wrigley
Director
Carl Vinson Institute of Government

Contents

INTRODUCTION

Now That You've Been Elected . . .

Politics has been defined as the pursuit of power and as such can exist in any setting with two or more people. In the context of government, politics is the struggle to determine public policy and spending. James Madison once mused that if men were angels, government would be unnecessary. It can also be argued that if everyone agreed on what was best for Georgia, there would be no need for the General Assembly. Of course, everyone does not agree on such issues as taxes, education, health care, economic development, and the environment. In a pluralistic society of differing—and often competing—interests, someone must make decisions regarding public policy and state spending. In Georgia, that responsibility lies with members of the General Assembly.

Despite the way the editorial page of the newspaper sometimes reads, many still regard public service as one of the highest callings that one can aspire to. In fact, the motto of Georgia's Trustees—"not for self but others"—could describe why some candidates continue to seek election to the General Assembly. Whatever selflessness may motivate someone to seek office, he or she does so hoping to influence public policy. And competition for that influence is what makes the legislature a political body.

Serving in the General Assembly can be a frustrating experience, particularly when one finds that not all legislators share one's vision for Georgia's future. At the same time, it can be an exciting, rewarding, and memorable experience. Legislators frequently speak with pride about the good feeling that comes with knowing they helped make a difference in the lives of the people of their district and state.

BICAMERAL REALITIES

Compounding the political nature of the General Assembly is the fact that it is a bicameral body, one in which each house has a potential veto over the other in the passage of legislation. As a result, legislative sessions involve a struggle for influence between the two houses, further antagonized by partisanship and the efforts of the governor to promote his or her legislative agenda. With rare exception, any important bill introduced in one house will be amended in the other. Often, a bill is held in committee to keep it from coming up for a floor vote. Toward the end of the session, the legislative process becomes a game of brinkmanship between the two houses. Eventually, however, almost every important bill ends up in conference committee, where three representatives and three senators seek to fashion a compromise. In the waning hours of a session, time simply runs out for many bills that have not made it through both houses. Still, however imperfectly, the process does work for most important legislative measures.

ROLES OF THE GENERAL ASSEMBLY

Some of the functions and responsibilities of the General Assembly are spelled out in the state constitution. Foremost is the lawmaking power for Georgia (which is discussed in Chapter 6). This handbook examines in detail the powers and limitations of the General Assembly and the requirements and procedures for enacting laws as spelled out by the state constitution and statutes and by House and Senate rules.

Related to the lawmaking function, but still distinct, is the legislature's budgetary power. Each year, the General Assembly authorizes funding for all agencies and programs of state government, and no money can be spent unless authorized by the appropriation act. How the state budget is distributed directly affects more Georgians than any other decision the legislature makes and may be the single most important function of the General Assembly. However, the budget is a shared responsibility in Georgia. Georgia's constitution gives the governor the exclusive power to set the revenue estimate for the coming fiscal year, which determines how much money can be spent. Furthermore, the governor has the exclusive power to propose the state budget, designating how much money will be appropriated to each agency. The General Assembly's power over the state budget is further limited by the fact that most of the state budget goes to state and federal entitlement and other formula-based programs that must be funded. Still, the ultimate power to approve or not approve the state budget rests in the hands of the General Assembly. Should the legislature fail to adopt an appropriation act, state government (at least nonvital services) would shut down on July 1 of the new fiscal year. Although this has never happened in Georgia, it has happened most recently in New Jersey.

Another important function of the General Assembly is to serve as custodian of the Georgia Constitution. No change in the current constitution or proposal for a new constitution can be initiated except by agreement of two-thirds of the total membership of each house. Once proposed, constitutional amendments must be ratified in the next general election by a majority of those voting on the amendment.

The state constitution also authorizes the General Assembly to serve as custodian of local governments in Georgia. For example, no counties can be consolidated or new counties created without action of the legislature. No city can be created or abolished without legislative action. City-county consolidations require legislative approval. Cities and counties cannot change their forms of government or sources of tax revenue without legislative action. While Georgia's constitution allows cities and counties limited home rule, in many cases local governments are subject to the oversight of the state legislature. In part, this is because local governments are not sovereign levels of government but rather are considered to be creatures of the state. In Georgia, counties serve as arms of state government, performing numerous services on behalf of state agencies, such as conducting elections and issuing license plates.

One important responsibility of the General Assembly is partly spelled out and partly implied in the state constitution: oversight of the executive branch. Although checks and balances give each branch of government certain powers over the other two branches, the legislature is often viewed as the first branch of government. The constitution has given it extensive powers over the other two branches, particularly the executive branch. Additionally, implied from its power to make the laws and enact the budget is the authority to create and abolish executive agencies (excluding those provided for in the constitution), spell out their powers, authorize funding levels, conduct audits and investigations, and perform a number of other functions designed to oversee the executive branch.

In addition to legislative powers and functions specified in the state constitution, the General Assembly has more general functions. The General Assembly is the primary vehicle at the state level for representative government. Although some states allow citizens to participate directly in the governing process through petitions and referendums, Georgia does not. Georgia's Supreme Court has ruled that the constitution entrusts the lawmaking power exclusively to the General Assembly.

At the district level, representation of constituents is a responsibility of each legislator, though what fulfilling this responsibility means and how it is achieved is not always easy to determine. Political scientists and philosophers have long debated what representation means. Does it mean voting according to what constituents say (or what you believe they might say if they were fully informed) or what seems in their best interest, no matter what some outspoken constituents might say? One concept of representation is the instructed delegate model, which assumes that the people of a district elect someone to represent them who will vote as they instruct. A fallacy of this model is that regarding the great majority of votes on the floor and in committee, legislators will not hear from a single constituent. Moreover, rarely are constituents in complete agreement on the issues. The other model of representation—the trustee model—assumes that constituents elect someone whose knowledge and judgment they respect to represent them and therefore expect the legislator to act wisely on their behalf. However, few legislators who routinely follow their own judgment exclusively and ignore constituent opinion will have a long career in the General Assembly. Generally, most legislators follow a practical rather than philosophical approach, acting as delegates on controversial and highly visible matters in their districts and as trustees on most everything else.

Another function of the General Assembly—and one that can be performed only by individual legislators—is constituent service. If faithfully performed, it can take up more time than any other function. Legislators will hear complaints and requests for everything imaginable, from getting help from a state agency, to having a road paved or a bridge named for someone, to making sure a son or daughter gets into a university, to appearing in a parade or dedication ceremony, to speaking to a civics class or at a Rotary luncheon. The request for help may not have anything to do with the General Assembly or state law. Frequently, constituents contact members because they are having problems with Social Security or other federal programs. Even though the request may involve something totally unrelated to state government, legislators usually feel compelled to act lest they lose a vote. In the end, constituent service can become a full-time duty for most state lawmakers.

PRESSURE ON LEGISLATORS' PERSONAL LIVES

Serving in the legislature involves multiple roles and responsibilities. Also, with only 40 days in a session, everyone is always watching the calendar and the clock. Then there's always concern about family and business back home. As a result, life during a session can be a stressful, exhausting, frustrating, and expensive experience. There are always more demands on a legislator's time than hours in the day, meaning that the successful ones learn to adopt time and stress management strategies to balance personal and family needs with the job of representing their district.

Being a legislator can also affect one's occupation or business. At one time, Georgia law firms, banks, and other businesses encouraged their employees to run for the General Assembly. Today, such support has become the exception rather than the rule. For one thing, public opinion polls show that state legislatures across the nation are held in low esteem. Some political scientists blame the public's negative perception of the state legislature on a negative bias in the media. As Alan Rosenthal, a recognized expert on state legislatures as an institution, notes in his recent study, "Conflict is newsworthy, so the media look for it. When they find conflict, they attribute it to partisan politics, campaign contributions, and political ambitions. Rarely do they portray it as simply legitimate disagreement over the merits of an issue; there is not much interest in such a story. The more negative, the more newsworthy."[1]

With their own careers at stake, state capitol journalists tend to be motivated by what will get attention in the newspaper or evening news. Thus, the positive things that legislators do, being generally less controversial and sensational, seldom make the news. Based on what it reads or hears, the public may generalize that the state legislature is a corrupt institution.

Georgia legislators serve two-year terms, so it seems they are always campaigning. Negative campaigning is now so commonplace that anything in a legislator's past or present is fair game, which can be embarrassing to the legislator as well as his or her family and employer. Also, the General Assembly is no longer a "citizen legislature" that allows farmers, lawyers, bankers, and insurance agents to take off six weeks from work once a year to attend to the people's business. The Georgia Constitution still limits a legislative session to 40 days—but with recesses, special sessions, interim standing committee work, constituent service, local legislation, speeches, and other legislative responsibilities, service in the General Assembly has become almost a year-round commitment. The dramatic increase in the cost of political campaigns also has precluded some citizens from running for the legislature. Low pay and the high cost of transportation and lodging in Atlanta further limit who can serve in the legislature.

THE CHANGING GEORGIA GENERAL ASSEMBLY

Until recently, it was not uncommon for legislators to serve for three or more decades. The all-time champion was Hugh Gillis, who served a total of 56 years in the House and Senate before retiring in January 2005. However, as of 2006, only a tiny handful of lawmakers in the House—and none in the Senate—had 30 or more years' seniority (the most-veteran lawmaker has served 32 years). In today's professional and political environment, the prospect of a legislator serving 40 or more years in the General Assembly seems remote. As a consequence, the House and Senate will have younger members and greater turnover. No doubt traditions will change.

In addition to declining member seniority (in terms of length of service), there have been other changes in the General Assembly in recent decades. Perhaps the most dramatic shift has been in composition. In 1957, there were no blacks, no women, and only four Republicans in the 259-member General Assembly. (The Republicans, incidentally, were not from metro-Atlanta counties but from Fannin and Gilmer Counties—two rural counties that have traditionally been Republican strongholds.) Additionally, 86 percent of the total membership had been born in Georgia, with another 12 percent born in a contiguous state. The formula for apportioning House seats guaranteed every county at least one representative, regardless of population. No county—no matter how large—was entitled to more than three representatives, thereby assuring that power would be in the hands of rural legislators.[2]

By 1977, the General Assembly (now with a total of 236 members) included 22 blacks, 10 women, and 31 Republicans. Federal court decisions in the 1960s requiring reapportionment effectively meant that the legislature was no longer controlled by rural counties. Twenty years later, in 1997, there were 39 blacks, 37 women, and 101 Republicans. In 2003, Republicans became the majority party in the Senate and two years later took control of the House, allowing the election of the first Republican Speaker of the House since 1870. By the 2006 session, the General Assembly included 47 blacks, 44 women, and

133 Republicans, with the majority of representatives and senators coming from metro areas. Georgia's changing demographics are also reflected in the fact that more and more lawmakers moved to Georgia from other states.[3]

Another important development in recent decades has been the modernization and professionalization of the General Assembly. As late as the 1980s, only legislative leaders had offices in the capitol. Most legislators shared a secretary and functioned without a private office. After the renovation of an old state office building across the street from the capitol in the 1980s, each legislator was given a private office (though secretaries are still shared). In 2000, the House and Senate chambers and the entire capitol complex were wired for Internet access, and legislators were given individual laptops to access both the Internet and an internal online information system. At the time, many veteran legislators had never used a computer. Today, the overwhelming majority of Georgia legislators access the Internet regularly by wireless connectivity throughout the capitol complex and from home. Both houses maintain Web sites that show the status of bills, committee schedules, and information on individual legislators and other topics. Citizens of Georgia can watch not only daily sessions of the House and Senate but also coverage of House committee meetings online.

FINAL WORD

In Georgia, the legislative process is actually three related things. First, it is a legal process involving requirements for enacting legislation that are spelled out in the state constitution and state statutes. Second, it is a procedural process involving parliamentary rules of procedure detailed in comprehensive House and Senate rules adopted at the beginning of each biennium. Third, because the General Assembly is of necessity a political institution, the legislative process is a political one involving different parties, personalities, and interests vying to determine policy and state spending.

This handbook examines in detail the first two aspects of the legislative process. The politics of the process, however, is constantly changing as new leaders, members, and majorities are elected, alliances are formed, and issues emerge. Rather than being teachable from the pages of a handbook, the political aspect is best learned firsthand in the chambers, committee rooms, offices, and lobbies of the state capitol.

Notes

1. Alan Rosenthal, *Heavy Lifting: The Job of the American Legislature* (Washington, D.C.: CQ Press, 2004), p. 3.

2. *Georgia Official and Statistical Register* (Atlanta: State of Georgia, 1955–56, 1977–78).

3. *Members of the Georgia General Assembly* (Atlanta: Senate and House Public Information Office, 1997–98).

CHAPTER 1

GEORGIA'S GENERAL ASSEMBLY

Georgia's constitution establishes three separate branches of government—the legislative, judicial, and executive—and declares that they are to remain forever separate and distinct.[1] Each, however, is given a number of checks over the other branches, so that "The separation is not, and, from the nature of things, cannot be total."[2] Nevertheless, in a republican form of government, the courts have said, the legislative authority necessarily predominates among the three coordinate branches of government.[3] Because of its closeness to the people and its powers over the other two branches, the legislature has been characterized as "the first branch of government."

In Georgia, as in 18 other states, the official name of the legislative body is "General Assembly."[4] In common usage, however, it is frequently referred to as the "Georgia legislature," and the two names are used interchangeably in this handbook.

Like all states except Nebraska, Georgia has a bicameral, or two-house, legislative body, consisting of a Senate and a House of Representatives. However, this has not always been the case. Georgia is one of four states to have experimented with a unicameral legislature.[5]

ORIGINS OF THE GENERAL ASSEMBLY

The origin of representative government in Georgia traces to 1750, two years before Georgia became a royal colony.[6] Prior to that time, Georgia's trustees, by virtue of their 1732 charter, exercised legislative, executive, and judicial powers to the extent that their actions conformed to English laws and met the approval of the King in Council.

Until 1750, the few governmental officials who functioned in Georgia were appointed by the trustees. There was no representative assembly.

The primary way for Georgia colonists to express concerns or petition for redress of grievances was by letter to the trustees. In March 1750, the trustees took the revolutionary action of allowing Georgia's colonists to hold an assembly of elected deputies in Savannah, with representation to be based roughly on population. Though waived for the initial assembly, qualifications for deputies included having at least 100 mulberry trees, plus proper fences on each 50 acres of land owned. By 1753, qualifications were extended to have at least one female in the family trained in reeling silk and to produce at least 15 pounds of silk on each 50 acres of land owned.

Although little is known about how they were elected to the assembly, 16 representatives met in Savannah for the first time on

IN 1911, WHEN THIS PHOTO OF THE GEORGIA HOUSE OF REPRESENTATIVES WAS TAKEN, THE GENERAL ASSEMBLY HELD A 50-DAY SESSION FROM JUNE 28 TO AUGUST 17.

January 15, 1751. They had no legislative powers, however, since the assembly had been created to advise the trustees on conditions in the colony and to report on various census data from each district. During the 24-day session, a variety of measures for improvement of the colony were debated, with grievances submitted to both local authorities and the trustees. Many grievances were favorably acted upon by local authorities, and while the trustees did not accept all of the assembly's recommendations, several were adopted. This assembly never met again, however, since the trustees surrendered their charter to the Crown the following year. Still, the seed of representative government—allowing citizens to elect delegates to represent their interests—had been planted in Georgia.

Under royal government, provision was made for a General Assembly, consisting of an elected lower house, called the Commons House of Assembly, and the Governor's Council (whose 12 members were appointed by the Crown), known as the Upper House of Assembly. The Commons House first met in January 1755, with 19 representatives elected by landowners of 50 or more acres within the colony.

Meetings of the General Assembly were called by the royal governor, with members' terms lasting until he dissolved the assembly. Laws passed by the body could be vetoed by the governor (with no legislative override) or by the British Privy Council. Despite its restrictions and the frequent dissolutions in later years, this assembly met at various intervals during the next 20 years, enacting important laws for the colony, including the levying of taxes, appropriation of money, limitation of interest on loans, and regulation of the Indian trade.

Incidentally, many of the legislative offices and procedures used by today's General Assembly can be traced back to the 1755 body. These include the practice of three readings of a bill, the requirement that money bills originate in the lower house, use of "the previous question," use of "Committee of the Whole," and such officers as the speaker and clerk of the House.[7]

As discontent with British rule grew in Georgia, a call was issued in January 1775 for convening a Provincial Congress in Savannah on the same date that the royal Commons House of Assembly was to open. However, since only five parishes sent delegates, it was ineffective as an alternate representative body.

The outbreak of hostilities against British forces in May 1775 again stirred sentiment for an end to royal government in Georgia,

REPRESENTATIVE GOVERNMENT AT WORK

Meeting in London on March 19, 1750, Georgia's trustees adopted a resolution that would plant the seed of representative government in Georgia: "That an assembly be formed and authorized to meet in the town of Savannah, in Georgia, every year, at the most leisure time, and such time as shall be appointed by the President and assistants; no such meeting to continue longer than three weeks, or a month at farthest. . . . That the power of making laws being, by his Majesty's charter, vested in the Trustees the assembly can only propose, debate and represent to the Trustees what shall appear to them to be for the benefit, not only of each particularly settlement, but of the province in general."

and a Council of Safety was established in June, followed by a call for election of members to a Second Provincial Congress. More than 100 delegates, representing every parish, met on July 4. In the months that followed, this one-house Congress assumed executive, legislative, and judicial functions, with the Council of Safety exercising governmental authority when the Congress was not in session. A Third Provincial Congress met in January 1776 and, though forced to flee Savannah in the face of British attack, reassembled in Augusta, where it adopted Georgia's first temporary constitution in April 1776.

The Constitution of 1777 provided for a legislature composed of representatives elected annually from each of the counties and from two cities. Seventy-two representatives were elected according to the apportionment plan. They then met to select a governor, and they elected from their own number 12 representatives to serve as an Executive Council. The remaining 60 members served as the House of Assembly.

Full legislative authority rested with the House of Assembly. The Executive Council could only recommend changes in proposed laws and had no formal legislative authority. Thus, Georgia joined two other states of the revolutionary period—Pennsylvania and Vermont—in providing for a unicameral legislative body.[8]

Following independence, Georgia continued its one-house legislative body until the Constitution of 1789 provided for a "General Assembly" composed of two separate houses—an arrangement that continued through all succeeding constitutions. Under this constitution, the legislature elected the governor, who did, however, now have veto authority over its acts, subject to override by two-thirds of both houses. In 1824, Georgia's constitution was amended to allow popular election of the governor.

CHANGES IN MEMBERSHIP AND SESSIONS

Since 1789, Georgia's legislative body has undergone a number of changes affecting its size, basis for apportionment, frequency of meetings, length of sessions, and terms of office for members.

Changes in Terms of Office

Except for the periods 1789–95 and 1868–77, senators and representatives have been elected for identical terms. This has meant that the entire General Assembly has usually been before the voters for reelection at one time, resulting in the reorganization of the legislature following every election.

Initially, representatives served one-year terms, with three-year terms for senators. In requiring more extensive qualifications for the Senate than the House, Georgia is reputed to be the first state to so discriminate between the two houses.[9] In 1795, however, senatorial terms were reduced to one year, and the entire General Assembly was elected annually, a practice continued until an 1841 constitutional amendment extended terms to two years for both houses, beginning in 1843.

During Reconstruction, terms for senators were increased to four years, but they were returned to two years in 1877 and have remained at this length to the present.

One interesting practice adopted by the state Democratic party earlier in this century and formalized by the General Assembly in 1939 was that of rotating senators at each biennium among the different counties composing a district.[10] All but two senatorial districts were made up of three counties each, and a procedure was instituted whereby each county within a district took a turn at electing the senator for that district. The senator had to reside in the county whose turn it was under the rotation, and in the Democratic primary only voters of that county could vote on the office. Occasionally, a county would defer and allow an incumbent to stay in office, but usually there was a wholesale turnover in the Senate every two years. Georgia's rotating senatorial scheme was declared unconstitutional, however, by a federal district court in 1962,[11] and the General Assembly subsequently abolished the practice at a special session that year.

Changes in Frequency and Length of Sessions

Sessions of the General Assembly have been held on an annual basis since 1777, except for the periods of 1843–57 and 1925–43, when biennial sessions were held. (See Table 1.)

The current session length—40 days—was first set by a 1955 constitutional amendment, later amended in 1962 to authorize 45 days in odd-numbered years. The 1962 change also instituted a split session in odd years whereby the legislature convened in January for no more than 12 days to organize and receive a general appropriations bill from the governor. Afterwards, the legislature adjourned for a budget recess of several weeks, reconvening in February for no more than 33 additional days. Even though a 1972 constitutional change provided for annual appropriations acts, the 45/40-day limit associated with the former biennial appropriations process remained in effect through 1976. The Constitution of 1976 reinstituted the 40-day session limit for both odd and even years, effective with the 1977 General Assembly, and abolished the formal split session in odd years.

Table 1. Legislative Sessions since 1777

Year Instituted	Session Held	Length of Session
1777	Annually	No limit
1843	Biennially	No limit
1857	Annually	40 days[a]
1880	Biennially[b]	40 days[a]
1893	Annually	50 days
1925	Biennially	60 days
1933	Biennially	70 days[c]
1944	Biennially[d]	70 days
1955	Annually	40 days
1963	Annually	45/40 days
1977	Annually	40 days

[a] This limit could be extended (and often was) by two-thirds vote of both houses. In the 1869–70 biennium, for example, the General Assembly was in session for a total of 328 days, and in 1889, for 140 days. (McElreath, A Treatise on the Constitution of Georgia, pp. 169–74.)

[b] Although biennial sessions were formally dictated, in practice the legislature was in session at some time during every year between 1880 and 1893.

[c] This is based on a split session of 10 days for organizing in January and 60 days for a regular session later in the same year.

[d] Though biennial sessions were formally dictated, the legislature could adjourn during the first year and reconvene the following year, as long as the total 70-day limit was not exceeded. From 1944 to 1955, the legislature met in regular sessions every year except 1944, 1948, and 1954.

Changes in the Size of the General Assembly

Historically, apportionment of House and Senate membership has been based on counties, population (sometimes roughly apportioned), or a combination of both. The size of these bodies—especially the House of Representatives—usually has been free to fluctuate (invariably upward) as new counties were created and populations increased, although there have not always been direct correlations between population and representation in the legislature. During some periods, precise sizes have been constitutionally set; this has necessitated redrawing apportionment districts or further amending these constitutional limits as counties were added or as populations shifted.

House Size

Until House elections in 1965, every apportionment plan for the House in the state's history has given each county then in existence at least one representative, with some formula for giving additional representation based on population. Table 2 illustrates the changes in House size, the number of counties in existence with each change, and the representation possible to each county.

TABLE 2. Changes in the Size of the Georgia House of Representatives since 1789 (year size became effective)

Year	Size	Number of Counties at Time of Session	Representatives Allowed per County
1789	34	11	2–5
1795	41	16	2–4
1798	58	23	1–4
1838	208	92	1–4
1844	130	93	1–2
1851	133	95	1–2
1859	169	132	1–2
1868	175	132	1–3
1905	183	137	1–3
1909	184	146	1–3
1915	189	148	1–3
1919	193	156	1–3
1921	206	160	1–3
1925	207	161	1–3
1932	205	159	1–3
1969	195	159	*
1972	180	159	*

*Representation not based on counties.

In 1868, a new state constitution set up a three-tiered system of county representation. The 6 most populous counties were entitled to three representatives; the next 26 most populous counties, two representatives each; and the remaining counties, one representative each. A constitutional amendment in 1920 changed the formula, giving the 8 largest counties three representatives each and the next 30 largest counties two representatives each. This system continued until 1964, when a federal district court declared this provision void and inoperative on the grounds that the system violated the voters' equal protection under the Fourteenth Amendment to the U.S. Constitution.[12] Under court directive to reapportion on the basis of population alone, the General Assembly adopted a new plan for the House in 1965. While the court rejected this method of apportionment because of population variances among districts, it allowed the plan to operate until further redistricting could be accomplished.[13]

At the 1967 session, both houses adopted new apportionment plans, with the House reducing its membership from 205 to 195. Court objections to some districts led to further reapportionment at the 1968 session, but the new 195-member size was allowed to go into effect in 1969.

The 1970 census necessitated further reapportionment, resulting in a 1971 reduction of House size to 180 members, effective with the 1972 session. The Constitution of 1983 added a constitutional mandate that the House of Representatives consist of *not fewer than* 180 members. However, since 1972, the size has remained set at 180—the minimum now allowed by the state constitution. Reapportionment acts could increase the size in the future should legislators so choose.[14]

Senate Size

Creation of the Senate in 1789 included provision for equal representation of counties within that body, a plan similar to the equal representation of states in the U.S. Senate adopted the same year. Each county—regardless of population—was to be entitled to one senator.

As the number of counties increased, so did the size of the Senate, and by 1838 it had 92 members. (See Table 3.) An 1844 constitutional amendment instituted a plan of 47 single-member districts, but in 1852 the former basis of representation—one senator from each county—was restored. By 1859, the Senate totaled 132 members, leading to a return to single-member districts and a reduction to 44 members in 1861.

TABLE 3. Changes in the Size of the Georgia Senate since 1789 (year size became effective)

Year	Size	Year	Size
1789	11	1859	132
1800	24	1861	44
1829	76	1919	51
1838	92	1939	52
1845	47	1947	54
1855	98	1969	56

Since 1861, the Georgia Senate has been apportioned on the basis of single-member districts, though federal courts in the 1960s ruled that these districts must be based solely on population and not on counties.

From time to time, constitutional amendments have not only reduced but enlarged the Senate's size. A 1968 amendment provided that the body consist of not less than 54 or more than 56 members; the precise number is set by the General Assembly. The Constitution of 1983 dropped the minimum size requirement, stating that the Senate will consist of *not more than* 56 members elected from single-member districts.[15]

NOTES

1. GA. CONST. art. 1, §2, ¶3.
2. Beall v. Beall, 8 Ga. 210 (1850). See discussion of separation of powers in Chapter 5.
3. Walker v. Whitehead, 43 Ga. 538 (1871); Myers v. U.S., 272 U.S. 52 (1926). See Chapter 5 of this handbook.
4. Two states use the term "Legislative Assembly"; two states use the name "General Court"; and the remainder use the term "Legislature" as the official designation of their legislative bodies. See *The Book of the States, 2006*, Vol. 38 (Lexington, Ky.: Council of State Governments, 2006), Table 3.1, p. 67.
5. In addition to Georgia, Pennsylvania and Vermont used a unicameral legislature during the revolutionary period. Georgia abandoned a one-house legislature in 1789, followed the next year by Pennsylvania. However, Vermont continued its unicameral legislature until 1836. In 1934, Nebraska voters approved a constitutional amendment to replace their bicameral legislature with a unicameral body, and its first session was held in 1937.
6. For a discussion of the historical background of legislative bodies in Georgia, see Albert B. Saye, *A Constitutional History of Georgia, 1732–1968* (Athens: University of Georgia Press, 1970); Walter McElreath, *A Treatise on the Constitution of Georgia* (Atlanta: The Harrison Co., 1912); and Robert Gerwig, "Colonial Georgia: Path to Self-Government," 12 *Georgia State Bar Journal* 130 (February 1976).
7. Saye, *A Constitutional History of Georgia*, p. 61. Many of the practices adopted by this early body, of course, were adapted from British parliamentary rules and tradition.

8. It has been argued that Georgia did not have a true unicameral legislative body because even though the Executive Council could not veto actions of the other house, it did play an important role in the lawmaking process. See Henry Luce, *Legislative Assemblies* (New York: Houghton Mifflin Co., 1924), p. 24.

9. McElreath, *A Treatise on the Constitution of Georgia*, p. 88.

10. Ga. Laws 1939, p. 311; Ga. Laws 1946, p. 44; Ga. Laws 1950, p. 165. For a discussion of this system, see William G. Cornelius, *Southeastern State Legislatures* (Atlanta: Emory University School of Law, 1967), p. 58; and Doyle Mathis, "Georgia's Reapportionment History and Process," in Brett W. Hawkins (ed.), *Reapportionment in Georgia* (Athens: Institute of Government, 1970), pp. 6–7.

11. Toombs v. Fortson, 205 F. Supp. 248 (N.D.Ga. 1962).

12. Toombs v. Fortson, (N.D. Ga., June 30, 1964).

13. Toombs v. Fortson, 241 F. Supp. 65 (N.D.Ga. 1965).

14. GA. CONST. art. 3, §2, ¶1(b).

15. GA. CONST. art. 3, §2, ¶1(a).

CHAPTER 2

MEMBERSHIP

COMPOSITION OF THE GENERAL ASSEMBLY

Georgia's legislature is composed of a 56-member Senate and a 180-member House. The General Assembly is free to enlarge (but not reduce) the size of the House by general statute.[1] The Senate consists of not more than 56 members, with the exact number to be set by the General Assembly.[2]

With a total membership of 236, Georgia's General Assembly is the third-largest state legislature in the United States. The Georgia House ranks third in size among lower houses of state legislatures, and the Georgia Senate fourth among state senates.[3]

QUALIFICATIONS FOR MEMBERSHIP

Formal Qualifications

The constitution of Georgia requires members of both houses of the General Assembly to be United States citizens, Georgia citizens for at least two years, and legal residents of their district for at least one year.[4] Should a senator or representative move from the district from which elected, that seat is automatically declared vacant.[5]

The only difference in qualifications between the two houses is that a senator must be at least 25 years of age, while a representative need only be 21.[6]

Other Provisions Relative to Membership

In addition to the specific qualifications for office, a number of constitutional and statutory provisions bear on eligibility to seek and/or hold office in the General Assembly.

Registered voter. Georgia's constitution contains a general mandate that only registered voters may hold public office or be appointed to any position of honor or trust in the state.[7]

Criminal record. Any person who has been convicted and sentenced for any felony involving moral turpitude is prohibited from holding any public office in the state, unless the State Board of Pardons and Paroles has restored that person's civil rights and at least 10 years have elapsed from the completion of the sentence without a subsequent conviction of another felony involving moral turpitude.[8] In a 1983 opinion to the board, Georgia's attorney general interpreted this constitutional provision to mean that, with respect to holding public office, (1) a person is not disqualified by virtue of a nolo contendere plea; (2) all felonies should be considered as involving moral turpitude; and (3) even if the sentence has been served, the board must specifically restore a convicted felon's civil rights before he or she can hold office in Georgia.[9]

THE WOMAN IN THIS 1911 PHOTO OF THE GEORGIA SENATE
WOULD NOT HAVE BEEN A SENATOR SINCE WOMEN
COULD NOT YET VOTE OR RUN FOR OFFICE.

Tax defaulters. The constitution prohibits anyone who has defaulted on any federal, state, county, municipal, or school system taxes from holding public office.[10]

Holder of public monies. By both constitution and statute, public office is denied any person illegally holding public funds.[11]

Incapacity. Although there is no mandatory retirement age for members of the General Assembly, Georgia law provides that persons of unsound mind or those who, from advanced age or bodily infirmity, are unfit to discharge the duties of public office are ineligible to hold it.[12] According to the constitution, any person who has been judicially determined to be mentally incompetent is disqualified from being a registered voter, and hence from holding public office.[13]

Should a court determine that any state officeholder has abandoned that office, has ceased performing his or her duties, or has become incapacitated or ineligible to continue (whether by voluntary act or misfortune of the incumbent), that office will be declared vacant.[14] Failure of an elected member of the General Assembly to obtain the proper commission for that office is also sufficient grounds for vacating the office.[15]

Qualifying for election. All candidates for the General Assembly seeking their party's nomination in a primary must qualify with their state political party in accordance with the procedural rules of their party.[16] Also, all candidates—whether seeking office through party primary, as members of a political organization, or as independents—must qualify within time periods and according to procedural requirements of the state election code.[17]

A candidate for the General Assembly may not seek nomination in the primary of one political party while seeking that or any other office in the primary of another party. The office of any state, county, or municipal elected official will be declared vacant when that elected official qualifies as a candidate in a general primary or election or a special primary or election for any state, county, or municipal elective office or for election to the House of Representatives or Senate of the United States if the term of the office which such official is being qualified for begins more than 30 days prior to the expiration of the official's current term of office.[18]

Special rules apply to any person seeking election to the legislature as a write-in candidate. A write-in candidacy is only allowed in a general or special election. No person can seek a write-in candidacy if that person sought the same office in the immediately preceding

REPRESENTATIVE GOVERNMENT AT WORK

Until 1835, property ownership remained a qualification for serving in the General Assembly. Early constitutional provisions, such as this one from 1777, set strict eligibility requirements for legislators: "The representatives shall be chosen out of the residents in each county, who shall have resided at least twelve months in this State, and three months in the county where they shall be elected . . . and they shall be of the Protestant religion, and of the age of twenty-one years, and shall be possessed in their own right of two hundred and fifty acres of land, or some property to the amount of two hundred and fifty pounds" [GA. CONST. of 1777, art. 1, §6].

primary. Also, between January 1 and the Tuesday after the first Monday in September before a general election or at least 20 days prior to a special election, the candidate (or one or more qualified voters acting in his or her behalf) must notify the secretary of state of the write-in candidacy and supply an affidavit stating that notice of the candidacy has been published in a newspaper of general circulation in Georgia.[19]

Restrictions on holding other offices. No person on active duty with any branch of the United States armed forces may hold a seat in the General Assembly, unless otherwise provided by statute.[20] Also prohibited from holding a seat in the General Assembly is any person holding any other compensated appointive or elective public office in the government of Georgia, any other state, or the United States.[21] According to a 1908 Georgia Supreme Court decision, this provision would invalidate the election to the General Assembly of one already holding state office, but it would not prohibit the person continuing in the prior-held position.[22]

In addition, no one seeking membership in the General Assembly may also run in the same primary or election for constitutional officer in the executive branch (e.g., commissioner of labor, secretary of state, etc.) or for any of the following offices: U.S. senator or representative, public service commissioner, justice of the supreme court, judge of the court of appeals, judge of superior court, or district attorney.[23] Further, no elected county or municipal official is eligible to serve as a member of the General Assembly.[24] There are no specific exclusions, however, applying to local government-appointed officials or employees (such as those of public schools).[25]

The Georgia Constitution declares that the legislative, judicial, and executive branches remain separate and distinct, and no one discharging the duties of one may, at the same time, exercise the functions of either of the others, except as the constitution specifically allows.[26] For example, no judge of a court of record or a judge's clerks or assistants may hold office in the legislature, nor may officers or employees of the executive branch.[27]

This prohibition has been construed by the Georgia Supreme Court to preclude a member of the General Assembly from holding any office or employment in the executive or judicial branches, including membership on boards and commissions (including authorities) involved in executive functions.[28] (However, this preclusion apparently does not apply to legislative memberships on various *advisory* boards and councils in the executive branch.) Georgia's high court also has refused to allow an employee of the executive branch—in this case a state college faculty member—to take an unpaid leave of absence while serving as a member of the General Assembly.[29] While a public school teacher can hold both jobs, a college teacher—if employed by the State Board of Regents—cannot.

A senator or representative cannot be elected by the General Assembly, or appointed by the governor, to any office that has an emolument during the period for which he or she has been elected unless first resigning from the legislature.[30] This provision, however, does not prevent a senator or representative from being elected by the General Assembly or appointed by the governor, with additional compensation, to certain legislative offices—such as the speaker of the House, the House and Senate majority leaders, and the administration floor leaders. Further, no legislator, during the term for which elected, can be appointed to any civil office that has been created during that term.[31]

REQUIRED OATH OF OFFICE AND COMMISSION

Required Oath

The Georgia Constitution requires that each member of the General Assembly, before taking his or her seat, take an oath of office as prescribed by law. Until adoption of the Constitution of 1983, the oath was specifically detailed in the constitution. Now a part of Georgia statutes, the oath reads:

> I do hereby solemnly swear or affirm that I will support the Constitution of this state and of the United States and, on all

questions and measures which may come before me, I will so conduct myself, as will, in my judgment, be most conducive to the interests and prosperity of this state.[32]

Georgia statutes also require an oath from every public officer that the officeholder does not hold any public money due the state or any political subdivision or authority that has not been accounted for; is not a holder of any office of trust under the government of the United States, any other state, or any foreign country that state laws prohibit holding; is qualified to hold the office; will support the constitutions of the United States and Georgia; and, if elected from a circuit or district, has been a resident for the period of time required by the constitution and laws of Georgia.[33]

A 1949 Georgia statute still remains on the books requiring every elected officeholder in the state to take a loyalty oath stating that he or she is not a member of the Communist party.[34] According to an opinion by Georgia's attorney general, the portion of Georgia's loyalty oath disavowing membership violates the First and Fourteenth amendments to the U.S. Constitution and should not be administered.[35] A check of the oath used in swearing-in ceremonies shows that the House continues to use the Communist party provision, while the Senate has dropped it.[36]

Rather than administer these oaths of office separately, the General Assembly practice has been to combine and administer them as one.

Commission

Each member of the Georgia General Assembly is entitled to a commission after taking the oath of office. It is the secretary of state's duty to prepare and furnish to the legislator this commission, which bears the Great Seal of the state. The commission recognizes that the person is a duly elected member of the General Assembly of Georgia for the term specified and notes any prior service that may have been performed in either house.[37]

ELECTIONS

Terms

Members of both the House and the Senate are elected at the general election held on Tuesday following the first Monday in November of even-numbered years. Both serve two-year terms of office, which begin on the second Monday in January following election (the time for convening the regular session) and end with the convening of the General Assembly following the second year of the term.[38] Neither house provides for staggered terms, and each member of the General Assembly must face reelection every two years.

Contested Elections

The Georgia Constitution vests in each house the authority to be judge of the eligibility and qualifications of its members.[39] Nevertheless, there are some instances (e.g., voting fraud or error) in which the results may be contested in state or federal court. To judicially contest an election, a petition is filed in superior court, where after notice to the defendant, the judge hears and decides the case alone (unless a jury is requested and the issues are such as could be determined by a jury). Such judgment may be appealed to a higher court within 10 days.[40]

Filling Vacancies

Georgia relies on the special election, rather than gubernatorial appointment, to fill vacancies that occur in the General Assembly.[41] Should a seat become vacant during a session of the General Assembly, or at a time when legislators would have to meet prior to the next general election, the governor issues within 10 days of such vacancy (or after the calling of a special session) a writ of election to the secretary of state. An election to fill the vacancy then takes place as authorized by the writ, no less than 30 or more than 60 days after its issuance.[42]

House and Senate Districts

The Senate consists of 56 members elected from single-member districts.[43] The House consists of 180 members elected from single-member districts.[44]

Reapportionment acts in 1972 brought a major change in the composition of the Georgia House and Senate by creating legislative districts, which are no longer drawn strictly according to county lines. They may instead be composed of either a portion of a county, a whole county, several counties, or any combination of these. Appendixes 1 and 2 contain maps of current House and Senate districts.

According to the Georgia Constitution, the House and Senate must be reapportioned as necessary at the first session after each U.S. decennial census becomes official.[45] However, in June 2006 the

U.S. Supreme Court ruled that state legislatures are not limited to just one reapportionment effort after each census.[46] Federal courts have held that reapportionments in both houses be conducted strictly on the basis of population, with minimum deviation among similar legislative districts.[47] The courts also require that three principal criteria be considered in drafting reapportionment plans: the U.S. Constitution, the Voting Rights Act, and neutral principles of redistricting such as compactness, contiguity, minimizing splits of counties and municipalities, recognizing communities of interest, maintaining the cores of existing districts, and using well-defined boundaries as district lines as long as those polices do not conflict with the one-person, one-vote principle and the Voting Rights Act. Single-member districts are preferred over multimember districts.[48] The U.S. Voting Rights Act requires that all reapportionment plans (as well as other election changes) for the Georgia General Assembly be submitted to the U.S. Department of Justice or the federal district court in the D.C. circuit.[49]

SALARY, ALLOWANCES, AND BENEFITS

Effective January 8, 2007, the annual base salary for members of the General Assembly is $17,341.68, paid in 12 monthly installments.[50] According to Georgia law, the annual salary for members of the General Assembly, the speaker of the House, the president pro tempore, and the speaker pro tempore may be increased by the General Assembly in the general appropriations act as a cost-of-living adjustment by a percentage that does not exceed the average percentage of the general increase in salary granted from time to time to employees of the executive, legislative, and judicial branches of government. The cost-of-living increase determined by the Legislative Services Committee and based on objective economic criteria will become effective for members and member-officers at the same time funds are made available for the increase for such employees. The balance of the increase for members and member-officers of the General Assembly will become effective on the convening of the next General Assembly in January of the next odd-numbered year. The Office of Planning and Budget will calculate the average percentage increase.[51]

There is no additional remuneration for any further service as a legislator—including special sessions—except for expense, mileage, travel, and office allowances as provided by law.

Salaries for Legislative Officers

In recognition of the greater demands placed on their offices, those in certain legislative leadership positions in the General Assembly are authorized to receive supplemental amounts over their basic $17,341.68 salaries. The speaker of the House of Representatives is paid an additional supplement, adjusted at the convening of each new term, plus an amount of salary over $30,000 per annum paid to the lieutenant governor. The speaker's salary for FY 2007 is $99,082.92. The speaker pro tempore in the House and president pro tempore in the Senate each receive a $4,800 supplement. The majority leader, minority leader, administration floor leader, and the assistant administration floor leaders in both houses each receive additional amounts provided by resolution in each house but not greater than the amount provided for the speaker pro tempore of the House.[52]

In 1987, the salary of the lieutenant governor was set at $54,920, and that is the official salary provided for in the code.[53] Though serving as president of the Senate, he or she is a member of the executive branch and thus entitled to the full cost-of-living adjustment granted state employees. Given those increases, the lieutenant governor's adjusted salary for FY 2007 is $88,941.24. He or she receives no additional compensation, though during sessions the president also receives the standard daily allowance of $173, plus reimbursement for actual transportation costs while traveling by public carrier or 44.5 cents per mile for use of a personal automobile.[54]

The secretary of the Senate and clerk of the House receive such salary, expenses, and allowances as provided by resolution of their respective houses.[55] Additionally, both officials are entitled to the same expense, mileage, and travel allowances as legislators for each day of official services.

Expense Allowance

Legislators are entitled, by law, to a standard expense allowance of $173 per day for

1. each official legislative day of a regular or special session (which can include Saturdays and Sundays, unless both houses have adjourned by joint resolution for a weekend or other period of time);
2. each day's service as a member of a standing committee or an interim committee created by, or pursuant to, a resolution of one or both houses; and

3. each day's service as a member of a statutory or constitutional committee, board, bureau, commission, or other agency.[56]

During formally invoked adjournments—including the customary budget recess—legislators are not entitled to the expense allowance unless involved in committee work under the second provision.

Depending upon the housekeeping resolution adopted in each house, legislators may also collect the $173 daily allowance during the interim between sessions while serving as a "committee of one."

For performing official duties out of state, legislators receive actual expenses (e.g., food, lodging, taxis, etc.) as an expense allowance—in lieu of the $173 daily rate—plus travel expenses outlined below. Members are also reimbursed for registration fees to attend approved legislative conferences or meetings, whether in or out of state.[57]

Prior to out-of-state travel at state expense, a senator or Senate staff member must have prior approval in writing by the Senate Administrative Affairs Committee. House members must have prior approval under procedures established by the speaker.[58]

Mileage and Travel Allowances

Each member of the General Assembly is provided a mileage allowance of 44.5 cents per mile for one round-trip each week or portion of a week during a regular or special session. Mileage reimbursement rates are the same as those set by the U.S. General Services Administration for federal employees. The round-trip mileage is calculated "by the most practical route." If the member travels by public carrier for any part of the round-trip, the reimbursement for that part is the actual expense in lieu of the mileage allowance.[59]

For authorized legislative travel, a member may receive a mileage allowance of either 44.5 cents per mile or actual transportation costs if traveling by air, bus, or other public carrier.[60] Reimbursement for commercial airfare is limited to the amounts provided for in the statewide contract for airline travel incorporated in the state travel regulations established by the state accounting office.[61] (Certain exceptions are outlined in O.C.G.A. §45-7-30.) These allowances or reimbursements will be paid upon submission of proper vouchers.[62]

Expense and Travel Vouchers

As noted above, during a regular or special session, legislators are automatically paid the daily $173 expense allowance and the round-trip mileage allowance to their home city once a week.

MARBLE STAIRS LEAD FROM THE SECOND (MAIN) FLOOR
OF THE CAPITOL TO THE THIRD FLOOR, WHERE THE
HOUSE AND SENATE CHAMBERS ARE LOCATED.

For any other expense, mileage, or travel reimbursements, a legislator must sign and submit a voucher to the legislative fiscal officer certifying (1) that he or she has personally performed the service and personally incurred the expense for mileage and travel covered by the voucher, and (2) that the information contained on the voucher is correct and true.[63] Penalties for knowing and willful submission of false information on a voucher by a legislator include a fine of not more than $1,000, imprisonment of not less than one or more than five years, or both.[64]

At least once every two months, the House Journals Committee and a special audit subcommittee designated by the Senate Rules Committee must examine and review legislative expenditures including all vouchers submitted by members of their respective houses.[65]

Office and Other Allowances

In addition to any other allowances authorized by law, each member of the General Assembly may receive reimbursement up to $7,000 each year for the following expenses: lodging, meals, postage (specifically excluded from reimbursement is postage for a "political newsletter"), personal services, printing and publications, rents, supplies (including software), telecommunications, transportation, utilities, and per-diem differential.[66] If purchased equipment depreciates in value to $100 or less when the member leaves office, it does not need to be returned to the state.

Georgia's attorney general has issued an official opinion to the lieutenant governor stating that when funds from this allowance are used to purchase items that are not fully consumed (e.g., office equipment, computers, and cellular telephones), the items become state property and cannot be retained as personal property by the legislator.[67]

Any amounts remaining in expense accounts at the end of the first year of a biennium may be used for expenses in the second year of the biennium. The "year" for the expense account begins on the convening date of the General Assembly and ends the day before the convening date of the General Assembly in the next calendar year. Members have until April 15 immediately following the end of such year to submit claims for expenses.[68]

Other expenses will be reimbursed to the $7,000 limit upon submission to the Legislative Fiscal Office of sworn vouchers accompanied by supporting documents showing payment.

Sickness and Death

If a member becomes unable to attend a session of the General Assembly because of personal or family sickness, or if granted leave by his or her legislative house, the member is entitled to the same daily expense allowance as attending members.[69] Regardless of the length of sickness, a legislator continues to receive the salary of his or her office as long as it is held—even if forced to miss part or all of a session.

Should a member die during or after a session without having received all or any part of his or her daily expense allowance, the amount due for the entire session (minus any portion already paid) is paid to the surviving spouse or, if none, to the children; and if there are no children, to the estate of the deceased legislator. The legislator's salary for the full calendar month in which he or she died is paid in the same manner.[70]

Restrictions on Additional Compensation

Georgia law prohibits any member of the General Assembly from receiving any compensation, salary, per diem, contingent expense allowance, longevity pay, or allowance of any kind for service as a legislator other than that specified by law.[71] One exception is that legislators may be reimbursed by the executive or judicial branches for service on advisory or investigatory boards and committees. For such service, legislators can claim (1) actual expenses or (2) actual travel expenses and the standard per diem allowance for legislators. However, no claims for reimbursement can be paid for days a legislator receives compensation or reimbursement from the legislative branch of government.[72]

Georgia's attorney general has issued an opinion stating that these restrictions do not apply to a legislator who continues to receive his or her regular salary and benefits during a legislative session from a full-time employer—as long as the paying of salary and benefits is not done for the purpose of influencing the legislator or the legislator's reelection campaign.[73]

As will be discussed in Chapter 3, the ban on additional compensation or allowances applies not only to receipt of public monies but private as well. The Georgia Supreme Court has held that, "Other than those emoluments of public office that are expressly authorized by law, *no* holder of public office is entitled to request or receive—from any source, directly or indirectly—anything of value in exchange for the performance of any act related to the functions of that office."[74]

INSURANCE AND RETIREMENT BENEFITS

Health Insurance

Legislators and the administrative and clerical personnel of the General Assembly, and their dependents, are authorized to participate in a group health insurance plan for state employees.[75] Administration of this plan is vested in the board of the state Department of Community Health. Payments into the health insurance fund are made by both employer and employee, with the legislative fiscal officer making employer payments for all legislators and legislative personnel.

Retirement

In 1967, the Georgia Legislative Retirement System (LRS) was established to provide retirement benefits for legislators, the secretary of the Senate, and the clerk of the House.[76] Five years later, membership eligibility was extended to the messenger and doorkeeper for each of the two houses.

In 1971, the state Employees' Retirement System (ERS) was extended to cover General Assembly members. Legislators who were members of LRS prior to May 1, 1971, could continue to claim benefits as outlined in the LRS, while all new members of the legislature received benefits as provided by ERS. The assumption was that, in time, LRS would be phased out, with ERS taking over administration of retirement benefits for legislators.

In 1979 and 1980, legislators elected since 1971 were given a chance to withdraw from ERS and join LRS. Any member of the General Assembly as of April 13, 1979, could elect to withdraw from ERS and join LRS or choose not to be a member of either system. This decision had to be made prior to the convening of the 1981 session of the General Assembly and once made was irrevocable.

General Assembly members elected after April 13, 1979, but before July 1, 1984, could join LRS or ERS, but they had to decide within 60 days from the date of becoming a member of the General Assembly. The decision once made was irrevocable. Since July 1, 1984, all persons elected to the General Assembly become members of LRS upon taking office.

Members of LRS may retire at age 62 with eight years of *membership service* (service as a member of the General Assembly) or at age 65 with eight years of *creditable service* (service as a member of the General Assembly plus service in the military during wartime and/or service in the General Assembly prior to January 1, 1954). Military service rendered prior to January 1, 1954, does not require a contribution, but military service after January 1, 1954, requires making the employee contribution plus 7 percent interest compounded annually. Up to five years of military service may be purchased at the rate of one year for every five years served in the legislature.

The monthly retirement allowance is calculated at $36 times the number of years of creditable service. Early retirement is available at age 60 with eight years of membership service and with normal benefits reduced 5 percent for each year below age 62.

A 100 percent or 50 percent joint and survivor annuity is available for a named beneficiary, but LRS does not provide a disability retirement option. If an LRS member ceases to be a member of the General Assembly before reaching age 60, he or she may continue as a noncontributing member, retaining membership service credits. If contributions are withdrawn, membership credits are irrevocably lost and cannot be reestablished even if the person is reelected to the General Assembly.[77]

Under ERS, a member may retire at age 60 with 10 years' service, although members can continue working beyond this age and increase their benefits. Benefits are based on a member's age at retirement, years of service, and highest average monthly compensation over eight consecutive quarters.[78]

For legislators who belong to ERS, employee contributions to the system are paid by the legislative branch. For LRS members, the legislative branch contributes an amount equivalent to that paid for legislators in ERS, with the difference (employee contributions required by LRS are higher than ERS) deducted from each member's salary. Since 1986, LRS members contribute an additional 1 percent of salary.[79]

OFFICE SPACE AND ADDITIONAL ADMINISTRATIVE RESOURCES

Office space. The General Assembly and other components of the legislative branch are housed in the state capitol and in the Coverdell Legislative Office Building across the street from the capitol. Individual offices in the capitol are provided for the president and president pro tempore of the Senate, the speaker and speaker pro tempore of the House, and the majority leaders and administration floor leaders of both houses. A majority of the House committee chairs have capitol offices, as do a majority of Senate committee

THE PAUL COVERDELL LEGISLATIVE OFFICE BUILDING
PROVIDES OFFICE SPACE FOR LEGISLATORS AND COMMITTEES.

chairs. Remaining legislators have private offices in the Coverdell Legislative Office Building.

Committee space. Certain rooms are designated at the capitol and Coverdell Legislative Office Building for committee use in each house. During a session and in the interim, Senate committees rely on the secretary of the Senate to schedule a room for their meetings. Likewise, the House Communications Office reserves rooms year-round for committee meetings. Representatives may make reservation requests through the communications office Web site.

Clerical assistance. Legislative leaders and some committees are provided with individual secretarial and clerical help. Every member has access to a secretary who may work for several legislators.

Computers. Beginning with the 2000 session, members of both houses of the General Assembly have been able to extensively use computers in conjunction with their legislative duties. After being sworn in, new legislators may select a laptop or a desktop computer

LEGISLATORS CAN ACCESS THE INTERNET FROM THEIR DESKS
ON THE FLOOR OR ANYWHERE IN THE CAPITOL COMPLEX.

issued by the General Assembly's information technology department. These computers are specially configured for legislative use whether a member is at the capitol, on the road, or at home. Direct access to the Internet and the General Assembly's local area network is provided at each legislator's desk on the floor as well as in that member's legislative office. All laptops are equipped with a secure virtual private network (VPN) to access the General Assembly from remote locations. The legislature also has secure wireless connectivity throughout the capitol complex.

The General Assembly's information technology department maintains a separate Web page for the House and Senate. Each Web page has a variety of information on that house and the legislative session, including a public Web page on each member. In addition to biographical information provided by legislators, each member's Web page contains contact information, political party and district information, committee memberships, and links to bills and resolutions sponsored or cosponsored by that legislator.

Telephones. Legislators may make long-distance calls for legislative matters using their office telephones at the state capitol or in the Coverdell Legislative Office Building. As part of a service through the Georgia Technology Authority, they may select billing at a per call rate as a payroll deduction. Legislators are allowed 40 calls per month. Calls above the limit are charged to the legislator but can be reimbursed out of the annual expense allowance.

Long-distance calls and telephone service pertaining to legislative business and incurred away from the capitol qualify for reimbursement from each legislator's annual $7,000 office expense allowance.

Legislative license plates. Each member of the General Assembly is entitled to a custom license plate that shows a capitol dome, identifies the member as a representative or a senator, and shows the member's district number. After an election, the special tags section of the Motor Vehicle Division of the Georgia Department of Revenue sends a letter and an order form to the member. The initial cost of the tag is $70, and the annual renewal fee is $45. Once the tag is manufactured, it is mailed to the local tag office in the member's county. The legislator must pay the annual ad valorem taxes.

Parking. Parking spaces in the state capitol complex are usually at a premium, and although legislators are assured of a space, this is not always true for aides, interns, and constituents.

The parking lot east of the capitol on Capitol Avenue is known as parking Lot #1. Here, for a fee of $10, each legislator is assigned a reserved space for use during the session only. The Georgia Building Authority, which has responsibility for the capitol complex parking lots, will issue the legislator a permit, which must be displayed at all times when the car is in Lot #1. If a legislator is not going to be using the reserved space on a particular day during the session, he or she can authorize someone else to use the parking space for the day by giving written permission for the borrower to present to the Lot #1 parking attendant.

During the remainder of the year, between sessions, legislators can pay $20 for use of Lot #1 for official business, or they can pay the standard $5 daily parking fee each time they use the lot. During the interim, parking spaces are not reserved, and a legislator's parking permit is nontransferable—only the legislator can use it. In fact, the legislator must be in the vehicle for the permit to be valid. Interim parking permits are only valid during normal office hours at the capitol and cannot be used for sporting events or at any of the other parking lots in the capitol complex area.

The parking situation for a legislator's aides, interns, and constituents sometimes becomes difficult. On a space-available basis, the Georgia Building Authority will assign permits for legislators' aides to park at the Archives Building Lot at the same rates full-time state employees pay for monthly parking, in addition to a nonrefundable $10 parking card deposit. However, limited spaces are available, and these are allocated on a first-come, first-served basis. Several public parking facilities allow visitor parking on a limited basis, including the Pete Hackney Parking Deck located on the corner of Jesse Hill Jr. Drive and Decatur Street, two blocks northeast of the capitol. Daily parking fees at the lots in the capitol complex area range from $5 at the state lots to $8 at the Underground Atlanta lots.

NOTES

1. GA. CONST. art. 3, §2, ¶1(b).
2. GA. CONST. art. 3, §2, ¶1(a).
3. *The Book of the States: 2006*, Vol. 38 (Lexington, Ky.: Council of State Governments, 2006), Table 3.3, p. 72.
4. GA. CONST. art. 3, §2, ¶3.
5. GA. CONST. art. 3, §4, ¶5.
6. GA. CONST. art. 3, §2, ¶3.
7. GA. CONST. art. 2, §2, ¶3.
8. Ibid.; *see also* OFFICIAL CODE OF GEORGIA ANNOTATED (O.C.G.A.) §45-2-1(3).
9. 1983 Op. Att'y Gen. 83-33.
10. GA. CONST. art. 2, §2, ¶3.
11. GA. CONST. art. 2, §2, ¶3. *See also* O.C.G.A. §45-2-1(2).
12. O.C.G.A. §45-2-1(5).
13. GA. CONST. art. 2, §1, ¶3(b).
14. O.C.G.A. §45-5-1.
15. Ibid.
16. O.C.G.A. §§21-2-111, 21-2-153.
17. O.C.G.A. ch. 21-2 provides most of these procedures.
18. O.C.G.A. §21-2-137; GA. CONST. art. 2, §2, ¶5.
19. O.C.G.A. §21-2-133.
20. GA. CONST. art. 3, §2, ¶4. *See also* O.C.G.A. §45-2-1(4).
21. Ibid.
22. McWilliams v. Neal, 130 Ga. 733, 61 S.E. 721 (1908).
23. O.C.G.A. §21-2-136.
24. *See also* 1977 Ops. Att'y Gen. U77-26, U77-40; 1985 Op. Att'y Gen. U85-33; O.C.G.A. §§28-1-13, 21-2-136.
25. *See, e.g.*, 1977 Op. Att'y Gen. 77-47; 1968 Op. Att'y Gen. U68-169.
26. GA. CONST. art. 1, §2, ¶3.
27. O.C.G.A. §16-10-9.

28. Greer v. State, 233 Ga. 667, 212 S.E.2d 836 (1975); Murphy v. State, 233 Ga. 681, 212 S.E.2d 839 (1975). *See also* 1974 Op. Att'y Gen. 74-109.

29. Galer v. Regents of the University System, 239 Ga. 268, 236 S.E.2d 617 (1977).

30. GA. CONST. art. 3, §2, ¶4(c).

31. Ibid. Also, in what appears to be the only appellate court decision considering these two prohibitions, the Georgia Supreme Court sustained the governor's appointment of the speaker of the House of Representatives to the State School Building Authority—an authority that the speaker, as a member of the General Assembly, had helped to create. The court based its holding upon the establishing act's express declaration that the authority members were to receive no compensation (thus no emolument was annexed), and upon its determination that the authority did not constitute a civil office because it did not perform "government functions." In making this latter determination, the court disregarded the act's express provision that governmental functions would be exercised by the authority. *See* Sheffield v. State School Building Authority, 208 Ga. 575, 68 S.E.2d 590 (1952). *See also* McLucas v. State Bridge Building Authority, 210 Ga. 1, 77 S.E.2d 531 (1953); Greer v. State, 233 Ga. 667, 212 S.E.2d 836 (1975); 1974 Op. Att'y Gen. 74-109.

32. O.C.G.A. §28-1-4.

33. O.C.G.A. §45-3-1.

34. O.C.G.A. §§45-3-11 through 45-3-14.

35. 1985 Op. Att'y Gen. 85-19.

36. Georgia *House Journal* 2005, reg. sess., 25; Georgia *Senate Journal* 2005, reg. sess., 18.

37. O.C.G.A. §28-1-5.

38. GA. CONST. art. 3, §2, ¶5; O.C.G.A. §21-2-502.

39. GA. CONST. art. 3, §4, ¶7.

40. O.C.G.A. §§21-2-520 through 21-2-529.

41. GA. CONST. art. 5, §2, ¶5; art. 3, §4, ¶5. *See also* 1969 Op. Att'y Gen. 69-59.

42. O.C.G.A. §21-2-544.

43. GA. CONST. art. 3, §2, ¶1; O.C.G.A. §§28-1-1, 28-2-2.

44. GA. CONST. art. 3, §2, ¶1; O.C.G.A. §§28-1-1, 28-2-1.

45. GA. CONST. art. 3, §2, ¶2. See Chapter 1 of this handbook for a brief history of reapportionment efforts in Georgia.

46. League of United Latin American Citizens v. Perry, 126 S.Ct. 2594 (2006).

47. Toombs v. Fortson, 205 F. Supp. 248 (N.D. Ga., 1962); Gray v. Sanders, 372 U.S. 368 (1963); Reynolds v. Sims, 377 U.S. 533 (1964); Kilpatrick v. Preisler, 394 U.S. 526 (1969); Wells v. Rockefeller, 394 U.S. 542 (1969); Georgia v. United States, 411 U.S. 526 (1973). For a history of reapportionment in Georgia prior to 1970, see Brett W. Hawkins (ed.), *Reapportionment in Georgia* (Athens: Institute of Government, 1970).

48. Larios v. Cox, 306 F. Supp. 2d 1214 (N.D. Ga. 2004).

49. 42 U.S.C.A. §§1971, 1973.

50. O.C.G.A. §45-7-4. *See also* O.C.G.A. §28-1-8.

51. Ibid.

52. O.C.G.A. §28-1-8. These amounts are set in the "housekeeping resolution" adopted by each house at the beginning of a biennium.

53. O.C.G.A. §45-7-4(a)(2).

54. O.C.G.A. §§45-7-20, 50-19-7.

55. O.C.G.A. §28-3-23.

56. O.C.G.A. §28-1-8.

57. Ibid.

58. O.C.G.A. §28-1-8(b)(2).

59. O.C.G.A. §28-1-8.

60. Ibid.

61. Ibid.

62. Ibid.

63. Ibid.

64. Ibid.

65. Ibid.

66. O.C.G.A. §45-7-4.

67. 1992 Op. Att'y Gen. 92-33.

68. O.C.G.A. §45-7-4.

69. O.C.G.A. §28-1-8.

70. Ibid.

71. O.C.G.A. §45-7-3.

72. Ibid.

73. 1992 Op. Att'y Gen. 92-27.

74. State v. Agan, 259 Ga. 541, 544, 384 S.E.2d 863 (1989).

75. O.C.G.A. §§45-18-1, 45-18-2.

76. O.C.G.A. §47-6-1.

77. O.C.G.A. ch. 47-6.

78. O.C.G.A. §§47-2-28, 47-2-110, 47-2-120, 47-2-121.

79. O.C.G.A. §47-6-60.

CHAPTER 3

STANDARDS OF LEGISLATIVE CONDUCT

A number of constitutional and statutory provisions, as well as House and Senate rules, apply to the behavior and ethics of members of the General Assembly. Some of these set privileges, immunities, or standards of conduct only apply on the floor of a member's house, while other standards have a broader application.

PRIVILEGES AND IMMUNITIES

Georgia law extends several privileges and immunities to members of the General Assembly.

Freedom of speech. Georgia's constitution provides that no legislator is liable to answer in any other place for anything spoken on the floor or in committee in either house.[1] In other words, a legislator cannot be sued for slander for remarks made during floor debate or in committee. Freeing legislators from the threat of suit presumably fosters a climate of free and open debate in the General Assembly. Nevertheless, there are other limitations that do restrict what a legislator may say.

Immunity from arrest. The Constitution of Georgia establishes an immunity (except for treason, felony, or breach of the peace) for members of the General Assembly in providing that they will be free from arrest while attending, going to, or returning from meetings of the legislature or legislative committees.[2]

Immunity in court proceedings. Members are also granted certain immunities in relation to state court and administrative agency proceedings that occur while they are attending sessions of the General

Assembly. Any legislator who is summoned to serve as a witness or a juror in a case is excused from service while attending a session of the General Assembly.[3] In all civil cases, either party has the right to take depositions from any legislator who is needed as a witness during a legislative session.[4]

Any legislator who is a party or attorney for a party in any court or administrative agency proceedings is granted a continuance in the case during the legislative session and for a period of three weeks following any recess or adjournment, including adjournment *sine die*. In such instances, it is not necessary that the legislator or attorney be present in court for the call of the case.[5]

Questions of privilege. In both houses, members are permitted to make certain personal statements as a matter of privilege. These are called "questions of privilege" or "points of personal privilege." House and Senate rules specify two types of questions that members can address to the full body on a point of personal privilege:

1. questions affecting the rights of the body collectively—its dignity, safety, and the integrity of its proceedings; and

2. questions affecting the conduct of members individually but in their representative capacity only.

In the Senate, questions of personal privilege have precedence over all questions; in the House, they have precedence over all questions except a motion to adjourn. However, in neither body can a member rise on a point of personal privilege when another matter is pending on the floor.[6] When speaking from the well on a point of personal privilege, senators are limited to five minutes.[7] In the House, a member is limited to five minutes if the point of personal privilege is raised during "Morning Orders" (i.e., the period immediately prior to third reading of bills and resolutions). If raised during "Evening Orders" (i.e., the period immediately following third readings), the amount of time a member can speak is determined by the speaker.[8]

Protests. Should a member of the Senate disagree with an action taken by that body, he or she may prepare a written protest against the action not to exceed 250 words for inclusion in the Senate journal. The protest may not impugn the motive of the Senate or of any member.[9]

House rules make no provision for members entering a protest against a House action. However, if a member disagrees with a ruling of the speaker on any point, that member can rise and state,

REPRESENTATIVE GOVERNMENT AT WORK

Georgia's Constitution of 1789 was the first in the state to authorize each house of the General Assembly with power to expel or punish members for disorderly behavior. After the Yazoo Land Fraud, a new constitution expanded the authority to punish members: "Each house shall be judge of the elections, returns, and qualifications of its own members; with powers to expel or punish, by censuring, fining, and imprisoning, or either, for disorderly behavior; and may expel any person convicted of any felonious or infamous offense." [GA. CONST. of 1798, art.1, §13]

"I appeal from the decision of the chair." Such appeal must be made immediately following the speaker's ruling and before any other business transpires. Debate on the correctness of the speaker's ruling is limited to five minutes, followed by a vote by the full House. To overrule the speaker requires approval by a majority of the House membership.[10]

MISCONDUCT, CRIMES, AND ETHICS

Some standards of conduct and ethics apply to all branches of state government; others apply only to members of the General Assembly and employees of the legislative branch; and still others apply only to members of the General Assembly.

Disorderly conduct. Under Georgia's constitution, each house of the General Assembly has the power to punish its members for disorderly behavior or misconduct.[11] Although this kind of power has been part of the state constitution since 1789, the question of what constitutes "disorderly behavior" or "misconduct" has never been defined, in part because this provision of the constitution has never been argued before Georgia's appellate courts. However, this definition likely includes flagrant abuse of House or Senate rules and refusal to accept rulings of the chair or orders by the entire body. In terms of misconduct, Georgia's recall statute defines misconduct for recall purposes as "an unlawful act committed willfully by an elected public official or a willful violation of the code of ethics for government service contained in Code Section 45-10-1."[12]

Punishment for disorderly conduct can involve censure, a fine, imprisonment, or expulsion. A motion to expel a member requires approval of two-thirds of the entire house to which that member belongs.[13] In practice, though, these punishments are very seldom invoked.

Disruptions. House rules direct members to refrain from private conversations and preserve silence when another member has the floor and is speaking from the well.[14] Senate rules direct members to refrain from audible private conservations that disrupt the business of the Senate.[15] In actual practice, these rules are commonly violated in each house, forcing the presiding officers repeatedly to gavel their chambers to order during debate. A legislator may be in the well addressing the membership on a particular bill while related and unrelated business is transpiring on the chamber floor. In addition to talking with each other, legislators may be talking with staff, interns, pages, members of the other house, and others who have been admitted to the floor.

Although only the House has a specific rule, both houses prohibit applause or hisses in their chambers, galleries, or lobbies during any speech or legislative proceeding.[16] Exceptions are applause by legislators to recognize a group in the gallery or someone invited to address the House or Senate and standing applause for the governor before and after he addresses a joint session of the General Assembly.

To help maintain order, each house has a sergeant-at-arms. In the Senate, this officer is directed to aid in the enforcement of order as directed by the president and the Decorum Committee.[17]

House rules provide that the sergeant-at-arms is to maintain order in the House chamber, gallery, anterooms, lobbies, and halls adjacent to the House. Additionally, the speaker can direct members of the Georgia State Patrol assigned to the capitol to assist the sergeant-at-arms.[18] If necessary, the speaker can order the House chamber, gallery, and adjacent areas cleared to preserve order and decorum.[19]

In either house, if a member violates the rules of the body during legislative proceedings, the presiding officer can call that member to order, at which time the member must immediately sit down unless allowed to explain his or her actions. The member may appeal the chair's order to the full house. If the member refuses to accept the decision of the full house, he or she may be reprimanded for the first offense and fined not more than $100 for subsequent offenses. If the member continues to abide by the action of the full house, that member can be expelled by a two-thirds vote of the membership.[20]

Obtaining recognition to speak. No member can address either house (except in the case of appeals in the House of Representatives) or question a member who is speaking unless he or she does so through the presiding officer. If the member who is speaking declines to be interrupted, no questions can be asked.[21]

Addressing or referring to members by name. Senate rules instruct senators to avoid calling each other by name during floor proceedings. Instead, they are to refer to each other by district or position on the floor, saying, for instance, "the senator from the 44th district" or "the gentleman (lady) in the well."[22] House rules allow the use of "Mr.," "Mrs.," "Miss," or "Ms." plus the member's last name or the member's title, position on the floor, or district, city, or county—for example, saying "Mr. Jones," "Mrs. Smith," "Miss Brown," "Ms. Black," "Mr. Majority Leader," "the gentleman from the 61st district," or "the lady from Fulton."[23] House rules direct members to use the term "Mr. Speaker" when addressing the presiding officer.[24] In the Senate, the presiding officer of that body is always addressed as "Mr. or Madam President" (even if someone other than the lieutenant governor is presiding).[25]

Privileged conversations. When debating, no senator or representative can refer to any private conversation with another member.[26]

Disparaging remarks. House rules direct members to be respectful of other members and to avoid references to personalities when addressing the House. Representatives are also directed to observe "decency of speech and gentleness of behavior at all times in the House."[27] Additionally, senators who are recording protests in the journal with respect to some action taken by the Senate may not impugn the motive of any senator.[28]

Securing a quorum. The speaker of the House and president pro tempore of the Senate can order the doors of their chambers closed in order to keep or secure a quorum. During a session, the doors of each chamber are always closed and may be locked so that no member may leave. Once the doors have been closed for quorum purposes, no member may leave the chamber without first obtaining permission from the speaker in the House and the membership in the Senate. If necessary, the speaker of the House can have the absentees arrested and brought before the House in order to secure a quorum.[29] In the Senate, the arrest of absentees can be ordered by the president pro tempore or a majority of the senators present.[30] In the event that a member is arrested and brought before the body, the full house determines under what conditions he or she is to be discharged from arrest.[31]

Floor decorum. During floor sessions, rules in both houses direct members to act at all times with dignity and in a manner to ensure decorum.[32] The presiding officer of each body is instructed to enforce decorum by calling members to order for such activities as eating at desks, reading newspapers and other materials not pertinent to legislation, unnecessary conversation, and inappropriate dress.[33] Although not defined in Senate rules, appropriate dress is defined by House rules as "coat and tie for male members and dignified dress for female members."[34]

Cell phones. House rules prohibit use of cell phones on the floor when another member is speaking from the well.[35] Senate rules forbid the use of cell phones in the chamber and during committee meetings.[36]

Laptop computers. Legislators are issued laptop computers for use at the chamber desk, office, and other settings. There are no House rules specifically addressing use of laptop computers. Senate rules provide that during Senate sessions and committee meetings, senators can only use their laptop computer for legislative business and necessary communication with their home and business.[37]

Smoking. Rules of the Senate prohibit smoking in the chamber while the Senate is in session or in committee rooms during committee meetings.[38] In the House, smoking is prohibited in the chamber, gallery, lobbies, anterooms, halls, or restrooms adjacent to the House.[39]

Intoxication. The House of Representatives has a specific rule forbidding members who are in an intoxicated state or under the influence of drugs listed in the Georgia Controlled Substances Act from entering the floor. The messenger and doorkeeper are charged with rigid enforcement of this rule.[40] Although there is no parallel rule in the Senate, that house follows the same practice of not allowing intoxicated members onto the floor.

Voting another member's machine. Because of the extensive use of electronic voting, rules in both houses prohibit any member or other person from voting in the place of another member on any question or proposition.[41] The rules are intended to prevent someone from using an absent colleague's machine to vote without his or her permission. Legislators often are not at their seat when an electronic vote is taken and, as a practical matter, will signal their seatmate to press the button on their behalf.

In the House, each member is issued a single electronic card to activate that member's voting console. Members are prohibited from duplicating the card and may not leave it in their voting console while they are away from their seat.[42]

Unless the speaker authorizes an exception, violation of the prohibition against voting in the place of another member can be punished by fine, censure, or other action ordered by the House.[43] In the Senate, violation of the prohibition is deemed to be disorderly behavior and subject to such punishment as provided by the state constitution and Senate rules.[44]

Refusing to vote. If a quorum is present and a member of either house refuses to vote on a measure, that refusal, unless excused by the body, is deemed a contempt of that house.[45] However, rules of both houses provide for instances in which a member should not vote, such as a bill that directly affects a legislator.[46]

Violating House and Senate Rules. In addition to violating House rules during legislative proceedings, members are prohibited from knowingly violating any rule of the House.[47] Senate rules prohibit any member or staff from knowingly circumventing the clear purpose or intent of laws or any Senate rule.[48] No specific penalty is provided, but such action likely would qualify as disorderly behavior or misconduct, in which case the state constitution allows each house to punish by censure, fine, imprisonment, or expulsion.[49]

Bribery. Bribery is committed when someone gives or offers to give anything of value to any person acting on behalf of the state for purposes of influencing that person in the performance of the duties of his or her office.[50] A legislator commits bribery when, directly or indirectly, he or she solicits, receives, accepts, or agrees to receive anything of value by inducing the reasonable belief that the giving of the thing will influence his or her performance or failure to perform any official action.[51] State law, however, specifically exempts the following as things of value in terms of the bribery statute:

1. food or beverage consumed at a single meal or event;
2. legitimate salary, benefits, fees, commissions, or expenses associated with a recipient's nonpublic business, employment, trade, or profession;
3. an award, plaque, certificate, memento, or similar item given in recognition of the recipient's civic, charitable, political, professional, or public service;
4. food, beverages, and registration at group events to which all members of the Georgia House, Senate, and their committees or subcommittees are invited;

5. actual and reasonable expenses for food, beverages, travel, lodging, and registration to allow a legislator to participate or be a speaker at a meeting;

6. a commercially reasonable loan made in the ordinary course of business;

7. any gift with a value less than $100;

8. promotional items generally distributed to the general public or to public officers;

9. a gift from a member of the legislator's immediate family; or

10. food, beverage, or expenses afforded legislators, members of their immediate families, or others that are associated with normal and customary business or social functions or activities.

Additionally, the receipt, acceptance, or agreement to receive anything not specified in this list of exclusions does not create the presumption that criminal bribery has been committed. However, if bribery is proven in a court of law, a legislator faces a fine of up to $5,000, imprisonment for 1 to 20 years, or both.[52]

Influencing the passage or defeat of legislation. Legislators may be charged with a separate felony crime similar to bribery should they ask for or receive anything of value in return for agreeing to procure (or attempting to procure) the passage or defeat of legislation by the General Assembly or for attempting to procure the signing or veto of legislation by the governor. The penalty for conviction is imprisonment for one to five years.[53]

Influencing state officials or employees. Legislators may be charged with another felony crime similar to bribery if they ask for or receive anything of value in return for attempting to influence official action by any state agency, official, or employee. Upon conviction, a legislator faces imprisonment for one to five years.[54]

Extortion. Extortion is committed when public officers unlawfully take, in their official capacity, any money or thing of value from any person that either is not due to them or is more than is due. Upon conviction of extortion, a legislator is dismissed from office.[55]

Conspiracy to defraud. A legislator commits conspiracy to defraud when agreeing with another to steal any property belonging to the state or under the control or possession of the legislator in his or her official capacity. The penalty for conviction is imprisonment for one to five years.[56]

Other crimes. It is also a crime (punishment for which includes fine, imprisonment, or both and/or removal from office) for a legislator to

1. willfully and intentionally violate the terms of his or her oath;[57]

2. enter into a contract, combination, conspiracy in restraint of trade, or free and open competition in any transaction with the state or any agency thereof, whether for goods, materials, or services;[58]

3. willfully and knowingly submit a false expense, mileage report, or travel voucher for purposes of reimbursement;[59]

4. accept any fee, money, gift, or any other thing of value in connection with any claim presented to the Claims Advisory Board.[60]

5. accept a monetary fee or honorarium over $101 for a speaking engagement, participation in a seminar or discussion panel, or other activities directly related to a legislator's official duties. (Exempted are actual and reasonable expenses for food, beverages, travel, lodging, and registration to allow a legislator to attend a meeting to speak or appear on a panel.)[61]

Conflict of interest. Few issues pose so difficult a problem as that of conflict of interest in so-called "citizen legislatures." One stance supports the belief that lawmakers should neither vote on issues in which they have a personal interest nor financially benefit by virtue of their office. An opposing view, however, recognizes that membership in a part-time legislature means that most lawmakers must pursue personal occupations or professions and may occasionally face business dealings with the state.

Georgia's constitution is silent on the issue of conflict of interest except to note that "public officers are the trustees and servants of the people and are at all times amenable to them."[62]

Each house of the General Assembly has adopted rules to discourage lawmakers from voting on issues in which they have a personal interest, but these restrictions have proven difficult to interpret and enforce. For instance, should a legislator who is a public schoolteacher be allowed to vote on the state appropriations act that, among other things, sets his or her salary? In the way of guidance, House rules provide that a representative may not vote on any question if he or she is "immediately and particularly interested" in its result; Senate rules stipulate the standard of "direct pecuniary interest."[63]

What should a legislator do in case of an actual (or perceived) conflict of interest when voting on a particular bill? Ordinarily, the rules of parliamentary procedure dictate that the member should abstain from voting. But rules of both houses in the General Assembly prohibit legislators from abstaining on a vote. The proper procedure is that before the vote begins, the legislator should request permission from his or her house to be excused from voting, briefly stating the reasons why. No debate is permitted on the request, and the body decides whether to excuse the legislator from voting.[64]

In 1968, the General Assembly enacted a Code of Ethics for Government Service as a guide for all state officials and employees.[65] According to this code, any person in government service should do as follows:

1. Put loyalty to the highest moral principles and to country above loyalty to persons, party, or government department.
2. Uphold the constitution, laws, and legal regulations of the United States and the state of Georgia and of all governments therein and never be a party to their evasion.
3. Give a full day's labor for a full day's pay and give to the performance of his duties his earnest effort and best thought.
4. Seek to find and employ more efficient and economical ways of getting tasks accomplished.
5. Never discriminate unfairly by the dispensing of special favors or privileges to anyone, whether for remuneration or not, and never accept, for himself or his family, favors or benefits under circumstances which might be construed by reasonable persons as influencing the performance of his governmental duties.
6. Make no private promises of any kind binding upon the duties of office, since a government employee has no private word which can be binding on public duty.
7. Engage in no business with the government, either directly or indirectly, which is inconsistent with the conscientious performance of his governmental duties.
8. Never use any information coming to him confidentially in the performance of governmental duties as a means for making private profit.
9. Expose corruption wherever discovered.
10. Uphold these principles, ever conscious that public office is a public trust.

Because the code is couched in terms of "should"—rather than legally enforceable "shall" or "shall not"—and because there are no legal penalties attached for violation, enforcement of the code is presumably left to the conscience of each individual. However, with the passage of the Recall Act of 1989, the willful violation of the Code of Ethics by an elected official now constitutes "misconduct in office" and is grounds for that official being recalled from office.[66]

Conflict of interest is clearer with regard to legislators' financial dealings with the state. Except for situations exempted by statute, legislators may not transact any business with any state agency for themselves or on behalf of any business. Likewise prohibited are financial transactions with state agencies by any business in which a legislator or family member has direct or indirect ownership of more than 25 percent in assets or stock. Among exceptions to this general rule are (1) transactions made according to sealed competitive bids, (2) single transactions not exceeding $250 (providing that $9,000 is not exceeded during the total per calendar year), (3) lease of real property to or from any agency if the transaction has been approved by the State Properties Commission or Space Management Division of the Department of Administrative Services, (4) transactions involving property or a service in which the legislator is the only party in Georgia, and (5) emergency purchases.[67]

A legislator is also prohibited from advocating for or causing the advancement, appointment, employment, promotion, or transfer of a member of his or her family to an office or position as a public employee that pays an annual salary of $10,000 or more or something of equal or greater value.[68]

In 1982 the Georgia Supreme Court ruled that as trustees of the people, legislators are prohibited from representing a client for financial gain in any civil transaction or matter in which the state or one of its agencies is an opposing party.[69] However, this ruling was overturned in 2001 in a case that involved a state senator and the Georgia Ports Authority. As a result, state legislators are not automatically disqualified under the conflict-of-interest principles from accepting fees to represent clients in civil cases against the state.[70]

Joint Legislative Ethics Committee. To address the many unsettled issues relating to conflict of interest, the General Assembly in 2005 created the Joint Legislative Ethics Committee.[71] This committee consists of four senators appointed by the president pro tempore and four representatives appointed by the speaker. In each case, half of the members from each house are from the majority party and half are from the minority party. Additionally, serving as nonvoting members are the president pro tempore and speaker, with the president pro tempore chairing the committee in odd-numbered years and the speaker in even-numbered years.

The committee is responsible for advising the General Assembly in establishing rules and regulations relating to conflict of interest for members of the legislative branch. Additionally, it is empowered to investigate written complaints charging a violation of these rules, or it may conduct an investigation on its own initiative.

The committee is directed to report violations of state law to the appropriate law enforcement authority. It also can investigate any written complaint against illegal involvement of state employees in political campaigns.

Upon written request, the committee can issue written advisory opinions based on a real or hypothetical set of circumstances.

For violations of law or regulations by employees of the legislative branch other than members of the General Assembly, the committee can order the violator to cease from further violations and may issue employment-related sanctions against the employee, including but not limited to reprimand, suspension, demotion, and termination. With respect to violations by members of the General Assembly, the committee can make recommendations to the respective house as to the type of punishment to be imposed.

To assist in its functions, the committee can hire an executive director and additional staff.

Senate ethics standards. In addition to state statutes, Georgia's Senate has adopted rules that prescribe and govern enforcement of ethical standards for members and employees of the Senate.[72] These standards are as follows:

- Senators and staff must refrain from using government positions to attain financial gain.
- Senators and staff must not use public resources or personnel for the purpose of conducting personal or private business. However, while serving in their public capacities, ordinary and necessary communications with their homes and business interests are permitted.
- Senators must not seek, accept, use, allocate, grant, or award public funds for any purpose other than that approved by law.
- Senators may not vote on any question if the senator or any family member has a direct pecuniary interest in the outcome

of the vote that is distinct or unique to the senator or his or her family.

- No senator or staff member may solicit a campaign contribution in a state office building or conduct political campaigns or fund-raising campaigns from state office buildings unless such space has been leased or rented for this purpose.

- Senators may not withhold, or threaten to withhold, political action or constituent services because of a person's decision to provide or not to provide a political contribution, charitable contribution, or support.

- Senators and staff must avoid financial conflicts of interest and close economic associations involving official action or decisions that are motivated not by public duty but by self-interest.

- No senator or staff member may seek, accept, or retain employment that makes it unreasonably difficult to fulfill legislative obligations or that requires the disclosure or use of nonpublic or confidential information acquired in the course of legislative service, improper use of government relationships or the prestige associated with legislative office, or compromise for any other ethical or legal duty.

- No senator or staff member acting as an attorney or representative of another may seek or accept any special treatment because of his or her legislative role not otherwise approved by law or court order.

- No senator or staff member may accept anything of value when the offer is conditioned on taking or withholding official action. Any offer must immediately be reported in writing to the chair of the Ethics Committee.

- No senator or staff member may knowingly commit any crime involving moral turpitude or knowingly possess, use, manufacture, or distribute any controlled substance, dangerous drug, marijuana, or alcoholic beverage in violation of state or federal law or municipal ordinance. Conviction of any such crime, acceptance of a plea of guilty or nolo contendere to any such crime, or mandated payment of a criminal or administrative penalty for any such crime constitutes a violation of this rule.

- Senators and staff are expected to discourage sexual harassment in the workplace and at events, professional meetings, seminars, or any activities that involve legislative business. Sexual harassment includes all conduct prohibited by federal and state law as well as verbal abuse of a sexual nature, graphic verbal comments about a person's body, physical touching of a sexual nature, sexual advances and propositions, sexually degrading words used to describe an individual, workplace display of any sexually suggestive object or picture, and any threat or insinuation, whether explicit or implicit, that an individual's refusal to submit to a sexual advance will adversely affect that person's employment evaluation, wages, duties, work shifts, or any other condition of employment or advancement. These rules apply to and complaints may be brought against senators, senate staff, senate aides, interns, and volunteers. Sanctions are proportionate to the seriousness of the offense, and any supervisor who does not take appropriate action when he or she knows or has reason to suspect harassment is also subject to sanctions.

- The Senate is committed to providing a work environment free from discriminatory harassment and intimidation of any kind, including harassment or discrimination based on race, color, religion, national origin, age, veteran status, disability, or gender. Discriminatory harassment includes any verbal or other conduct that disparages any individual or group and that creates an offensive, intimidating, or hostile work environment. Prohibited discriminatory harassment includes any form of pictures, cartoons, teasing, jokes, e-mail, epithets, slurs, negative stereotyping, name-calling, offensive gestures, or threatening, intimidating, or hostile acts. These rules apply to and complaints may be brought against senators, senate staff, senate aides, interns, and volunteers. Sanctions are proportionate to the seriousness of the offense, and any supervisor who does not take appropriate action when he or she knows or has reason to suspect harassment is also subject to sanctions.

- All contact with constituents, staff, lobbyists, representatives of the media, and others interested or involved in the process of government will be conducted in a courteous, professional, and discreet manner.

- No senator or staff member may knowingly circumvent the clear purpose or intent of these rules outlining standards of conduct.

- A senator or staff member may request in writing the opinion or advice of the Committee on Ethics regarding the interpretation of any section of the Senate's ethics rules. The Committee on Ethics must respond in writing in an expeditious manner. All requests as well as responses are confidential.

Complaints alleging violations of these rules are to be filed with the secretary of the Senate or if the person is supervised by the secretary of the Senate, with the president pro tempore. A complaint may be brought by senators, Senate staff, aides, interns, or volunteers. The complaint must specifically describe the alleged violation and name the party or parties involved. Further, it must be signed by the complainant and verified under oath. The secretary of the Senate or the president pro tempore will promptly refer the complaint to the chair of the Senate Ethics Committee, who schedules a meeting of the committee to investigate the complaint, assigning in-house staff and counsel and investigators as necessary. If the Ethics Committee chair is the subject of the complaint, then the chair must recuse himself or herself, and the investigation will be overseen by the vice-chair of the committee. The committee must promptly serve the named respondent with a copy of the complaint either personally or by certified mail, return receipt requested.

The Committee on Ethics may also initiate its own investigation by majority vote. Following such an initiation, a majority of the committee must sign within a reasonable period of time a complaint specifically describing the nature of the alleged violation and the party or parties involved. The named respondent must be promptly served the complaint either personally or by certified mail, return receipt requested.

Any complaint brought by or before the committee must remain confidential until the committee has determined that substantial cause exists to believe that a violation has occurred. If the committee determines that substantial cause does not exist, the complaint remains confidential.

Upon completion of an investigation, the investigators must detail their findings in a written report and present the report to the committee. If there is insufficient evidence of a violation, the complaint can be dismissed, with notice given to the complaining party and respondent. If the committee finds that a violation has occurred, it may attempt to negotiate a settlement with the respondent or set the matter for a hearing.

Any settlement reached is a matter of public record and is filed with the secretary of the Senate. If no settlement is reached, the committee is required to hold an open hearing, at which attendance of witnesses and the production of materials can be required. The respondent is entitled to receive reasonable notice of the hearing and copies of all materials not exempt from disclosure under the Georgia Open Records Law. The senator or staff member being investigated has the right to counsel of his or her own choosing and the right to call witnesses and present evidence. The respondent may also examine witnesses who are called by the committee. The committee must record all hearings. The committee and the respondent are entitled to rebuttal. When the hearing is finished, the committee must issue a report of its findings and recommendations to be filed with the secretary of the Senate.

The burden of proof is on the committee, which must find "clear and convincing evidence" in order to conclude that a violation of these rules has occurred. If a senator is in violation of the ethics rules, the committee may recommend a sanction or penalty, including a letter of reprimand to the Senate. The Senate can independently initiate action against a senator pursuant to the Georgia Constitution. If the committee finds that a Senate staff member, aide, intern, or volunteer is in violation of the rules, it may recommend a sanction or penalty up to and including dismissal to the Committee on Administrative Affairs. The Administrative Affairs Committee has the authority to take any action on the Ethics Committee's recommendation.

No person who reports alleged violations to the Ethics Committee can be subjected to any reprisal, retaliation, harassment, discrimination, or ridicule by senators or staff.

House ethics standards. The House of Representatives has a similar set of rules that prescribe and govern enforcement of ethical standards for its members and employees.[73] These rules are as follows:

- No House member or employee may unlawfully use his or her office or official position for personal financial gain. However, while serving in an official capacity, members or employees are not prevented from engaging in business or professional pursuits or necessary business or professional communications.
- No House member or employee is entitled to compensation for official duties beyond the pay and allowances attached to that office or as may otherwise be provided by law.
- No House member or employee may use state funds, facilities, equipment, services, or other state resources for nonlegislative purposes, the private benefit of any person, or the solicitation of campaign funds. This rule does not prohibit limited use of public resources for personal purposes if the use does not interfere with the member's performance of public duties and the

cost or value is nominal. The use of mailing lists, computer data, or other information lawfully obtained from public resources and available to the general public is not prohibited. The use of telephone, fax, or other communications that is necessary in order for the member to conduct ordinary business is permitted. The use of the individual House member's office for nonlegislative purposes is permitted if it does not interfere with the performance of public duties and no cost is incurred to the state. In addition, the storing and maintenance of campaign finance and election records in a legislative office, participation in normal and customary caucus activities, and any other use not inconsistent with public service is permitted.

- House members and employees cannot seek, accept, use, allocate, grant, or award public funds for a purpose other than approved by law or make any false statements in regard to public funds.

- No House member or employee can directly or indirectly perform or withhold any official action or constituent service as a result of a person's decision to provide or not provide a political contribution.

- No House member or employee can improperly retaliate against any state employee or other person for reporting to an authority any conduct believed to be unlawful or improper.

- Unwelcome sexual advances, requests for sexual favors, and other verbal or physical conduct of a sexual nature constitutes sexual harassment when (a) submission to such conduct is made (explicitly or implicitly) a term or condition of an individual's employment, (b) submission to or rejection of such conduct by an individual is used as a basis for employment decisions affecting an individual, or (c) such conduct interferes with an individual's work performance or creates an intimidating, hostile, or offensive work environment.

- House members and staff may not knowingly violate any rule of the House, including without limitation the provisions of these rules relating to confidentiality of proceedings of the committee on ethics.

- No House member or employee can remain in office if he or she commits a felony or crime involving moral turpitude related to his or her position as a public officer or employee.

Any House member or employee can file a written complaint alleging violations of these rules. The complaint is presented to the chair of the House Ethics Committee, unless the chair is involved in the complaint. In that instance, House rules detail how a replacement committee member is chosen. The complaint remains confidential unless otherwise requested by the subject of the complaint or otherwise provided for in the rules. A subcommittee made up of the majority and minority leaders and whips conducts a preliminary inquiry. The subcommittee considers all complaints and determines by majority vote if there is substantial evidence to proceed. If not, the determination of the subcommittee is the final disposition of the complaint.

The Committee on Ethics is empowered to investigate the complaint, hold hearings, and compel the attendance of witnesses and production of documents relevant to the investigation. Any House member or employee being investigated has the right to full notice of the alleged charges, the right to counsel, the right to cross-examine committee witnesses, the right to present witnesses and evidence, and the same rights as the committee to call witnesses and present evidence.

Should the committee conclude that a violation of House ethics standards has occurred and that disciplinary action is warranted, it is directed to report these findings to the speaker of the House, clerk of the House, Legislative Services Committee, or any other officer or agency of the General Assembly. Should the Ethics Committee find strong evidence that a House member or employee has committed a criminal violation, such evidence is to be reported to the appropriate law enforcement agency.

The Ethics Committee can among other things issue advisory opinions that address questions of ethical and proper conduct by House members and employees. The committee is authorized to determine on a case-by-case basis which of its meetings will be open to the public. Such determinations are made on the basis of balancing the need for openness in government with the need to preserve confidential sources and protect the privacy rights of witnesses. The Ethics Committee is also empowered to educate House members with respect to proper and ethical conduct by providing for the annual compilation, publication, and distribution of a manual containing provisions of rules and laws relevant to ethical conduct of members. House rules provide that all newly elected members of the House who have not previously served in that body complete a course of training related to proper and ethical conduct of members. The Committee on Ethics is to cooperate with the Georgia General Assembly Training Institute and Carl Vinson Institute of Government at the University of Georgia to make such training available. The course may be completed at the Biennial Institute for Legislators following the November general election or by other appropriate means. However, a member will not be prevented from serving if he or she does not take ethics training.[74]

REGULATION OF LOBBYING

Prior to 1983, Georgia's constitution declared "lobbying" to be a crime, a prohibition dating back to 1877. However, the constitution left it to the discretion of the General Assembly to define lobbying by statute and provide for its penalties. Because lobbying was entirely regulated by statute, framers of the Constitution of 1983 deleted reference to lobbying from the new constitution.

Until 1992, Georgia statutes continued to declare lobbying to be a crime but defined it in terms of attempting to influence a legislator's vote by means "not addressed solely to the judgment" (e.g., bribery or coercion). State law required anyone who attempted to influence the legislative process to register with the secretary of state and pay a $5 annual fee. Legally, the lobbyist was then known as a "registered agent."

In passing the Public Officials Conduct and Lobbyist Disclosure Act of 1992, the General Assembly acknowledged that lobbying was not a crime in Georgia. The law made important changes in the definition of lobbying and instituted new registration and disclosure procedures for lobbyists.[75]

Georgia law now defines lobbying as any effort by anyone (including members of the executive and judicial branches) to promote or oppose passage of legislation in the General Assembly (including committees) or the approval or veto of legislation by the governor if (1) such effort is conducted for compensation (either individually or as an employee of someone else) or (2) more than $250 is spent on lobbying activities in a calendar year (not including the cost of that person's own travel, food, lodging, or informational material).[76]

On the issue of compensation, Georgia's attorney general has ruled in an unofficial opinion that it is not necessary that a person be employed for compensation solely for the purpose of lobbying in order to be subject to the requirements for registration: "As long

Lobbyists follow floor proceedings and wait to speak with legislators on the third floor of the Capitol near the entrance to the House and Senate chambers.

as an individual is compensated to represent the general business or purpose of a corporation, association, or agency, and that individual contacts a member of the General Assembly for the purpose of promoting or opposing the passage of legislation on behalf of such group, then that individual must register as a lobbyist and comply with the provision of Article 4 of O.C.G.A. Chapter 21-5."[77] At issue in the opinion was whether compensated officers of unions and business organizations who attempt to influence legislation on behalf of their organization come under the lobbyist registration requirements, which the opinion held that they did.

The State Ethics Commission has given some guidance on determining whether someone who as "an employee of another person" is lobbying "for compensation" and thus is subject to the registration requirements. Foremost, there must be a connection between the promoting or opposing of legislation and the job for which the employee is paid. In making that determination, the following are among the factors that should be considered:

- the nature and extent of the activity (For example, is the activity a pure "appeal to reason" through a letter or telephone conversation discussing the merits of legislation? Is it the cultivation of goodwill through some social event or through some other form of payment designed to encourage or influence? Is it a gift of anything of value?);
- whether the subject matter of the legislation would affect the business of the employer;
- whether the lobbying effort is known to the employer;
- whether the employer has a policy as to who is and is not authorized to lobby on behalf of the employer;
- whether the lobbying effort is approved by the employer;
- whether the lobbying effort is encouraged by the employer;
- whether the lobbying effort is directed by the employer;
- whether the lobbying effort is undertaken during hours for which the employee is being paid;
- whether the employee routinely, or when needed, handles lobbying or "governmental relations" functions for the employer;
- whether any equipment, property, or facilities of the employer are used in the lobbying effort;
- whether the employer reimburses or pays directly any expenses incurred by the employee during the lobbying effort;

- whether the parties had some previous relationship outside the lobbying context;
- how the contact or activity was initiated;
- the ability of the individual by virtue of his or her position or other factors to influence a legislative decision;
- the number of times of contact or activity; and
- the number of persons contacted or involved in an activity.[78]

The following types of expenditures do count against the $250 threshold for nonpaid lobbyists:

- any purchase, payment, distribution, load, advance, deposit, or conveyance of money or anything of value made for the purpose of influencing the actions of any public officer or employee;
- any form of payment that can be reasonably construed as designed to encourage or influence a public officer;
- any gratuitous transfer, payment, subscription, advance, or deposit of money, services, or anything of value, unless something of equal or greater value is received; and
- food or beverage consumed at a single meal or event by a public officer or employee or a member of the immediate family of such public officer or employee.[79]

Not counted against the $250 threshold are

- the value of personal services performed voluntarily and without compensation;
- gifts received from a member of a public officer's family;
- legal compensation or expense reimbursement provided to public officers and employees in the performance of their duties;
- promotional items generally distributed to the public or public officers;
- foods and beverages produced in Georgia;
- awards, plaques, certificates, mementos, or similar items given in recognition of the recipient's record of service;
- legitimate salary, benefits, fees, commissions, or expenses associated with a recipient's nonpublic business, employment, trade, or profession;
- food, beverages, and registration at group events to which all members of a state or local agency (including the House, Senate, and the committees and subcommittees of either house) have been invited;

- campaign contributions or expenditures that must be reported as required by O.C.G.A. Article 2 of Chapter 5 of Title 2;
- commercially reasonable loans made in the ordinary course of business; or
- food, beverage, or expenses given to public officers, members of their immediate families, or others who are associated with normal and customary business or social functions or activities.[80]

Registration of lobbyists. No person may engage in lobbying as defined by law unless he or she is first registered with the State Ethics Commission. All lobbyists must register annually, at which time they must provide information about themselves and the person, firm, association, or agency they represent.[81]

Once registered, the lobbyist receives an identification badge with the word "LOBBYIST" and the name of the lobbyist and a color photograph. If the lobbyist represents a single client, the name of that client is also listed on the badge. In the case of multiple clients, client names are omitted. Lobbyists must display their identification badges in a readily visible manner whenever they are lobbying in the state capitol or any governmental facility.[82]

Exemption from registration requirements. State law exempts the following persons from having to register as lobbyists:

- any individual who on his or her own behalf expresses personal views to any public official;
- any person not otherwise required to register as a lobbyist who appears before a government agency, committee, or hearing to testify;
- any public employee who appears before a government agency or committee at that entity's request;
- any licensed attorney appearing on behalf of a client in any adversarial proceeding before a state agency;
- any person employed or appointed by a registered lobbyist whose duties and activities do not include lobbying;
- elected public officials performing their official duties; and
- any public employee who performs services at the discretion of a member of the General Assembly, including such services as bill drafting, taking testimony, collecting facts, preparing arguments and submitting them to legislative committees or other legislators, and "other services of like character intended to reach the reason of legislators."[83]

Lobbyist disclosure reports. Each registered lobbyist must file a disclosure report current through the end of the preceding month on or before the fifth day of any month in which the General Assembly is in session. A disclosure report current through the end of the six-month period ending July 31 must be filed by August 5, and a similar report for the six-month period ending December 31 must be filed by the following January 5.[84]

Disclosure reports must include a description of all expenditures made by a lobbyist or his or her employees, including the name and title of the public officer to whom the expenditure was made; the amount, date, and description of the expenditure; and, if applicable, the number of the bill or resolution for which the lobbying expenditure was made.[85]

Other regulations. No person, firm, corporation, or association may retain or employ an attorney-at-law or an agent to aid or oppose legislation for compensation that is contingent in whole or in part upon the passage of any legislative measure.[86]

State law prohibits any registered lobbyist or any other unauthorized person, except as authorized by the rules of the House or Senate, from entering the chamber of either house of the General Assembly while it is in session to discuss privately measures that are pending in the legislature.[87]

Lobbyists and the legislative process. Many states have what is termed a "professional legislature," which is characterized by long sessions and provision of aides for each legislator and professional staffing for each committee. In contrast, Georgia's General Assembly historically has functioned more as a "citizen legislature," with brief sessions, few aides and committee staff, and extremely limited office space. Over the last two decades (particularly since the acquisition of the Coverdell Legislative Office Building in the 1980s), these forms have been changing. Each house now has a small research office and public information office, and the two houses share 30 college interns during the session. But except for those who work in the research and public information offices, Office of Legislative Counsel, House and Senate Budget Offices, and Budgetary Responsibility Oversight Committee, most legislators and committees still must function without aides or professional staff.

Given the fact that the General Assembly may consider 3,000 or more bills and resolutions in a single session, many Georgia legislators have come to depend on lobbyists for information on potential legislation. Although the General Assembly has taken strides to improve legislative staffing, the number of registered lobbyists has grown steadily, from 280 in 1971, to 917 by 1994, to 1,437 in 2006.[88]

Ambiguities in what is allowed. Georgia law provides some clear answers about what types of expenditures lobbyists can make in attempting to influence legislation. But there are many gray areas regarding what a lobbyist can offer and what a legislator can accept.

Unfortunately for both lobbyist and legislator alike, there is no comprehensive compilation of do's and don'ts covering every possible situation that might arise. State law does not specify exactly what is and is not permissible because much depends on the total circumstances of the offer or acceptance.

As a final caution, even if the acceptance of a gift or expenditure proves to be entirely legal, legislators should remember that state law requires the lobbyist to report the offer to the State Ethics Commission, at which time it becomes a matter of public record available to the press and political opponents. Officials must keep in mind that there may be both legal and political ramifications when a legislator accepts a gift.

FINANCIAL REGULATIONS

Campaign contribution requirements. Contributions to any candidate seeking office in the General Assembly must be made directly to the candidate or to the candidate's campaign committee. Every campaign committee must have a chair and a treasurer, although the candidate may serve both roles.[89]

Before the candidate or campaign committee can accept any contributions, the name and address of the chair and treasurer must be filed with the State Ethics Commission. No contributions may be accepted if there is a vacancy in either office. Once a legislator is elected to the General Assembly, his or her campaign committee does not have to be re-registered unless the legislator creates a new committee.[90]

Contributions of money for use in a campaign for election or reelection must be deposited in a separate account opened and maintained by the candidate or campaign committee. The account may earn interest, but that interest can only be used for campaign purposes.[91]

Should separate contributions of less than $101 be received from a common source (such as the legislator's family, firm, partnership, or employees), those contributions are to be aggregated for reporting purposes. Excluded from this requirement is the purchase of tickets for a fundraising event that do not exceed $25 each.[92]

Acceptance of anonymous contributions is prohibited, and a candidate is required to turn those monies over to the Office of Treasury and Fiscal Services and to report the contribution to the State Ethics Commission.[93] Candidates and campaign committees cannot accept any direct or indirect campaign contribution from any state or local government agency.[94]

Each candidate or campaign committee treasurer must keep detailed accounts, current within not more than five business days after receipt of a contribution or making an expenditure, of all contributions received and all expenditures made. Also required are detailed accounts of all deposits and withdrawals made to the separate campaign depository and interest earned on the deposits. Such records must be kept for three years after the race.[95]

Funds from a campaign account may only be used for ordinary and necessary expenses associated with a campaign for election or reelection, which may include any loan from a candidate to the campaign committee or any expenses incurred in connection with fulfillment or retention of elected public office. Any monies left over in the account after the election may only be used to donate to charitable organizations or to any committee of any political party or candidate, to reimburse donors up to the amount of their contributions, or to repay any prior campaign obligations incurred by the candidate. Additionally, any unspent funds may be used in future campaigns but only for the elective office for which they were originally given.[96] Thus, a legislator campaigning for reelection could use unspent funds collected in a previous race for the legislature but could not spend them in a campaign for any other office. In other words, a member of one house of the General Assembly would be prohibited from using leftover funds from a previous race in a future race for a seat in the other house.

Any candidate for a seat in the General Assembly or officer of his or her campaign committee must file with the State Ethics Commission a contribution disclosure report (along with a copy to the election superintendent of the county in which the candidate resides) listing

- the amount of the contribution and date of receipt, along with the name, mailing address, occupation, and employer of any person making a contribution of $101 or more;
- a list of separate contributions of less than $101 (but identification of the donor would be required should additional contributions push the total to $101 or more);

- the name, mailing address, occupation, and place of employment of any person to whom a contribution of $101 or more is made, including the amount and general purpose of the expenditure;
- name of the lending institution or party if the contribution consists of a loan, advance, or other extension of credit; the names, mailing addresses, occupations, and places of employment of all persons having any liability for repayment of such contribution; and the fiduciary relationship (if any) of the person making the contribution to the lending institution or party advancing or extending credit; and
- the corporate, labor union, or other affiliation of any political action committee making a contribution of $101 or more.

The campaign contributions report must be filed

- in each nonelection year, on June 30 and December 31.
- in each year a candidate qualifies to run
  - on March 31, June 30, September 30, October 25, and December 31;
  - six days before any runoff primary or election in which the candidate is listed on the ballot; and
  - between the date of the last report due prior to the statewide primary or the statewide election and the primary and the election (all contributions of $1,000 or more must be reported within two business days of receipt).
- 15 days prior to the special primary and 6 days prior to the special primary runoff.
- 15 days prior to a special election and 6 days prior to a special election runoff.

Only the initial and final reports must be filed if a candidate has no opposition in either a primary or general election and receives no contribution of $101 or more.[97]

Candidates seeking election to the General Assembly must use electronic means to file their campaign contribution disclosure reports with the State Ethics Commission upon having raised or spent $10,000 in an election cycle. If this threshold is not met, electronic filing is permitted and encouraged but not required.[98]

Contributions prohibited during legislative session. No member of the General Assembly or that member's campaign committee is allowed to seek or accept any contribution during a legislative session. This restriction, however, does not apply to the receipt of a contribution by a political party from the proceeds from a dinner, luncheon, rally, or similar fundraising event in which a member of the General Assembly participates.[99]

Financial disclosure statements. Between January 1 and July 1 of each odd-numbered year, each member of the General Assembly is required to file with the State Ethics Commission a financial disclosure statement for the preceding calendar year that identifies

(1) Each monetary fee or honorarium which is accepted by a public officer from speaking engagements, participation in seminars, discussion panels, or other activities which directly relate to the official duties of the public officer or the office of the public officer, with a statement identifying the fee or honorarium accepted and the person from whom it was accepted;

(2) All fiduciary positions held by the candidate for public office or the public officer, with a statement of the title of each such position, the name and address of the business entity, and the principal activity of the business entity;

(3) The name, address, and principal activity of any business entity and the office held by and the duties of the candidate for public office or public officer within such business entity as of December 31 of the covered year in which such candidate or officer has a direct ownership interest which interest:

(A) Is more than 5 percent of the total interests in such business; or

(B) Has a net fair market value of more than $10,000.00;

(4)(A) Each tract of real property in which the candidate for public office or public officer has a direct ownership interest as of December 31 of the covered year when that interest has a fair market value in excess of $10,000.00. As used in this paragraph, the term "fair market" value means the appraised value of the property for ad valorem tax purposes. The disclosure shall contain the county and state, general description of the property, and whether the fair market value is between (i) $10,000.00 and $100,000.00; (ii) $100,000.01 and $200,000.00; or (iii) more than $200,000.00;

(B) Each tract of real property in which the candidate for public office's spouse or public officer's spouse has a direct ownership interest as of December 31 of the covered year when that interest has a fair market value in excess of $10,000.00. The disclosure shall contain the county and state, general description of the property, and whether the fair market value is between (i) $10,000.00 and $100,000.00; (ii) $100,000.01 to $200,000.00; (iii) or more than $200,000.00;

(5) The filer's occupation, employer, and the principal activity and address of such employer;

(6) The filer's spouse's name, occupation, employer, and the principal activity and address of such employer;

(7) The names of the filer's dependent children;

(8) The name of any business or subsidiary thereof or investment, exclusive of the individual stocks and bonds in mutual funds, in which the filer, jointly or severally, owns a direct ownership interest which interest:

(A) Is more than 5 percent of the total interests in such business or investment, exclusive of the individual stocks and bonds in mutual funds; or

(B) Has a net fair market value of more than $10,000.00;

(9) If the filer has actual knowledge of such ownership interest, the name of any business or subsidiary thereof or investment, exclusive of the individual stocks and bonds in mutual funds, in which the filer's spouse or dependent children, jointly or severally, own a direct ownership interest which interest:

(A) Is more than 5 percent of the total interests in such business or investment, exclusive of the individual stocks and bonds in mutual funds; or

(B) Has a net fair market value of more than $10,000.00

or in which the filer's spouse or any dependent child serves as an officer, director, equitable partner, or trustee;

(10) All annual payments in excess of $20,000.00 received by the public officer or any business entity identified in paragraph (3) of this subsection from the state, any agency, department, commission, or authority created by the state, and authorized and exempted from disclosure under Code Section 45-10-25, and the agency, department, commission, or authority making the payments, and the general nature of the consideration rendered for the source of the payments.[100]

SUSPENSION AND REMOVAL FROM OFFICE

In addition to being subject to censure, fine, imprisonment, expulsion, and impeachment, legislators may be suspended under certain circumstances. By virtue of constitutional amendments in 1984 and 1986, lawmakers and other state officials face suspension if indicted for certain offenses.

If a legislator is indicted for a felony by a state or federal grand jury, the indictment is reviewed by a special committee consisting of the attorney general and one member from each house. (If the attorney general has prosecuted the indictment, the governor names a retired supreme court justice or court of appeals judge to sit on the committee instead.) The committee has 14 days to conduct its investigation and hold a hearing. If it determines that the indictment relates to and adversely affects the legislator's duties and that the interests of the public are adversely affected, it informs the governor, who may immediately suspend the legislator (with pay). If the suspended lawmaker is subsequently convicted in a trial court, the pay is stopped. If the conviction is overturned on appeal, the suspension is lifted and the withheld pay returned. If the decision is not overturned or if no appeal is filed, the office is declared vacant immediately.[101]

RECALL

State legislators (as well as every other public official who holds elected office in Georgia) are subject to recall from office by the registered voters of their respective districts.[102] There are statutory grounds for recall if, while in office, an elected official

1. has conducted himself or herself in a manner that relates to and adversely affects the administration of that office and the rights and interests of the public,
2. has committed one or more acts of malfeasance,
3. has violated his or her oath of office,
4. has committed an act of misconduct (defined by statute as an unlawful act committed willfully by an elected public official or a willful violation of the Code of Ethics for government service contained in O.C.G.A. §45-10-1),
5. is guilty of a failure to perform duties prescribed by law, or
6. has willfully misused, converted, or misappropriated, without authority, public property or public funds entrusted to or associated with the elective office. (However, discretionary performance of a lawful act or a prescribed duty shall not constitute grounds for recall).[103]

In order for a state legislator to be recalled, a petition must first be filed identifying the official sponsors and chair of the recall drive and the specific statutory grounds for the legislator's recall. The petition must be signed by at least 30 percent of the number of registered voters in the legislator's district at the last general election. No petition may be filed during the first 180 days or the last 180 days of a legislator's term of office.[104]

If these conditions are met, the legislator can ask a superior court judge to review the legal sufficiency of the recall grounds and the alleged facts upon which such grounds are based. If the judge rules that the grounds and facts are sufficient, the recall proceedings can continue.[105]

Within 10 days of receiving a certification of sufficiency, the governor must call a recall election to be held not less than 30 or more than 45 days after the call. At that election, if more than 50 percent of the votes cast are in favor of recall, the legislator's office is immediately declared vacant, and a special election to fill the office is called within 10 days. The date of such election is to be at least 30 days and not more than 45 days from the date of vacancy. The legislator who was recalled is eligible to run in that election.[106]

NOTES

1. Ga. Const. art. 3, §4, ¶9.
2. Ibid.
3. Official Code of Georgia Annotated (O.C.G.A.) §§9-10-159, 17-8-28, 15-12-2.
4. O.C.G.A. §§9-10-159, 17-8-28.
5. O.C.G.A. §§9-10-150, 17-8-28.
6. Senate Rule 8-1.13; House Rule 40.3.
7. Senate Rule 8-1.7(c).
8. House Rule 40.1.
9. Senate Rule 8-1.12.
10. House Rule 30.
11. Ga. Const. art. 3, §4, ¶7.
12. O.C.G.A. §21-4-3(8).
13. Ga. Const. art. 3, §4, ¶7.
14. House Rule 1.10.
15. Senate Rules 8-1.4 and 9-1.2.
16. House Rule 8-1.1.
17. Senate Rule 1-1.6.
18. House Rule 4.
19. House Rule 19.
20. Senate Rule 9-1.16; House Rule 82.
21. Senate Rule 8-1.3; House Rule 84.

22. Senate Rule 8-1.5(b).
23. House Rule 86.
24. House Rule 79.
25. Senate Rule 8-1.1.
26. Senate Rule 8-1.5; House Rule 85.
27. House Rule 1.1 and 1.2.
28. Senate Rule 8-1.12.
29. House Rules 45 and 46.
30. Senate Rules 5-1.2 and 5-1.10.
31. Senate Rule 5-1.10; House Rule 46.
32. Senate Rule 9-1.2; House Rule 1.1.
33. Senate Rules 9-1.2 and 9-1.14; House Rules 1-4, 1-7, and 1-8, 19.
34. House Rule 1.4.
35. House Rule 1.10.
36. Senate Rule 9-1.14.
37. Ibid.
38. Ibid.
39. House Rule 1.8.
40. House Rule 7.10.
41. Senate Rule 5-1.8; House Rule 136.
42. House Rule 138.1.
43. House Rule 135.
44. Senate Rule 5-1.8; GA. CONST. art. 3, §4, ¶7 provides for punishment for disorderly behavior and misconduct.
45. Senate Rule 5-1.10; House Rule 131.
46. Senate Rule 5-1.8(c); House Rule 133.
47. House Rule 171.7.
48. Senate Rule 10-1.1.
49. GA. CONST. art. 3, §4, ¶7.
50. O.C.G.A. §16-10-2.
51. Ibid.
52. Ibid.
53. O.C.G.A. §16-10-4.
54. O.C.G.A. §16-10-5.
55. O.C.G.A. §45-11-5.
56. O.C.G.A. §16-10-21.
57. O.C.G.A. §16-10-1.
58. O.C.G.A. §16-10-22.
59. O.C.G.A. §28-1-8.
60. O.C.G.A. §28-5-62.
61. O.C.G.A. §21-5-11.
62. GA. CONST. art. 1, §2, ¶1.
63. Senate Rule 5-1.8; House Rule 133.
64. Senate Rule 1-2.2; House Rule 133.
65. O.C.G.A. §45-10-1.
66. O.C.G.A. §21-4-3(8).

67. O.C.G.A. §§45-10-20(11), 45-10-24, 45-10-25; 1983 Ops. Att'y Gen. U83-48 and U83-63.

68. O.C.G.A. §45-10-80.

69. Ga. Dept. of Human Resources v. Sistrunk, 249 Ga. 543, 291, S.E.2d 524 (1982).

70. Georgia Ports Authority v. Harris, 274 Ga. 146, 549 S.E.2d 95 (2001).

71. O.C.G.A. §§45-10-90 through 45-10-94.

72. Senate Rules Section 1, Part 4.

73. House Rules 164 through 173.

74. House Rule 172.2.

75. O.C.G.A. §§21-5-70 through 21-5-73.

76. O.C.G.A. §21-5-70 (7). "Lobbying" is also defined to include attempts to influence the passage of ordinances and resolutions by local governments or the approval or veto of such measures (where applicable).

77. 1993 Op. Att'y Gen. U92-2.

78. *Information Concerning Lobbyist Registration and Reporting* (Atlanta: State Ethics Commission, 1993), pp. 3–4.

79. O.C.G.A. §21-5-70(1). In §21-5-70(1)(E)(x), the law includes a provision exempting "[f]ood, beverage, or expenses afforded public officers, members of their immediate families, or others that are associated with normal and customary business or social functions or activities" from the definition of "expenditure." However, this apparent exemption is overridden by §21-5-70(1)(D), which states, "Notwithstanding division (x) of subparagraph (E) of this paragraph, includes food or beverage consumed at a single meal or event by a public officer or public employee or a member of the immediate family of such public officer or public employee." The position of the State Ethics Commission is that food and beverage expenses do count when calculating whether a person qualifies as a lobbyist by virtue of having spent more than $250 in attempting to influence legislation. Also, by virtue of §21-5-73(e)(1)(C), food and beverage expenditures must be listed in the disclosure forms that lobbyists must file with the commission.

80. Ibid.

81. O.C.G.A. §21-5-71.

82. Ibid.

83. Ibid.

84. O.C.G.A. §21-5-73.

85. Ibid.

86. O.C.G.A. §28-7-3.

87. O.C.G.A. §28-7-4. Similarly, Senate Rule 9-1.5 and House Rule 7.9 prohibit any person engaged in lobbying or otherwise attempting to influence legislation from going on the floor of either house.

88. Figures compiled by the Office of Secretary of State and the State Ethics Commission.

89. O.C.G.A. §21-5-30(a).

90. O.C.G.A. §21-5-30(b).

91. O.C.G.A. §21-5-30(c).

92. O.C.G.A. §21-5-30(d).

93. O.C.G.A. §21-5-30(e).

94. O.C.G.A. §21-5-30.2(c).

95. O.C.G.A. §21-5-32.

96. O.C.G.A. §21-5-33.

97. O.C.G.A. §21-5-34.

98. O.C.G.A. §21-5-34.1.
99. O.C.G.A. §21-5-35.
100. O.C.G.A. §21-5-50.
101. Ga. Const. art. 2, §3, ¶1–2.
102. O.C.G.A. ch. 21-4.
103. O.C.G.A. §21-4-3.
104. O.C.G.A. §§21-4-4(a), 21-4-5(a).
105. O.C.G.A. §21-4-6.
106. O.C.G.A. §21-4-13.

CHAPTER 4

CONVENING AND ORGANIZING

SESSIONS OF THE GENERAL ASSEMBLY

Regular Sessions

Members of Georgia's House and Senate are elected in the November general election in even years for a two-year term of office that begins with their swearing in the following January and concludes two years later with the swearing in of a new House and Senate. Known as a *biennium*, the two-year life of each General Assembly begins and ends on the second Monday in January of odd-numbered years.

Regular sessions of the General Assembly are held annually. Legislative matters pending at the end of the first session of a biennium are carried over automatically to the second. Any business still pending at the end of the second session, however, dies.

Between 1963 and 1976, the constitution provided for a split session in each odd-numbered year, whereby the legislature convened in January for no longer than 12 days, during which time it organized, began consideration of legislation, and received the governor's proposed appropriations bill. Thereafter, the General Assembly adjourned for a "budget recess" to study the appropriations bill. On the second Monday in February, it reconvened in regular session for no more than 33 additional days, permitting sessions of 45 days in odd years. In even years, there was no provision for a budget recess, and the regular session was limited to 40 days.

This difference in session length traces to the practice of biennial appropriations acts that were adopted in odd-numbered years. Before a 1972 constitutional amendment formalized annual appropriations,

With 180 members, the Georgia House of
Representatives is the third-largest lower House
among the 50 state legislatures.

the General Assembly appropriated money by passing a biennial budget in odd years and amending that budget in even years. The 45-day split session, however, was not provided for in the Constitution of 1976, and now all sessions are the same length.

Session length. Georgia's constitution limits a regular session of the General Assembly to "40 days in the aggregate each year."[1] Compared with other states, Georgia has one of the shortest session lengths—particularly in view of the fact that many states have no mandated limit on session length.[2] But it is difficult to predict a session's actual length because regular sessions are measured by *legislative* days, which are synonymous with *calendar* days, unless both houses adopt a concurrent resolution to adjourn, in which case the count of legislative days is suspended during the recess. Since formal adjournments are common, annual sessions always exceed 40 calendar days, with final adjournment usually occurring between late March and early May. Although Georgia's constitution does not require the General Assembly to use all 40 days, it always has. There has been a single exception in modern Georgia history: in 2005, the General Assembly adjourned on the 39th day of the session.

Unless both houses formally adjourn, Saturdays and Sundays count in the 40-day limit for a session, regardless of whether the legislature is actually in session. Saturday sessions, although not common, do sometimes occur, while Sunday sessions rarely happen.

Adjournment by concurrent resolution. Georgia's constitution provides that the General Assembly may adjourn a regular session and set a time for reconvening by concurrent resolution.[3] The effect of formally adjourning by joint action of both houses is to suspend the count of session days during the period.

Early in a session, each house typically concludes legislative activity Friday afternoon and adjourns over the weekend by simple resolution, so Saturday and Sunday count as legislative days. As the workload escalates, however, both houses will adjourn, by a concurrent resolution, and stop the count of days over a weekend. Also, early in the session both houses will adjourn by joint resolution so that their respective appropriations committees can hold joint hearings on the governor's proposed budget.

Simple adjournment. At the conclusion of legislative activities or at any time during the day, either house may terminate or suspend proceedings through a motion to adjourn. A simple motion to adjourn—which is not debatable and takes precedence over all other motions in either house—terminates proceedings for that day, which

REPRESENTATIVE GOVERNMENT AT WORK

The position of Georgia's speaker of the House of Representatives traces to the office of speaker of the Commons House of Assembly, created in 1755. Georgia's colonial speaker, in turn, traces to 1377 when the position of speaker of the House of Commons was created in England. In contrast, the office of lieutenant governor is a Georgia government newcomer. From 1789 to 1945, Georgia's constitution provided for a president of the Senate to be elected by the members from that body. It was not until the Constitution of 1945 that the office of lieutenant governor was created and given responsibility for serving ex officio as president of the Senate.

resume at 10:00 a.m. the next legislative day.[4] A motion also may be made to adjourn to a particular day or time (sometimes called a "motion to adjourn to a time definite"). This motion is both debatable and amendable as to the day or time proposed and ranks fourth in precedence for motions in both house.[5]

It should be noted that these motions—unless jointly undertaken through concurrent resolutions—do *not* have the effect of suspending the count of days authorized for a session.

The constitution prohibits either house from adjourning for more than three days or meeting at any other place without the approval of the other house. Also, during special sessions, neither house may adjourn more than twice, and each adjournment may not exceed seven days.[6]

After the 30th day of any session, if one house adopts a resolution to adjourn for a specified period of time and the other house has not concurred by the end of the day set for such adjournment, the governor may adjourn both houses for not more than 10 days.[7]

Adjournment sine die. At the conclusion of a session, the final adjournment is accomplished through a joint resolution for adjournment *sine die*, which literally means "adjournment without a day [for reconvening]." The House and Senate chambers are located on opposite sides of the state capitol. Traditionally, when the time for final adjournment comes, the presiding officers of both houses order the doors to their chambers be opened. Looking across through the open rotunda to the other chamber, the two presiding officers attempt to gavel adjournment *sine die* simultaneously.

Carry-over legislation. All business pending in either house at the adjournment of the first session of a biennium is carried over to the second session of the same General Assembly and taken up again at the point to which the measure had progressed at the close of the previous session. But bills and resolutions (or other business) pending at the adjournment of the second regular session of a biennium die and cannot be carried over to the newly elected legislature that meets the following January unless they are reintroduced as new legislation.

Special Sessions

Should important matters arise between regular sessions, Georgia's governor may call the General Assembly back into special session (once termed "extraordinary session"). Since 1900, 29 separate special sessions have been convened, most recently in 2004 and 2005. In recent years, most have been called to deal with reapportionment or with state budget crises.

To convene a special session, the governor issues an executive proclamation stating the subjects to be considered. The decision to call a special session is not reviewable by the courts, nor is there a limit as to how many subjects may be included in the proclamation.[8]

Any time prior to the opening of the special session, the governor may amend the call to add or delete subjects. However, once the session is under way, the governor may amend the call only with approval of three-fifths of the members of each house.[9]

No law may be enacted at a special session that does not relate to the purposes stated in the governor's proclamation.[10] Although in some states the subjects to be dealt with must be stated *specifically* in the governor's call, Georgia courts have ruled that the state constitution only requires that enactments *relate* to subject matter set forth in the call.[11] Should the General Assembly pass a law at a special session not related to these matters, the bill would not be valid, regardless of whether the governor signs it.[12]

Statutes have been held invalid when the court thought that they clearly did not meet this requirement. For example, a statute purporting to require the equipping of automobiles with brakes, horns, headlights, and the like and regulating the speed at which drivers may approach bridges was held not to relate to the governor's call for a special session for the purposes of amending the automobile license tax.[13]

Self-convening sessions. Since 1937, the legislature has been empowered to convene itself in special session. This authority resulted from the refusal of a governor to call a special session after the regular session had failed to approve an appropriations bill for the state.

Now, a governor must convene a special session within three days (excluding Sundays) of receipt of a petition signed by three-fifths of the members of each house stating that in their opinion an emergency exists in the affairs of the state. If the governor refuses, the legislature may convene itself.[14]

Length of special sessions. However called, special sessions are limited to 40 days unless a resolution to extend the length is approved by three-fifths of each house and the governor. Should an impeachment trial be under way at the expiration of 40 days, the House must adjourn, leaving the Senate in session until the impeachment trial has been completed.[15]

Emergency Sessions

In the event of an emergency or disaster resulting from man-made or natural causes or enemy attack upon Georgia, the legislature may meet in an emergency session. The emergency meeting would be held at the new location of state government as designated by the governor. It could take place either upon the call of the governor or, if no call is issued, by initiative of the legislators themselves following the emergency or disaster. At this emergency meeting, the General Assembly is not controlled by constitutional limitations upon length of sessions, and it can suspend operations of constitutional rules governing the procedures of both houses.[16]

ORGANIZING THE TWO HOUSES

At 10:00 a.m. on the second Monday in January of odd-numbered years, newly elected and reelected members of the General Assembly gather in their respective chambers for swearing-in ceremonies.[17] The first task after the oaths are taken is to organize the two houses.

Organizing officials. State law provides that the task of organizing the two houses is to be performed by the secretary of the Senate and the clerk of the House of Representatives and that each serve as presiding officer of his or her house until a presiding officer is elected.[18] However, this statue was enacted before the office of lieutenant governor was created in 1945. In practice, an incumbent lieutenant governor who has been reelected or is in the middle of a term presides over the organization of the Senate. If a newly elected lieutenant governor has not yet been sworn in and the incumbent lieutenant governor chooses not to preside for the remainder of the term, the secretary of the Senate of the previous biennium presides. In the House of Representatives, the clerk of the last biennium presides until a speaker is elected.

Oath. Before taking a seat, each senator and representative must take an oath or affirmation. The oath used in the House of Representatives states,

> I do hereby solemnly swear or affirm that I will support the Constitution of this State and of the United States, and on all questions and measures which may come before me, I will so conduct myself, as will, in my judgment, be most conducive to the interests and prosperity of this State.

> I further swear or affirm that I am not the holder of any public money due this State, or any political subdivision or authority thereof, unaccounted for, that I am not the holder of any office of trust under the government of the United States, nor of any one of the several States, nor of any foreign state, that I am otherwise qualified to hold said office according to the Constitution and laws of Georgia and that I am not a member of the Communist party, so help me God.[19]

The oath in the Senate is nearly identical, except that reference to membership in the Communist party has been deleted.[20]

The oath may be administered to legislators by any supreme court justice or by any court of appeals, superior court, or state court judge. Arrangements for the justice or judge are made by the organizing officer of each house.[21] All members take the oath as a group.

Assignment of seats. Assignment of seats to members in the House is the express duty of the speaker.[22] In the Senate, senators are entitled to choose their seats in the following order: president pro tempore, majority leader, minority leader, senators with over 20 years' continuous service, majority whip, minority whip, administration floor leader, chair of the Rules Committee, two deputy whips chosen by the majority whip, and one deputy whip chosen by the minority whip. All other senators are seated by district number in ascending numerical order, beginning with the lowest permanently numbered available seat. Only on the first day of the first regular session, and at no other time, any two senators may mutually agree to exchange their assigned seats. This agreement must be given in writing to the secretary of the Senate.[23]

Contested elections. The state constitution empowers each house to be judge of the election and qualifications of its members.[24] Georgia appellate courts have ruled that the power to judge the eligibility of members belongs exclusively to each house, and these courts have refused to take jurisdiction of controversies involving these matters.[25] However, election contests can be based on other issues and thus be properly handled by the courts.[26]

Senate rules are silent on the procedure for handling contested elections. House rules specify that a contest may be filed only by a person certified as having won an election to the House or by the challenger(s) for that contested seat. The contest is filed with the clerk, who reports the matter to the speaker, who in turn refers it to the Rules Committee. As soon as possible, that committee must notify the person whose seat is being challenged that he or she will have the right to speak, have counsel, and compel the production of evidence. Then a hearing is held by the committee; a decision on the contest follows. The action of the committee is considered to be the action of the House until the next legislative day, when the House votes on whether to sustain or reverse the committee's decision or take other action.[27] Rules of both houses require the member who is being challenged and the challenger to leave the chamber before a vote by the full body is taken.[28]

ELECTION OF OFFICERS IN THE TWO HOUSES AND THEIR POWERS AND DUTIES

After members have been sworn in and have taken their seats, each house of the General Assembly elects its respective officers for the session.

Georgia's constitution provides for a speaker, a speaker pro tempore, and a clerk in the House of Representatives and for a president, a president pro tempore, and a secretary in the Senate.[29]

Elected officers of each house are formally selected by recorded vote or unanimous consent in each house as the second order of business in a new biennium. However, because the speaker, speaker pro tempore, and president pro tempore are selected at caucuses of the majority party of the House and Senate prior to the session, the floor election is a formality for these officers.

President of the Senate

The office of president of the Senate was first established in the Constitution of 1789. From that date to 1945, the office was filled by a senator elected by the membership. A new state constitution

GEORGIA'S LIEUTENANT GOVERNOR SERVES EX OFFICIO
AS PRESIDENT OF THE SENATE.

---

adopted in 1945, however, created the office of lieutenant governor to exercise executive power in case of the death, resignation, or disability of the governor. Following the federal model, the 1945 constitution directed that the lieutenant governor serve ex officio as president of the Senate. In the half-century that followed, the lieutenant governor's primary role developed within the legislative rather than the executive branch. Through changes in Senate rules, the lieutenant governor was given most of the powers of the speaker of the House, including appointing members and officers of standing committees and assigning bills to committee. In contrast to the vice president (who seldom presides over the U.S. Senate), Georgia's lieutenant governor became the full-time presiding officer of the state Senate. Although the lieutenant governor has some executive duties (primarily serving on boards and appointing members to boards in the executive branch), the office is funded through and considered a de facto part of the legislative branch.

As president of the Senate, the lieutenant governor presides over that body throughout the session, except when the Senate resolves itself into the Committee of the Whole. When that happens (such as when appropriation bills are considered), the president must yield the chair to the president pro tempore (or his or her designee).[30]

At any time during a day's session, the president may turn the chair over to the president pro tempore or to the designee of the president, but only for that day.[31]

Any senators wishing to ask a question from their desk—either to the chair or to another senator speaking from the well—must do so through the president.[32] Should two or more senators rise at the same time, the president determines which senator may speak.[33]

During floor sessions, the president rules on points of order and a variety of procedural questions that arise. To appeal the chair's decision, a senator must signify immediately before the Senate moves on to the next item of business. Appeals to the chair's ruling are decided by a majority vote of the total membership of the Senate.[34]

Questions about the germaneness of amendments to bills that are under consideration on the Senate floor are decided by the president.[35] If a point of order is made, the president also rules on the germaneness of conference committee reports to the original bill or resolution.[36]

All questions as to the priority of pending business in the Senate not otherwise provided for by Senate rules are decided by the president.[37]

One of the most important powers of the president is the power to decide which standing committee will consider each bill and resolution.[38]

After a vote on the Senate floor and a member gives notice of intention to move for reconsideration at a later time, the president sets the time when that motion will be taken up. The time is at the president's discretion but must be at least 10 minutes.[39]

The president has the power to compel attendance of senators in order to keep or secure a quorum, to order the doors of the Senate closed, and to order the sergeant-at-arms to arrest absentees and bring them to the chamber in order to secure a quorum.[40] The president also has the power to suspend the sergeant-at-arms for misconduct or neglect of duty.[41]

The president can suspend irrelevant debate, command silence during debate, and call senators to order for engaging in behavior that is disruptive to the decorum and dignity of the Senate.[42] The president also can order the galleries and lobbies of the Senate closed, and in case of disturbance or disorderly conduct, order the sergeant-at-arms to arrest the offending party and bring him or her before the Senate to be charged with contempt of that body.[43]

The presiding officer may require the third reading of a bill in its entirety rather than by title alone and may order a roll call vote on any matter before the Senate.[44] Should a quorum not be present during Senate consideration of a subject, the president can either direct the secretary of the Senate to call the roll or use the electronic voting machine for a roll call.[45]

Unlike the U.S. Constitution, which allows the vice president while serving as president of the U.S. Senate to vote in case of a tie, Georgia's constitution makes no similar provision for the lieutenant governor. While Senate rules do not specifically prohibit the president from voting, they do so by implication when they provide for the voting rights of a presiding senator. A presiding senator can vote only in the case of a tie or when his or her vote, if cast with the minority, would result in a tie vote.[46]

In contrast to the House, there is no provision in the Senate for the president to yield the chair in order to participate in debate. The president will frequently address the Senate briefly with respect to announcements and other matters affecting the body. However, Senate custom is that such remarks must be made from the president's podium (and not from the well or a senator's seat) and cannot be part of substantive debate on a bill or amendment.

All acts and resolutions passed by the Senate, as well as all writs, warrants, and subpoenas issued by its order, must be signed by the president.[47]

The president serves ex officio as chair of the Senate Committee on Assignments and as a member of the Senate Committee on Administrative Affairs.[48] The president also serves as an ex officio member of the Legislative Services Committee (the joint committee responsible for the operation and supervision of the General Assembly),[49] the Senate Fiscal Affairs Subcommittee,[50] the Code Revision Commission,[51] and the Georgia Criminal Justice Improvement Council.[52] The president also appoints members to the latter three bodies, the Budgetary Responsibility Oversight Committee,[53] and various joint legislative oversight committees.[54]

Also appointed by the president are up to 40 Senate pages during a session.[55]

Senate rules provide that the president establish a program of familiarization with state government to be used in training Senate pages.[56]

Although the lieutenant governor's principal role in state government historically has been in the legislative branch, he or she has several executive functions—foremost, serving ex officio on a number of state boards and commissions and appointing members to many others in the executive branch.[57] Georgia's constitution allows the governor to prescribe the executive duties of the lieutenant governor (although this rarely if ever happens).[58] Perhaps the most important functions of the lieutenant governor are to exercise the executive powers in case of the temporary disability of the governor and to become governor in case of a sitting governor's death, resignation, or permanent disability.[59] Interestingly, since the office was created in 1945, only one lieutenant governor has ever been called on to perform this duty.[60]

President Pro Tempore

The origin of the office of president pro tempore is obscure, but almost certainly it was created by Senate rules after the office of president of the Senate was first established in 1789, when a new state constitution was adopted providing for a bicameral legislature. There had to be some provision for presiding when the president was not available, so internal Senate rules likely created the position.

The office of president pro tempore first appeared as a constitutional position in the Constitution of 1945 and has remained as such. The president pro tempore is elected by a majority vote of senators voting, provided the total vote constitutes a quorum.[61]

The constitutional role of the president pro tempore is to serve as president of the Senate in the event of the temporary disability of the president. In event of the president's death, resignation, or permanent disability, or should the president have to become governor, the president pro tempore becomes president.

When the president yields the chair or is unable to preside for whatever reason, the president pro tempore serves as presiding officer. If the president pro tempore is unable or chooses not to preside, then the president designates who will serve in his or her place.[62]

When the Senate resolves itself into the Committee of the Whole, the president yields the chair to the president pro tempore (or that officer's designee).[63]

While presiding, the president pro tempore (or any other senator called on to preside) does not vote except (1) in cases of tie or when his or her vote, if given to the minority, would create a tie; (2) in all cases in which a fixed constitutional vote is required to pass a measure under consideration and the measure is lacking one vote to meet that requirement; and (3) in all Senate elections.[64]

The president pro tempore serves ex officio on the Senate Committee on Assignment and on the Committee on Administrative Affairs.[65] The president pro tempore also is an ex officio member of two joint legislative bodies: the Legislative Services Committee[66] and the Joint Legislative Ethics Committee, to which he or she also appoints four senators as members.[67]

In addition to serving in the legislative branch, the president pro tempore is an ex officio member of, or appoints members to, several boards in the executive branch.[68]

Speaker of the House

The position of Georgia's speaker of the House of Representatives traces to the office of speaker of the Commons House of Assembly, created in 1755. Georgia's colonial speaker, in turn, traces to 1377, when the position of the speaker of the House of Commons was created in England.

With the outbreak of the American Revolution, Georgia adopted its first state constitution in 1777. That document provided for a unicameral legislature—the House of Assembly—which was empowered to choose its own speaker. It was not until the Constitution of 1861 that the office of speaker was specifically designated as the presiding officer of the House.

The speaker has broad discretion over legislative proceedings in the House—not only on the floor but in committee as well. The speaker has full power to recognize which representative will be accorded the right to the floor,[69] to suspend irrelevant debate and command silence,[70] and to call to order any member who violates the rules of the House (in which event the offending member must immediately sit down).[71]

All questions on the priority of business before the House are decided by the speaker.[72] Bills that are ready for the third reading and floor action may be called from the daily rules calendar at the discretion of the speaker.[73]

The speaker may direct that the third reading of general bills be in their entirety rather than by title only.[74] Amendments and motions may be ruled out of order by the speaker if not considered germane to the subject under consideration.[75] Also, the speaker may order a roll call vote at any time on any question.[76]

The speaker rules on points of order and other questions that come before the House. Because House rules do not provide for a parliamentarian, the speaker also decides on interpretation of rules.

THE HOUSE SPEAKER HAS EXTENSIVE AUTHORITY OVER
FLOOR AND COMMITTEE PROCEEDINGS.

In the event a member is dissatisfied with the ruling of the chair, that member can appeal the decision to the body. Overruling the chair's decision requires a majority of the House membership.[77]

During a day's session, the speaker may name any representative to perform the duties of the chair for any part of that day's session.[78] Whenever the speaker is not presiding, he or she may participate in debate or otherwise act as a member. House rules allow the speaker to be recognized at any desk on the floor.[79]

During floor action, the speaker can vote (1) when the House is equally divided; (2) when a fixed constitutional vote is required to pass some bill or measure and one more vote is needed for passage; (3) when the speaker's vote, if given to the minority, would result in an equal division of the House on a particular question, thereby defeating it; and (4) when the House is conducting an election.[80]

Although the House can resolve itself into a Committee of the Whole, the speaker can take this action without a motion.[81] Once the Committee of the Whole is established, the speaker appoints a chair to preside and then can take part in the proceedings, including voting (unless he or she is excused).[82]

In addition to floor proceedings, the speaker has extensive power over the committee system in the House. The speaker is authorized to appoint all members and officers of House standing committees,[83] to reassign committee assignments of members on request,[84] and to remove officers of committees, subcommittees, and special committees as the speaker sees fit.[85] In addition to having exclusive power over committee assignments and officers, the speaker is allowed under House rules to appoint a Committee on Assignments to exercise this responsibility.[86] If such a committee is appointed, the speaker serves on it and is given three votes on all decisions (and a fourth in case of a tie). If the speaker objects to any committee action, he or she can veto that action within 48 hours.[87]

The speaker serves as an ex officio member of all standing committees and subcommittees in the House and has a vote in all but the Committee on Rules.[88] Additionally, the speaker can appoint one or more members to the position of hawk. Hawks are ex officio members of all committees and subcommittees and have a right to vote on any committee or subcommittee actions.[89]

In addition to the standing committee provided for in House rules, the speaker can create special committees at any time. These ad hoc committees are created to consider a particular bill or bills. They have the same power as a standing committee, except that they cease to exist after taking final action on any bill assigned to them.[90]

The speaker also appoints House members to conference committees.[91]

The speaker has sole discretion to refer bills and resolutions that are introduced in the House or sent from the Senate to the appropriate standing committee without debate.[92] Or the speaker can choose to send a measure to a special committee designated specifically for that measure.[93]

The speaker also has the power to

1. grant special access to the House floor for special recognitions;[94]
2. allow prominent persons or others to address the House on significant occasions;[95]
3. authorize members to introduce visitors in the gallery;[96]
4. appoint the House sergeant-at-arms;[97]
5. suspend the sergeant-at-arms, messenger, or doorkeeper for misconduct or neglect of duty;[98]

6. sign all acts and joint resolutions passed by the House, as well as any writs, warrants, and subpoenas ordered by that body;[99]

7. determine which persons are to be allowed to sit in the House gallery;[100]

8. clear the galleries and lobbies and order the arrest of any person for disturbance or misconduct, directing that the person be brought before the House for contempt;[101]

9. compel the attendance of members in order to keep or obtain a quorum and, if necessary, order the arrest of absentees to secure their attendance;[102]

10. assign seats and offices to members of the House;[103]

11. create interim study committees.[104]

The speaker serves as ex officio chair of the Legislative Services Committee[105] and is an ex officio member of the House Fiscal Affairs Subcommittee,[106] Code Revision Commission,[107] and Georgia Criminal Justice Improvement Council.[108] The speaker serves as a non-voting member and chair in even years of the Joint Legislative Ethics Committee.[109] Also, the speaker appoints one or more members to the House Fiscal Affairs Subcommittee, Code Revision Commission, Georgia Criminal Justice Improvement Council, Joint Legislative Ethics Committee, Budgetary Responsibility Oversight Committee,[110] and various joint legislative oversight committees.[111] The speaker also serves ex officio on several boards in the executive branch[112] and appoints members to a number of boards in the executive branch.[113]

Georgia's constitution provides that in the event of the death, resignation, or permanent disability of the governor and lieutenant governor, the speaker of the House exercises the powers of the governor until the election of a governor to fill the unexpired term. This special election must be held within 90 days from the date the speaker becomes acting chief executive.[114] So far, no speaker has been called upon to serve as acting governor in Georgia.

Speaker Pro Tempore

The origin of the office of speaker pro tempore is not clear but likely was created along with the office of speaker to address the need for someone to preside in the speaker's absence. The office first appears as a constitutional position in the Constitution of 1976.

Georgia's constitution provides for a speaker pro tempore to be elected from the membership of the House.[115] The speaker pro tempore becomes speaker in case of the death, resignation, or permanent disability of the speaker. In such case, House rules provide that within 120 days of such transition, an election for a new speaker must be held (unless there are 120 days or less remaining in the biennium).[116]

The speaker pro tempore presides if the speaker is absent at the beginning of a daily session. If both are absent, the clerk of the House presides until an acting speaker pro tempore can be elected.[117]

The speaker pro tempore serves as an ex officio voting member of all standing committees in the House and the joint Legislative Services Committee.[118] However, because the presiding officer of the House will always be a member of the majority party, the speaker pro tempore does not have the extensive powers of the president pro tempore in the Senate.

Clerk of the House and Secretary of the Senate

The clerk of the House traces to the clerk of the House of Commons, which originated in England in the early 14th century. The post existed in the colonial Commons House of Assembly and throughout subsequent legislatures after statehood.

The counterpart of the clerk in the other house—the secretary of the Senate—traces to the creation of a bicameral legislature in the Constitution of 1789. The term "secretary" rather than "clerk" appears to be based on usage in the U.S. Senate, which elected the first secretary of the Senate on April 8, 1789, two days before the first official meeting of that body. In Georgia, the offices of clerk of the House and secretary of the Senate first appear in the Constitution of 1868.

The clerk and secretary are the chief administrative officers of their houses, serving as full-time officers and having responsibility for many important functions during and between sessions. Despite the differences in titles, they have similar duties, contributing much to the orderly process of business in the respective houses.

The clerk and secretary are elected by a recorded vote or unanimous consent of the majority of the members of his or her respective house. Their terms of office are the same as those of the members of the General Assembly, and they serve until a successor is elected. Before assuming their duties, the clerk and secretary must take an oath to discharge their duties faithfully and to the best of their skill and knowledge.[119]

In the event of a vacancy in the office of clerk, the speaker appoints a qualified person to serve for the remainder of the term. In case of a vacancy or permanent disability in the office of the secretary of the Senate during a session, the Senate elects a successor for the remainder of the unexpired term. If the Senate is not in session, the president pro tempore appoints a qualified person to serve until the next session. Any question as to permanent disability is determined by the president pro tempore, with the concurrence of a majority of standing committee chairs.[120]

The "housekeeping resolution" adopted by each house at the beginning of a biennium authorizes the secretary and clerk to select staff to assist in carrying out the duties of the two officers.[121]

Any bill or resolution introduced in the House of Representatives must be filed through the office of clerk, and in the Senate, through the office of secretary.[122] Once introduced, a measure is assigned a number and entered online as well as printed for distribution to members of both houses, the news media, and the public. The secretary and clerk prepare other materials vital to the legislative process, including status sheets showing the stage of legislation, calendars of bills ready for floor action, and first readers showing the titles of newly introduced measures. These are prepared daily during a session in printed format and online.

In each house, the clerk and secretary and their staff are always present during floor sessions. In the House, the clerk and staff are situated immediately below the speaker's podium, and the secretary and staff are below and to the right of the president's podium.

In each house, bills must be read aloud three times before floor action is taken. By tradition, the clerk does the reading in the House, and a member of the secretary's staff does the reading in the Senate. The clerk and secretary's staffs activate the microphones on legislators' desks once a member has been recognized to ask a question or make a motion. They also operate the electronic voting machines, tally hand votes, and keep copies of all recorded votes in each chamber.

All writs, warrants, and subpoenas issued by order of the House or Senate are attested to by the clerk or secretary. These officers must also certify all engrossed copies of bills for their houses.[123]

Should the president and president pro tempore be absent in the Senate or the speaker and speaker pro tempore be absent in the House, the secretary and clerk must call their respective houses to order and preside until a temporary replacement can be elected.[124] When there is a joint meeting of both houses, the secretary joins with the clerk to perform the duties required at the meeting.[125]

Within 10 days after a session adjourns, the secretary and clerk must file all papers and documents of their houses and deliver them to the secretary of state. After each session, the clerk and secretary respectively oversee compilation of the *House Journal* and *Senate Journal*, which constitute the official record of the session's legislative action.

The Georgia Court of Appeals has stated that the secretary and clerk officially owe no duty to citizens in general,[126] which suggests that they are answerable for their actions only to the Senate and House, respectively. Still, both offices serve the public as an invaluable source of information about legislation, committee meetings, and other matters during a session.

Other Officers

State law authorizes a doorkeeper and a messenger for the House and a sergeant-at-arms for the Senate, who are elected by the members to perform such duties as required.[127]

In the House, the doorkeeper is responsible for controlling access to the floor and has a special charge to rigidly enforce House rules regarding any member or other person entering the floor while in an intoxicated condition or while under the influence of controlled drugs.[128] The specific duties of the messenger are to attend to the wants of the House while in session, aid in the enforcement of order under the direction of the speaker, and execute the demands of the House along with all processes issued by its authority.[129]

House rules also authorize the speaker to appoint a sergeant-at-arms to maintain order in the House chamber, gallery, anterooms, lobbies, and halls adjacent to the House.[130] On order of the speaker, the sergeant-at-arms, doorkeeper, and messenger may arrest absent House members and bring them before the House in order to secure a quorum.[131] House rules also allow the speaker to direct any uniformed members of the Georgia State Patrol who are assigned to duty at the capitol to maintain order in the House chamber and to exercise any authority granted to the sergeant-at-arms by House rules.[132] Although there is no similar rule in the Senate, state law allows the Georgia State Patrol to enforce criminal law on state property[133] and to further provide security to both the lieutenant governor and speaker of the House.[134] Also, Georgia Building Authority law enforcement officers have statutory authority to enforce law and order in the capitol complex, including the power to make arrests.[135]

In the Senate, a sergeant-at-arms is to attend to the wants of that body while in session, including executing the demands of the Senate and all such processes issued under its authority.[136] Senate rules empower the sergeant-at-arms at the direction of the president to arrest any absent senators and bring them before the Senate in order to secure a quorum.[137] The sergeant-at-arms also is directed to aid in enforcing order under the direction of the president and the Decorum Committee.[138] Although Senate rules do not require the Georgia State Patrol to help the sergeant-at-arms to maintain order in the Senate chamber and galleries, state law authorizes members of both the patrol and Georgia Building Authority police to take action to help maintain order in either legislative chamber.

During a session, the Senate may employ up to 12 doorkeepers,[139] who are under the supervision of the sergeant-at-arms.[140]

Although many legislative bodies have the office of parliamentarian, there is no designated parliamentarian provided for in House or Senate rules. Therefore, the function is performed by the presiding officer, subject to appeal to the entire house.[141]

Pages

Members of both houses are served by pages. On the desk of each legislator is a button for use when the services of a page are desired. When the button is pressed, an electronic notification is sent to the page coordinator in the hallway. The coordinator sends the available page to the legislator who needs his or her services. An enactment of the General Assembly directs that schools grant excused absences to students who serve as pages and that on the days spent away from school, they be counted as present.[142]

By their rules, the Senate and House require pages to be at least 12 years of age. The rules of the Senate further provide that each senator may name up to 20 pages during a session. Any senator who does not use all of his or her pages or "page days" (that is, the service of one page on one day) may assign them to another senator. The lieutenant governor can name up to 40 pages during a session. To name a page, the president and each senator must file the name of the page and date of proposed service with the director of pages at least three days prior to the date requested. However, Senate rules limit the number of pages that can serve on any single day to 30, and these are selected by the director of pages in the order in which senators submit their requests. Prior to serving, pages must attend a program established by the president to learn about state government and their duties as pages.[143]

The rules of the House provide that each member is allowed a maximum of 10 page days during the session and may use these either on one or on separate legislative days. A member must make a reservation for each page at least one week before his or her selected page day.[144]

House and Senate Party Organization

A recognized party organization known as a caucus exists for both Democrats and Republicans in each house of the General Assembly. The officers and leaders of the party in power in each house are the "majority," and leaders of the party not in power are the "minority."

Republican Caucus. The House Republican Caucus was organized in 1966, and the caucus in the Senate was formed in 1969. All members elected as Republicans are considered members of the caucus, but participation is voluntary. Both the House and Senate Republican caucuses meet in November before the convening of the General Assembly following a general election. Caucus officers and party leaders are elected for two-year terms in each chamber. The officers chosen

PAGES ASSIST DURING FLOOR PROCEEDINGS BY DELIVERING
MESSAGES AND DOCUMENTS TO LEGISLATORS AT THEIR DESKS.

in both the House and Senate are the party leader, party whip, and caucus chair, vice-chair, treasurer, and secretary. The caucus leadership establishes policy for the caucus.

Democratic Caucus. A Democratic Caucus was established in the House in 1967 and in the Senate in 1970. Both the House and the Senate consider all members who are elected as Democrats to their respective houses as eligible caucus members, even though participation is voluntary. The House Democratic Caucus meets no earlier than 5 days and no later than 15 days after the general election. The Senate Democratic Caucus convenes within 15 days after the general election.

In the Senate, the Democratic Caucus elects a party leader, party whip, and caucus chair, vice-chair, and secretary. The House Democratic Caucus elects these same officers as well as a caucus treasurer. Officers are elected by the caucus for two-year terms. Caucus members are honor-bound to support their caucus nominees in the election of officers of their respective houses.

The rules for the Democratic Caucus in the House and the bylaws for the Democratic Caucus in the Senate establish a permanent policy committee composed of the caucus nominees for chamber offices, party leaders, caucus leaders, and several caucus members. The committees deal with organizational measures for each body. In addition, the committees may recommend party positions, which the party leader and party whip communicate to the membership.

COMMITTEES IN THE LEGISLATURE

After the session officers have been elected, the next important step in organizing the two houses is the appointment of House and Senate members to their respective standing committees. The standing committees of both houses are established by House and Senate rules adopted at the beginning of each session. It is through these committees (see Tables 4 and 5) that most of the work of the General Assembly is carried out.

House Standing Committees

Number. House rules provide the number and name of standing committees. During the 2007 session, there were 36 standing committees.[145] Additionally, House rules allow the speaker to appoint at any time a special committee for the purpose of considering any bill or bills he or she may assign. In all respects, the special committee acts as if it were a standing committee, except that it ceases to exist when final action is taken on bills assigned to it.[146]

Each representative must serve on at least two standing committees.[147] Unlike Senate rules, however, House rules do not specify the number of members appointed to each standing committee. During the 2007 session, the largest committee was Appropriations, with 73 members, and the smallest was Special Rules, with 3 members.

TABLE 4. Standing Committees in the Georgia House of Representatives

Agriculture and Consumer Affairs	Interstate Cooperation
Appropriations	Intragovernmental Coordination
Banks and Banking	Judiciary
Budget and Fiscal Affairs Oversight	Judiciary, Non-civil
Children and Youth	Legislative and Congressional
Code Revision	Reapportionment
Defense and Veterans Affairs	Motor Vehicles
Economic Development and Tourism	Natural Resources and Environment
Education	Public Safety and Homeland Security
Energy, Utilities, and Telecommunications	Regulated Industries
Ethics	Retirement
Game, Fish, and Parks	Rules
Governmental Affairs	Science and Technology
Health and Human Services	Special Rules
Higher Education	State Institutions and Property
Human Relations and Aging	State Planning and Community Affairs
Industrial Relations	Transportation
Information and Audits	Ways and Means
Insurance	

TABLE 5. Standing Committees in the Georgia Senate

Agriculture and Consumer Affairs	Natural Resources and the Environment
Appropriations	Public Safety and Homeland Security
Banking and Financial Institutions	Reapportionment and Redistricting
Economic Development	Regulated Industries and Utilities
Education and Youth	Retirement
Ethics	Rules
Finance	Science and Technology
Government Oversight	Special Judiciary
Health and Human Services	State and Local Governmental Operations
Higher Education	State Institutions and Property
Insurance and Labor	Transportation
Interstate Cooperation	Urban Affairs
Judiciary	Veterans and Military Affairs

Subcommittees. The speaker can create one or more subcommittees in any standing committee.[148] Subcommittee actions are subject to review by parent standing committees, and no bill can be reported to the House until it has been acted upon by the full standing committee to which it was referred. Additionally, House rules provide for eight subcommittees in the Appropriations Committee: Education, Higher Education, Health, Human Services, Public Safety, Economic Development, Special Appropriations Projects Oversight, and General. Each subcommittee is headed by a vice-chair appointed by the speaker or the Committee on Assignments.[149]

Appointment of Members and Officers. House rules authorize the speaker or the Committee on Assignments to appoint members of all standing committees.[150] The speaker also appoints members of subcommittees and special committees, as well as officers of all committees and subcommitties.[151]

The speaker has the express power to appoint committee members, and House rules allow him or her to create a Committee on Assignments to perform this function. This committee consists of the speaker, majority leader, and no fewer than five additional members appointed by the speaker. On all questions coming before the committee, the speaker has three votes, the majority leader has two, and the remaining members have one vote each. Decisions are reached by a majority vote of committee members who are present and voting. In case of a tie, the speaker is entitled to one additional vote. The speaker can veto any action by the committee within 48 hours of receiving written notice of such action.[152]

Hawks. The speaker may appoint one or more members of the House to the position of hawk. If more than one hawk is named, the speaker can designate one as senior hawk. Hawks are ex officio voting members of all standing committees and subcommittees in the House.[153]

Ex Officio Members. The speaker, speaker pro tempore, majority leader, majority whip, and hawks are ex officio members of all standing committees and subcommittees in the House. All are voting members, except the speaker can only vote on the Rules Committee.[154]

Additionally, the minority leader and minority whip serve as ex officio voting members of the Rules Committee. The chair and secretary of the Appropriations Committee serve as ex officio voting members of the Ways and Means Committee, and the chair and vice-chair of the Ways and Means Committee serve ex officio as voting members on the Appropriations Committee. The chair of the Ethics Committee serves as an ex officio voting member on the Judiciary Committee.[155]

Serving ex officio on the Ethics Committee are the speaker pro tempore, majority and minority leaders, majority and minority party caucus chairs, majority caucus vice-chair, minority caucus secretary, and the chair of the Judiciary Committee.[156]

Committee Seniority. There is no provision in House rules for seniority ranking status gained through continuous service on a standing committee.

Committee Tenure. At one time, House rules provided for committee tenure, giving representatives the right to remain on a committee as long as they remained a member of the House. This protection is no longer true, especially for members of the Rules Committee: the speaker can remove any member of that committee without cause.[157] There is a type of tenure for members of other committees during a biennium arising from the rule that says that once announcement of standing committees has been made, no other members will be assigned (except when a member requests a change or in case of a vacancy).[158] Should a member request a change, the speaker is authorized to make it. A requested reassignment is solely at the speaker's discretion, as House rules only stipulate "[i]f a change can be accomplished."[159]

There is no tenure for committee officers. House rules give the speaker the authority to remove any officer of a standing committee, special committee, or subcommittee without cause or explanation.[160]

Open Meetings. House rules provide that all meetings of any committee, subcommittee, or interim committee are open to the public. A majority of a quorum of a committee, however, can vote to close a meeting when (1) discussing the future acquisition of real estate; (2) discussing employment, dismissal, or disciplinary action against a public officer or employee; or (3) hearing complaints or charges against a public officer or employee unless that officer or employee requests that the meeting be open to the public.[161] House rules also provide that conference committees be open to the public.[162]

Excluded from the open meetings requirement are the Committee on Assignments[163] and certain meetings of the Ethics Committee.[164] No standing committee, subcommittee, or interim committee can meet officially in any place where a citizen is denied admittance or membership based on religion, race, creed, nationality, or gender.[165]

Committee Rules. In the House, rules are adopted within each committee, leaving each free to decide many procedural matters (such the requirements for a quorum). One exception is the Ethics Committee, for which many procedures and requirements are spelled out in House rules.[166]

Senate Standing Committees

Number. Senate rules provide for the number and names of standing committees. During the 2007 session, there were 26 standing committees.[167] Each senator is appointed to no more than four standing committees. Membership on the Ethics Committee, Reapportionment and Redistricting Committee, Government Oversight Committee, and Urban Affairs Committee do not count against this limitation (though serving as chair does). Also excluded from the limit of four committees is membership on the Committee on Assignments or Committee on Administrative Affairs.[168]

Subcommittees. The president is authorized to create subcommittees within any standing committee and to name the members and officers. If the president does not do so, the chair of a standing committee may appoint subcommittees.[169]

Appointment of Members and Officers. Members and officers of all standing committees and subcommittees are appointed by the president.[170]

In contrast to the rules of the House, in which the size of a committee is at the discretion of the speaker, Senate rules specify the number of members on each committee.[171] During the 2007 session, the size of Senate standing committees ranged from 5 to 30 members, the Appropriations Committee being the largest. These limits do not apply to senators who are elected in special elections to fill vacancies that arise during a biennium.

Ex Officio Members. In addition to regular committee members, the president of the Senate may appoint one or more temporary members to any standing committee.[172] Senate rules specifically designate such additional appointees as ex officio members (although "ad hoc members" would be more accurate because according to parliamentary practice, true ex officio members of a committee are not appointed but rather serve automatically by virtue of holding another office).

Although Senate rules do not specify the reason for or duration of ex officio appointments, a common reason is to allow a committee or subcommittee to establish a quorum in order to transact business. Such additional appointments do not count against Senate rules limiting committee size or the number of committees a senator can serve on. However, even though their appointments are temporary, ex officio members may vote on any matter coming before the committee.

Committee Seniority. Senate rules make no provision for length of service on a standing committee as a factor in determining officers.

Committee Tenure. Once appointed, a senator cannot be removed from a standing committee during a biennium, except for failure to attend three consecutive meetings (unless excused by the committee or having filed a statement that the missed meeting was due to attending another committee meeting).[173] One other exception is that the president can remove any member of the Rules Committee and any appointed member of the Committee on Assignments and Committee on Administrative Affairs at any time and for any reason.[174]

After the announcement of standing committees has been made at the beginning of a biennium, Senate rules prohibit the appointment of additional members. The president, however, may assign newly elected members to committees that have vacancies as well as fill vacancies of committee officers.[175]

Officers of standing committees and subcommittees can be removed at any time and for any reason by the president.[176]

Open Meetings. All meetings of Senate committees, including conference committees, are open to the public except when there is a majority of quorum votes to close the meeting when (1) discussing the future acquisition of real estate; (2) discussing employment, dismissal, or disciplinary action against a public officer or employee; or (3) hearing complaints against a public officer or employee, unless that officer or employee requests that the meeting be open to the public.[177] Excluded from the open meetings requirement are the Committee on Assignments and Committee on Administrative Affairs.[178]

As with the House, no Senate committee, subcommittee, or interim committee can meet officially in any place where a citizen is denied admittance or membership based on religion, race, creed, nationality, or gender. An exception is made should a committee visit a correctional facility and segregation of inmates is required to maintain security.[179]

The secretary of the Senate is responsible for posting a list of the times and locations of Senate committee meetings by 10:00 a.m. on the Friday preceding the week of the scheduled meetings. The chair of a committee may request additional meetings if a request is made to the secretary of the Senate at least 24 hours prior to the scheduled meeting. The chair may cancel a scheduled meeting by notifying the secretary of the Senate at least 24 hours prior to the meeting. A scheduled meeting can be canceled if no agenda for the meeting has been posted or distributed by notifying the secretary of the Senate an hour prior to the meeting.[180]

No standing committee can meet in the Senate chamber unless a scheduled public hearing is being held.[181]

Committee Rules. Unlike in the House, in which each standing committee adopts its own rules of procedure, standing committees in the Senate are subject to a number of uniform rules of procedure that govern committee powers, meetings, quorums, attendance, officers, testimony, motions, debate, voting, and decorum.[182]

Special Standing Committees

In each house, there are three standing committees to which bills and resolutions are referred that have special functions as well.

Rules Committee. In each house, the Rules Committee is responsible for setting the daily rules calendar, which determines the legislative agenda on the floor. In the Senate, the Rules Committee sets the floor agenda for the last 35 days of the session; in the House, it controls the agenda throughout the 40 days of the session.[183] The Rules Committee also proposes changes in the rules of each house.

Ethics Committee. In each house, the Ethics Committee is responsible for implementing ethics rules in that house. This committee conducts investigations when charges of unethical or improper conduct are filed; holds hearings, at which witnesses and documents can be compelled; and recommends punishment to the full house. Each committee can also issue advisory opinions with respect to ethical and proper conduct.[184]

Committee on Interstate Cooperation. Each house has a Committee on Interstate Cooperation. Together with the Governor's Committee on Interstate Cooperation, they form the Georgia Commission on Interstate Cooperation. This agency, created by statute in 1937, is responsible for overseeing Georgia's participation in the Council of State Governments and the Southern Legislative Conference.[185]

Joint Standing Committees

Each year, the Senate and House Appropriations Committees hold joint hearings to consider the governor's proposed budget for the next fiscal year as well as the proposed amended budget for the current fiscal year. From time to time, other committees in the House hold joint meetings or hearings, but there is no provision in state law or legislative rules requiring similar standing committees in both houses to hold joint hearings and meetings, except for the Fiscal Affairs Subcommittee.

Special or Interim Committees

Special or interim committees study issues and sometimes hold hearings between sessions. They are created by motion or resolution of one or both houses. In addition, the "housekeeping resolutions" in each house grant the speaker of the House and the president of the Senate authority to create special or interim committees as needed. Thus, there are joint interim committees representing both houses created by joint resolution, as well as special committees of either house.

Interim committees have no official power (other than to study a problem), cannot introduce legislation, and are dissolved upon the completion of their task. Members of interim committees are not necessarily on the related standing committee, which would be assigned legislation resulting from the committee's study. Despite these limitations, use of interim study committees does permit the legislature to respond overtly to matters of public concern, and such committees can provide valuable reports based upon serious investigation and study. Still, both houses rely more on the interim study of legislative matters by the appropriate standing committee.

Joint Statutory Committees

The General Assembly has provided by law for a number of special joint committees. None are involved in the consideration of bills and resolutions but rather exist to perform special functions.

Legislative Services Committee. This committee consists of officers and leaders of both houses. It is responsible for managing and overseeing operations of the General Assembly.

Budgetary Responsibility Oversight Committee. This joint committee was created to enhance the legislature's capacity to oversee state budgeting and planning. It may employ a full-time director and staff.

Fiscal Affairs Subcommittee. Once each quarter, the Fiscal Affairs Subcommittees of each house meet jointly as one committee to review and approve budget transfers recommended by the governor.

Joint Legislative Ethics Commission. This joint committee is responsible for advising the General Assembly in establishing rules governing conflict of interest for legislators, investigating complaints regarding those rules or state law, issuing advisory opinions, and performing other functions as provided by law. It may employ an executive director and staff.

Joint Oversight Committees. The General Assembly has created a number of joint committees to review and evaluate the operations of select state programs. Examples of these oversight committees are the MARTA Overview Committee, Georgia Technology Authority Overview Committee, and the HOPE Scholarship/Pre-K Legislative Oversight Committee.[186]

Other Types of Committees

Several other types of committees have special functions during the legislative process.

Upon passage of a motion on the floor, the speaker of the House and president of the Senate may appoint *conference committees* consisting of three members from their respective houses to meet and attempt to resolve differences between the two houses on a given piece of legislation.

To facilitate deliberations, or upon occasion as required by House or Senate rules, each house may resolve itself into a Committee of the Whole, whereby the total membership sits in a body as a committee.

In the Senate, the president appoints members and officers to all standing committees and subcommittees and names Senate members of all conference committees.[187] The Senate Committee on Assignments appoints members to statutory joint legislative oversight committees.[188] House rules vest committee appointment power in the speaker but allow discretion in creating a Committee on Assignments to make standing committee assignments.

Other special-purpose committees include the Committee on Senate Administrative Affairs, Audit Subcommittee in the Senate Rules Committee, and House Committee on Information and Audits. Custom also dictates other ad hoc committees, such as a Committee of Escort to accompany the governor to the House floor when giving a joint address to the General Assembly.

Through housekeeping resolutions, both houses currently authorize a unique type of committee: *the committee of one*. This special committee allows a single legislator to engage in official legislative business in Georgia—other than attending standing or interim committee meetings—and receive the standard per diem allowance. In the House, the speaker, speaker pro tempore, majority leader, minority leader, majority whip, minority whip, administration floor leader, and the assistant administration floor leaders may, with the authorization and approval of the administration floor leader, serve as needed; other representatives may serve up to 7 days a year.[189] In the Senate, the president pro tempore, majority leader, and minority leader serve as needed; other senators are permitted up to 15 days of service each year.[190]

NOTES

1. GA. CONST. art. 3, §4, ¶1.
2. See *The Book of the States, 2006*, Vol. 38 (Lexington, Ky.: Council of State Governments, 2006), Table 3.2, pp. 68–71.
3. GA. CONST. art. 3, §4, ¶1.
4. Senate Rules 6-2.2 and 6-2.4; House Rules 154 and 156.
5. Senate Rule 6-2.3; House Rule 155.
6. GA. CONST. art. 3, §4, ¶1.
7. Ibid.
8. Bunger v. State, 146 Ga. 672, 92 S.E. 72 (1917); affirmed by Busbee v. Georgia Conference of American Association of University Professors, 215 Ga. 752, 221 S.E. 2d 437 (1975).
9. GA. CONST. art. 5, §2, ¶7(a).
10. Ibid.
11. Mayes v. Daniel, 186 Ga. 345, 198 S.E. 535 (1938). Moreover, matters that are germane and incidental to purposes broadly stated in the proclamation will permit passage of ancillary legislation at a special session. In determining germaneness, the entire proclamation will be considered by the courts. Carroll v. Wright, 131 Ga. 728, 63 S.E. 260 (1908).
12. Jones v. State, 151 Ga. 502, 107 S.E. 565 (1921).
13. Bibb County v. Williams, 152 Ga. 489, 110 S.E. 273 (1921).
14. GA. CONST. art. 5, §2, ¶7(b).
15. GA. CONST. art. 5, §2, ¶7(c).
16. OFFICIAL CODE OF GEORGIA ANNOTATED (O.C.G.A.) §§38-3-52 and 38-3-53. *See also* GA. CONST. art. 3, §6, ¶2(a)(4).
17. O.C.G.A. §28-1-2.
18. O.C.G.A. §28-1-3.
19. This oath is a composite of the oath contained in O.C.G.A. §28-1-4 as well as the oaths required in O.C.G.A. §§45-3-1 and 45-3-11 through 45-3-14. Georgia *House Journal* 2005, 5.
20. Georgia *Senate Journal* 2005, 18.
21. O.C.G.A. §28-1-4.

22. House Rule 25.

23. Senate Rule 1-2.3.

24. Ga. Const. art. 3, §4, ¶7.

25. *See* Rainey v. Taylor, 166 Ga. 476, 143 S.E. 383 (1928); Fowler v. Bostick, 99 Ga. App. 428, 108 S.E.2d 720 (1950); Beatty v. Myrick, 218 Ga. 629, 129 S.E.2d 764 (1963); *but see* Bond v. Floyd, 251 F. Supp. 333 (1966), *rev'd,* 385 U.S. 166 (1966), in which the U.S. Supreme Court affirmed that even though a state constitution may declare that each house of the state legislature shall be the judge of the election and qualifications of its own members, such provision does not deprive federal courts of jurisdiction when a legislature's action or decision as to the qualifications of a member involves substantial federally protected rights. *See also* Powell v. McCormack, 395 U.S. 486 (1969).

26. O.C.G.A. §§21-2-520 through 21-2-529. Although contested elections for the General Assembly are infrequent, when they occur, they are variously dealt with by the appropriate house or by the courts, depending on the grounds upon which the election is being challenged.

27. House Rule 159.2.

28. Senate Rule 5-1.8; House Rule 133.

29. Ga. Const. art. 3, §3, ¶¶1 through 3.

30. Senate Rule 2-7.2.

31. Senate Rule 1-1.2.

32. Senate Rule 8-1.1.

33. Senate Rule 8-1.2.

34. Senate Rule 8-1.11.

35. Senate Rule 7-1.2.

36. Senate Rule 2-8.5.

37. Senate Rule 8-1.8.

38. Senate Rule 4-2.5.

39. Senate Rule 6-7.1(c).

40. Senate Rule 5-1.2.

41. Senate Rule 1-1.6(c).

42. Senate Rules 8-1.9 and 9-1.2.

43. Senate Rule 9-1.17.

44. Ga. Const. art. 3, §5, ¶¶6 and 7; Senate Rule 8-1.10.

45. Senate Rule 5-1.10(b).

46. Senate Rule 1-1.3.

47. Ga. Const. art. 3, §5, ¶10; Senate Rule 1-1.1(e).

48. Senate Rules 2-1.1 and 2-1.2.

49. O.C.G.A. §28-4-1(a).

50. O.C.G.A. §28-8-21(a).

51. O.C.G.A. §28-9-2(a).

52. O.C.G.A. §28-8-1(a).

53. O.C.G.A. §28-5-5(b).

54. Joint legislative oversight committees with one or more members appointed by the president of the Senate include the MARTA Overview Committee, Georgia World Congress Center Overview Committee, Georgia Rail Passenger Authority Overview Committee, Georgia Technology Authority Overview Committee, Georgia Tobacco Community Development Board Overview Committee, Georgia

Agricultural Exposition Authority Overview Committee, and OneGeorgia Authority Overview Committee.

55. Senate Rule 9-1.9(c).

56. Senate Rule 9-1.9(f).

57. Executive agencies and boards on which the lieutenant governor is an ex officio member include the Georgia State Financing and Investment Commission, One-Georgia Authority, Georgia Building Authority, Constitutional Amendments Publication Board, and State Commission on the Condemnation of Public Property. Additionally, the lieutenant governor appoints members to a variety of nonlegislative boards, including the State Properties Commission, State Commission on Compensation, Georgia Airport Development Authority, Power Alley Development Authority, Georgia Technology Authority, Georgia Environmental Training and Education Authority, Georgia Public Defender Standards Council, Georgia Child Care Council, Georgia Child Fatality Review Panel, Computer Equipment Disposal and Recycling Council, State Wastewater Privatization Oversight Committee, State Victim Services Commission, Southern Dairy Compact Commission, Georgia State Games Commission, Georgia Golf Hall of Fame Board, Georgia Commission on Women, and Georgia Commission on the Holocaust.

58. Ga. Const. art. 5, §1, ¶3.

59. Ga. Const. art. 5, §1, ¶5.

60. After the death of governor-elect Eugene Talmadge in December 1946, there were three contenders for the office. The controversy ended in 1947 when the Georgia Supreme Court ruled that lieutenant governor–elect M. E. Thompson should be acting governor until the next general election in 1948.

61. Senate Rule 1-1.2(a).

62. Senate Rule 1-1.2(c).

63. Senate Rule 2-7.2.

64. Senate Rule 1-1.3.

65. Senate Rules 2-1.1, 2-1.2, and 9-1.1.

66. O.C.G.A. §28-4-1.

67. O.C.G.A. §45-10-91(a).

68. Among the boards to which the president pro tempore appoints members are the Governor's Commercial Transportation Advisory Committee, State Commission on the Efficacy of the Certificate of Need Program, and Hotel Motel Tax Performance Review Board.

69. House Rule 20.

70. House Rule 21.

71. House Rule 82.

72. House Rule 23.

73. House Rule 52.

74. Ga. Const. art. 3, §5, ¶7.

75. House Rule 111.

76. Ga. Const. art. 3, §5, ¶6. *See also* House Rule 24.

77. House Rule 30.

78. House Rule 27.

79. Ibid.

80. House Rule 22.

81. House Rule 61.

82. House Rule 67.

83. House Rule 11.1.
84. House Rule 11.7.
85. House Rule 12.6.
86. House Rule 12.
87. Houses Rule 12.5.
88. House Rule 11.3.
89. House Rule 11.8
90. House Rule 10.2.
91. House Rule 146.1.
92. House Rule 54.
93. House Rule 10.2.
94. House Rule 7.12.
95. House Rule 7.13.
96. House Rule 7.11.
97. House Rule 4.
98. House Rule 5.
99. GA. CONST. art. 3, §5, ¶10; House Rule 151.
100. House Rule 9.
101. House Rule 8.3.
102. House Rule 45.
103. House Rules 25 and 163.
104. The "housekeeping resolution" adopted by the House at the beginning of a biennium authorizes the speaker to create interim study committees. *See, e.g.,* House Resolution 12, 2005 session.
105. O.C.G.A. §28-4-1(a).
106. O.C.G.A. §28-5-21(b).
107. O.C.G.A. §28-9-2(a).
108. O.C.G.A. §28-8-1(a).
109. O.C.G.A. §45-10-91.
110. O.C.G.A. §28-5-5.
111. In addition to the joint legislative oversight committees cited in note 54, the speaker appoints members to the General Oversight Committee for the Georgia Public Defender Standards Council and the HOPE Scholarship/Pre-K Legislative Oversight Committee.
112. Among the boards of which the speaker is an ex officio member are the Georgia State Financing and Investment Commission, Constitutional Amendments Publication Board, and Governor's Commercial Transportation Advisory Committee.
113. In addition to the boards cited in note 57, the speaker appoints one or more members to the State Commission on the Efficacy of the Certificate of Need Program, Hotel Motel Tax Performance Review Board, and Power Alley Development Authority.
114. GA. CONST. art. 5, §1, ¶5(c).
115. GA. CONST. art. 3, §3, ¶2(b).
116. House Rule 29.2.
117. House Rule 28.
118. House Rule 11.3; O.C.G.A. §28-4-1(a).
119. O.C.G.A. §§28-3-20(a) and 28-3-25.
120. O.C.G.A. §28-3-20.

121. *See, e.g.*, House Resolution 12 and Senate Resolution 5 for the 2005 "housekeeping resolutions."

122. Senate Rule 3-1.2; House Rules 48 and 49.

123. O.C.G.A. §28-1-11; Senate Rule 1-1.1(e); House Rule 151.

124. Senate Rule 1-1.2; House Rule 28.

125. O.C.G.A. §28-3-22.

126. Richter V. Harris, 62 Ga. App. 64, 7 S.E.2d 432 (1940).

127. O.C.G.A. §28-3-1.

128. House Rule 7.10.

129. House Rule 3.

130. House Rule 4.

131. House Rule 45.2.

132. House Rules 4 and 45.2.

133. O.C.G.A. §35-2-33(a)(2).

134. O.C.G.A. §35-2-73.

135. O.C.G.A. §50-9-9(f).

136. Senate Rule 1-1.6.

137. Senate Rule 5-1.2(c).

138. Senate Rule 1-1.6(b).

139. Senate Rule 9-1.6.

140. Senate Rule 1-1.6(b).

141. Senate Rule 8-1.11.

142. O.C.G.A. §20-2-392.

143. Senate Rule 9-1.9.

144. House Rule 160.

145. House Rule 10.1.

146. House Rule 10.2.

147. House Rule 11.2.

148. House Rule 11.1.

149. House Rule 11.9.

150. House Rule 11.1.

151. House Rules 11.1 and 11.5.

152. House Rule 12.

153. House Rule 11.8.

154. House Rule 11.3.

155. House Rule 11.4.

156. House Rule 165.

157. House Rule 12.6.

158. House Rule 11.7.

159. Ibid.

160. House Rule 12.6.

161. House Rule 14.1.

162. House Rule 146.3.

163. House Rule 14.2.

164. House Rule 167.1.

165. House Rule 16.

166. House Rules 164 through 172.
167. Senate Rule 2-1.3.
168. Senate Rule 2-3.1.
169. Senate Rule 2-1.1(b).
170. Senate Rule 2-1.1(a).
171. Senate Rule 2-1.3(a).
172. Senate Rule 2-3.2.
173. Senate Rule 2-3.3.
174. Senate Rule 2-3.1(c).
175. Senate Rule 2-3.1(b).
176. Senate Rule 2-2.1.
177. Senate Rule 1-5.1.
178. Ibid.
179. Senate Rule 2-1.7(c).
180. Senate Rule 2-1.7(a).
181. Ibid.
182. Senate Rules 2-1.5 through 2-6.2.
183. Senate Rule 2-1.10(a); House Rule 33.1.
184. Senate Rule 1-4.10; House Rule 164.8.
185. O.C.G.A. §§28-6-1 through 28-6-7.
186. See notes 54 and 111 for a list of joint legislative oversight committees.
187. Senate Rule 2-1.1(b).
188. For example, the Committee on Assignments appoints senators to the HOPE Scholarship/Pre-K Legislative Oversight Committee and the General Oversight Committee for the Georgia Public Defender Standards Council.
189. House Resolution 12 adopted January 10, 2005.
190. Senate Resolution 5 adopted January 10, 2005.

CHAPTER 5

POWERS AND LIMITATIONS

SEPARATION OF POWERS

The Georgia Constitution commands that "[t]he legislative, judicial, and executive powers shall forever remain separate and distinct; and no person discharging the duties of one shall at the same time exercise the functions of either of the others except as herein provided."[1] This is the celebrated "separation of powers" clause, and an understanding of its impact on the General Assembly is important to the legislator.

Generally speaking, the doctrine of separation of powers has been interpreted to mean that no branch—legislative, executive, or judicial—is subordinate to the others, but all are to be recognized as coordinate, independent, and coequal branches.[2] Without an express constitutional provision, no branch may infringe upon the power, jurisdiction, or ordinary functions of the others.[3] Furthermore, on numerous occasions, the court has demonstrated its commitment to protecting each branch from invasion by the others.[4]

Yet "this separation is not, and, from the nature of things, cannot be total."[5] First, under the concept of *checks and balances*, each branch has been given certain constitutional powers to limit the other branches, such as executive veto of legislation. Second, in a legal sense, the legislative branch is a first among equals by virtue of its broad lawmaking and funding powers over the other branches (except where constitutionally limited).[6] Third, it is impossible to draw a precise line to distinguish every governmental action as either *executive*, *legislative*, or *judicial*.[7]

THE RESTORED CHAMBER OF THE GEORGIA SENATE LOOKS
MUCH AS IT DID WHEN THE CAPITOL WAS DEDICATED IN 1889.

Regarding the third point, the Georgia Supreme Court occasionally has incorporated some variant of Chief Justice John Marshall's separation of powers maxim: "the legislature makes, the executive executes, and the judiciary construes the law."[8] Unfortunately, this offers little help in understanding the exact domain of each branch.

Defining when a particular function is "executive" in nature, and thus outside the limits of legislative exercise, has been particularly troublesome.[9] Courts have tended simply to conclude that if a particular activity is not "judicial" or "legislative" in the strictest sense, then it apparently falls within the executive branch.[10]

Several decisions of the Georgia Supreme Court help to more clearly define separation of powers. In 1975, the court looked at legislative membership on two statutory agencies—the World Congress Center Authority and the State Properties Commission—and ruled in both cases that since the agencies performed executive functions, legislative membership on these bodies violated the constitution's separation of powers mandate.[11] To allow the legislature to create an agency to implement specific legislation and then place legislators on that agency's governing body allowed the legislature to retain some control over implementation, the court added. This arrangement, if carried to the extreme, could allow the legislature to enact specific legislation and then appoint an ad hoc committee of its own members to implement it.[12]

As a result of the court's 1975 ruling, the General Assembly began the practice of creating joint legislative oversight committees to review designated projects, programs, and agencies in the executive branch.[13] Composed of members appointed from each house, the committees are not authorized any executive function; rather, they study how well a project, program, or agency is achieving its statutory function and report back to the General Assembly on their findings and any suggestions for changes in state law or funding.

It should be noted, however, that the court has not ruled out legislative participation in the executive branch in all situations. For example, it seems that no constitutional harm is incurred by legislative participation on "executive" boards and councils that perform advisory functions only and that in no way become involved in the executive or implementing process. Also, Georgia's supreme court has affirmed the right of members of the legislative branch—in this case, the speaker—to appoint nonlegislators to an executive commission without violating the separation of powers clause.[14]

REPRESENTATIVE GOVERNMENT AT WORK

Until 1825, members of the General Assembly elected the state governor. A constitutional amendment in 1824, however, turned the election over to the people of the state. In 1823, George M. Troup became the last governor named by the legislature, winning by a margin of 4 votes out of the total votes cast in both houses. In the election of 1825, Governor Troup became the first chief executive to win a popular election, this time winning just over half of the 40,000 votes cast.

In 1976, the court was faced with the question of whether the state auditor—who is elected by, funded through, and responsible to the General Assembly—was a member of the executive or legislative branch of government. The justices ruled that the auditor was part of the executive branch, "for he has no lawmaking powers."[15] The auditor's election by the legislative branch was, to the court, "simply a reflection of the system of checks and balances among the three branches of government."[16]

Thus, rather than being a rigid principle, "separation of powers" has and does assume a degree of flexibility to permit practical arrangements in a complex government.[17]

DELEGATION OF LAWMAKING POWERS

If the separation of powers clause prevents one branch from encroaching on the functions of the others, it also prohibits any branch from delegating its essential functions to another. Georgia's constitution specifically vests the legislative power of the state in the General Assembly.[18] The supreme court has interpreted this to mean that what the legislature has been granted cannot be delegated to anyone else—the so-called "nondelegation doctrine."[19] On numerous occasions, the court has used this theory to strike down laws that attempted to delegate legislative powers to another branch, local government, or nonpublic body.[20] For example, the Georgia General Assembly cannot confer on any person or any other body the power to determine what the law is in this state.[21] A statute will be declared unconstitutional as an improper delegation of legislative power if it is incomplete as legislation and allows an executive agency to decide what is and what is not an infringement of the law.[22] Following this principle, the supreme court has invalidated a statute that, in delegating certain powers to a state board, gave that board authority to determine which acts (for example, possession of depressant and stimulant drugs) would constitute a crime.[23]

Nevertheless, the legislature may confer upon administrative agencies "quasi-legislative functions which it itself might perform, but could not so adequately perform directly as it could by delegating them."[24]

> Thus, while it is necessary that a law, when it comes from the lawmaking power shall be complete, still there are many matters as to methods or details which the legislature may refer to some designated ministerial officer or board. [Cit.] The constitutional prohibition, therefore, does not deny to the lawmaking body "the necessary resources of flexibility and practicality, which will enable it to perform its function in laying down policies and establishing standards, while leaving to selected instrumentalities the making of subordinate rules within prescribed limits and the determination of facts to which the policy as declared by the legislature is to apply." [Cit.][25]

While repeatedly upholding the nondelegation doctrine, Georgia's supreme court has also recognized that in a complex society, the General Assembly cannot be aware of all facts and anticipate all situations that will arise in implementing legislative policy. Consequently, the court has approved numerous delegations of legislative authority in situations where the General Assembly has spelled out sufficient guidelines for the delegatee.[26]

Related to the nondelegation doctrine are questions about two devices used in some states to circumvent the concept that full lawmaking authority belongs to the legislature. One of these, *popular initiative*, allows the public directly to change state law without legislative involvement. While specifics vary in the 17 states that currently allow popular initiative, if a specified percentage of the voters (usually 5 to 10 percent of the votes cast in the last general election) sign a petition, a proposed measure is placed on a state ballot.[27] In all states, a majority of the popular vote is necessary to enact the proposal into law. Georgia's constitution does not provide for popular initiative, and in view of art. 3, sec. 1, para. 1, it would undoubtedly require a constitutional amendment to authorize the procedure.

The second device related to delegation of legislative power is the *referendum*. With this procedure, the legislature passes a law, but voters then have to approve the law before it can go into effect. Twenty-eight states have some type of referendum, though in many cases it is limited to certain types of laws (e.g., debt authorization).[28] Georgia's constitution specifically authorizes a public referendum on general laws in only one case—any law to exempt property from ad valorem taxes must be approved by two-thirds of each house of the General Assembly and by a majority of the qualified voters voting in a referendum on the exemption.[29] The constitution also directs that local referenda be held in conjunction with several types of local acts, such as those (1) changing the homestead exemption in any county; (2) exempting from ad valorem taxes inventories of goods in the process of manufacture or production, and inventories of finished goods; and (3) consolidating or reorganizing local governments.[30] From time to time, the General Assembly enacts other types of local acts that call for voters of the affected city or county to give their consent.

Clearly, there is no issue of delegation of legislative power when the state constitution specifically authorizes voter approval for designated laws. The constitutionality of referenda on other types of acts, however, could raise the delegation of legislative power question. Almost exclusively, referenda are associated with local legislation, and the supreme court has upheld the right of the General Assembly to require local approval for legislation affecting a named city or county. In fact, in several cases in which a local referendum was challenged as violating the delegation of legislative power provision of the constitution, the court has seemed sympathetic with the general concept of the referendum. For example, in a 1931 decision, the court observed, "This state has been committed for many years to the doctrine that the legislature may submit to the electorate the question whether legislation framed and approved by the General Assembly shall become operative." Similarly, a 1953 decision noted, "Such [a referendum] is not a delegation of legislative power, but is simply an exercise of that power, guided by the will of the people to be affected." At issue in each case was a local act in which the people of the community affected were called on to decide whether the act would become effective.[31]

The constitutionality of a statewide referendum on a general statute (other than one granting an exemption from ad valorem taxes) is not so clear—an issue the supreme court has carefully shied away from. Excluding laws creating agricultural commodity commissions (which only affect growers of particular commodities) and ad valorem tax exemptions, the General Assembly has called for a statewide referendum in only a few cases, with only one—a 1935 referendum on repealing prohibition—actually held.[32] In the few cases in which the constitutionality of a referendum on a general statute has been before the supreme court (including the prohibition referendum), the justices have avoided ruling on the issue.[33]

In 1993, Georgia's governor specifically asked the state attorney general whether the General Assembly could enact a general law that could only become effective upon approval of the voters in a statewide referendum. The attorney general's official opinion held that a binding referendum would be an abdication of the General Assembly's exclusive authority to enact laws as provided for in Article III of the Georgia Constitution. The opinion also held that a binding referendum would be unconstitutional for two other reasons: (1) it would amount to a limitation on the General Assembly's power (something also specifically prohibited in the constitution), and (2) it goes beyond the constitutional provision that "all bills and resolutions which have been passed by the General Assembly [that are] intended to have the effect of law shall become law if the [g]overnor approves or fails to veto the same. . . ." The attorney general's 1993 opinion noted that there are several instances in which a statewide referendum can be held (e.g., a general act exempting property from ad valorem taxation) and even more instances in which a local referendum must be held (e.g., a local act consolidating local school systems). However, in each case, there is an express constitutional provision authorizing the referendum. Without such specific authorization, a statewide referendum cannot be held to determine whether a general act will become law.[34]

In 2003, the question of a binding statewide referendum came before the General Assembly. The issue was whether to change Georgia's state flag. Two years earlier, the legislature had changed the state flag from the one adopted in 1956 to a new design. However, not only did the new flag design prove unpopular, but also there were calls for a return to the 1956 flag. A number of opponents to the 2001 flag change called for a statewide referendum to allow the people to select Georgia's state flag. By the 2003 session, however, another option was before the legislature: to replace the 2001 flag with a different design. In May 2003, the governor signed legislation permitting a new design.[35] The legislation also contained a provision for a statewide referendum on whether voters preferred the 2001 or 2003 flag (the 1956 flag was not a choice on the ballot). Because of constitutional concerns over a statewide binding referendum, the legislature deemed the results to be advisory; that is, they would be informational but not binding on the General Assembly. Subsequently, in a statewide

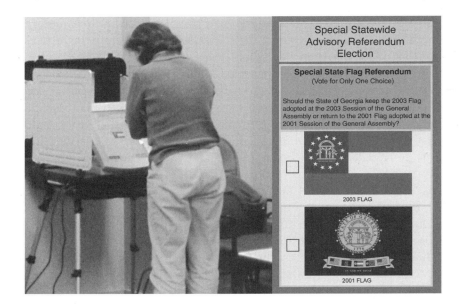

IN 2004, GEORGIA VOTERS PARTICIPATED IN AN
ADVISORY REFERENDUM ON GEORGIA'S STATE FLAG.

referendum held on March 2, 2004, Georgia voters had the opportunity to express their preference for either the 2001 or 2003 design. Support for the new design was overwhelming, with more than 73 percent of voters selecting the 2003 flag. Had the results gone the other way, the legislature would have been under no legal obligation to revisit the flag issue.

LAWMAKING POWERS

The Georgia Constitution confers broad lawmaking powers on the legislature, stating that "[t]he General Assembly shall have the power to make all laws not inconsistent with this Constitution, and not repugnant to the Constitution of the United States, which it shall deem necessary and proper for the welfare of the state."[36]

Nor are the powers of the General Assembly limited only to those expressly enumerated in the constitution. The Georgia Supreme Court has held that there are no restrictions on the General Assembly's power to legislate, so long as its laws do not violate the U.S. or Georgia constitutions.[37] The courts will assume that the General Assembly is authorized to enact a given law unless there is a stated or implied constitutional denial of legislative authority involved.

In addition to granting broad power to make laws, Georgia's constitution explicitly entrusts many lawmaking powers into the hands of the General Assembly, such as those to

1. tax for any purpose authorized by law (and for purposes that existed as of June 30, 1983, the day before the Constitution of 1983 became effective);[38]

2. appropriate public funds for the operation of all state agencies and to meet the expenses of the state (no state fund can be drawn from the treasury except by appropriation act);[39]

3. establish the jurisdiction of courts (except where otherwise provided within the constitution), as well as authorize administrative agencies to exercise quasi-judicial powers;[40]

4. create, abolish, or change superior court circuits, courts, and judgeships (so long as no circuit consists of less than one county);[41]

5. prescribe the duties, authority, and salaries of the executive officers of the state (unless otherwise provided by the constitution);[42]

6. provide for the state militia (National Guard);[43]

7. provide grants, scholarships, loans, and assistance for educational purposes;[44]

8. provide for the recall of elected public officials;[45]

9. provide for the regulation of insurance within the state;[46] and

10. waive or qualify the state's sovereign immunity from suit.[47]

The General Assembly has broad authority to legislate with regard to the powers, duties, and functions of city and county government in the state.[48] Also, exclusive power is given to the General Assembly to propose amendments to the existing constitution or to propose a new constitution (or provide for a convention or commission to propose a new constitution), though such proposals must be submitted to the voters of the state for ratification.[49]

No general obligation debt may be incurred by the state until the General Assembly has enacted legislation stating the purposes for which such debt is to be incurred, specifying the maximum principal amount of such issue and appropriating an amount at least sufficient to pay the highest annual debt service requirements for the issue. Similarly, guaranteed revenue debt may not be incurred until the General Assembly has authorized by legislation the guarantee of the specific issue, specifying the maximum principal amount of such issue and appropriating an amount at least equal to the highest annual debt service requirements for such issue.[50]

Except as provided by the constitution, the General Assembly has broad powers over public officers and employees in the executive branch. These powers cover matters of eligibility and qualifications for office; oaths; bonds; vacancies and resignations; inspection of books, papers, and reports; salaries; fees; counsel for state employees; open meetings; insurance; strikes; retirement; crimes; and various other matters.[51]

In addition to these specific powers, the constitution, in providing for many of the executive officers, boards, and departments, directs that their powers, authority, and duties will be provided by the General Assembly. Thus, there are a variety of "constitutional boards," or "constitutional agencies," whose memberships, terms of office, and appointments are constitutionally stipulated, but whose powers and duties are directed by statute. Currently, there are no executive agencies so constitutionally insulated as to be totally immune from at least some aspect of legislative control; certainly this is true regarding appropriations.

As will be discussed later, however, the constitution contains numerous restrictions on the General Assembly's lawmaking powers.

NONLAWMAKING POWERS AND FUNCTIONS

In addition to enacting laws and appropriating funds, the Georgia legislature performs a variety of other important functions.

Appointment of State Officers

Any state officer whose selection is not otherwise provided for is elected by the General Assembly in the same manner and at the same time it elects other officers.[52] (Currently, there are no state officials whose selection is unprovided for.) Under present law, the General Assembly selects the state auditor, who is elected by the House and confirmed by the Senate, for an indefinite term (until his or her successor is elected in a like manner).[53] Also, the senators and representatives in each of the state's congressional districts caucus to elect the member of the State Transportation Board from their district.[54]

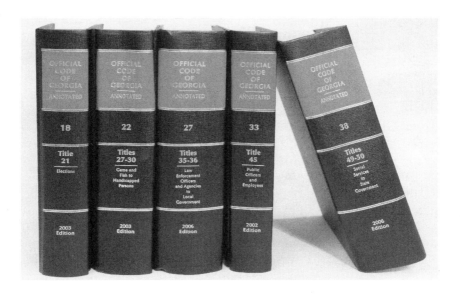

THE OFFICIAL CODE OF GEORGIA ANNOTATED IS A 54-VOLUME
COMPILATION OF GEORGIA STATUTORY LAW.

Confirming Appointments of the Governor

All appointments by the governor to boards, commissions, and bureaus created by the General Assembly are subject to confirmation by the Senate. If they are not confirmed, they may not hold office, and the name of another appointee must be submitted immediately by the governor.[55] With regard to this Senate power, the Georgia Supreme Court has observed that the Senate does not acquire the power to discharge officials once confirmed, and that the power of approving appointees does not include the power to later discharge that appointee.[56] Once the Senate has rejected an appointment of the governor to any office, that person may not be reappointed by the governor to the same office for a period of one year from the date of rejection.[57]

Appointments by the governor to boards and commissions established by executive order are not subject to Senate confirmation.

Recall of Elected Officials

The General Assembly may provide by general law procedures and grounds for the recall of any elected public official in the state.[58]

Special Oversight Powers

In addition to its other powers, the General Assembly possesses special authority to oversee the executive branch. First, all books kept by any public officer under Georgia laws are subject to the inspection of any legislator (as well as any citizen),[59] and the minutes of any meeting of any state agency at which official actions are taken must be recorded and open for similar inspection.[60] By law, the General Assembly is granted authority as complete and absolute as that granted to the attorney general to conduct investigations at any time into the affairs of the state, any agency, or of any person or organization to the extent that the person or organization has dealings with the state.[61] For purposes of conducting these investigations, the General Assembly may subpoena witnesses, require them to testify under oath, and require the production of books, records, and papers.[62]

Either the House or Senate Appropriations Committee (or the governor) may require the state auditor to make a special examination and audit of all books, records, accounts, vouchers, warrants, bills, and other papers and records, and the financial transactions and management of any agency at any time.[63] Additionally, the auditor is directed to cooperate with either appropriations committee and to furnish any information requested for its use.[64] Officers and employees of all state agencies are directed to produce and turn over to the auditor or his or her assistants for examination and audit—upon demand—all of their books, records, accounts, vouchers, warrants, bills, and other papers dealing with or reflecting upon the financial transactions and management of the agency, officer, or employee.[65]

Georgia's constitution authorizes the governor to give the General Assembly information on the state of the state at the beginning of each session and to recommend for its consideration such measures as deemed necessary.[66] In addition, state law requires the governor to furnish a written report to each legislator by the fifth day of each session outlining the governor's policies and goals on the major program areas of state government as well as any other subject matters.[67] State law also requires the governor, through the Office of Planning and Budget, to prepare an annual state strategic plan that addresses statewide goals, objectives, and opportunities and to transmit this to the General Assembly at the beginning of each session. A program budget report can satisfy this requirement.[68]

Legislative capacity to oversee the executive branch—particularly with respect to budgeting and planning—was greatly expanded when the General Assembly passed the Budget Accountability and Planning Act of 1993. This legislation created a Budgetary Responsibility Oversight Committee consisting of six members from each house with broad authority to review executive agencies and make recommendations to the General Assembly with respect to the budget.[69] To assist it in its responsibilities, the committee has a full-time director and staff.

Though not all agencies are so required, many executive departments and agencies are directed by statute to submit annual or other periodic reports to the General Assembly and governor, detailing accomplishments and activities, as well as recommendations for additional legislation.

Another oversight power of the legislature is that over rules and regulations adopted by executive agencies subject to the Administrative Procedures Act (APA) (see O.C.G.A. ch. 50-13). Because of legislative concern that executive agencies were adopting rules and regulations that either exceeded or violated legislative intent, a legislative review process was instituted in 1978. That process requires that any proposed rule or rule change subject to the APA must be sent to the legislative counsel at least 30 days prior to its adoption. (See Fig. 1, "Georgia's Administrative Rule-Making Process.") Within three days of receipt, the legislative counsel forwards it to the presiding officer of each house, who assigns the rule to the appropriate standing committee (and to any committee member who has requested notification) for review. If the committee objects to the proposed rule prior to its adoption, and the agency adopts the rule anyway, a resolution to void the rule may be introduced in that committee's house within the first 30 days of the next regular session. If that resolution is adopted, it is sent to the other house. If passed in both houses by a two-thirds vote, the resolution does not go to the governor, and the rule is voided after the second house passes the resolution. If less than a two-thirds vote is received, the resolution may be vetoed or sustained by the governor.[70]

Impeachment

Still another nonlawmaking power of the General Assembly is the power of impeachment. The Georgia Constitution specifically invests this power in the General Assembly.[71] Impeachment has been generally defined as calling for the removal from office of a public official charged with a crime, misconduct, or violation of the public trust, instituted by a written accusation called "articles of impeachment."[72]

In Georgia, the House of Representatives is given the sole power to vote impeachment charges against any person who has been, or

FIGURE 1. Georgia's Administrative Rule-Making Process

① Denotes steps in administrative rule-making process

ⓘ Denotes steps in legislative review of administrative rule-making process

❶ Agency Initiative / Statutory Mandate / Federal Mandate / Public Request

❷ Agency drafts proposed rule

❸ Agency gives at least 30 days' notice of proposed rule to "interested parties" on mailing list

Agency gives at least 30 days' notice of proposed rule to legislative counsel

❹ Agency holds public hearing and considers all written and oral comments

Agency decides not to adopt rule

❺ Agency modifies rule, if necessary

❻ Agency formally adopts rule

❼ Rule filed with Secretary of State

❽ Rule becomes final 20 days after filing (unless vetoed by legislature)

❾ Secretary of State publishes quarterly bulletin containing rule

❿ Rule codified and distributed as supplement to official compilation, "Rules and Regulations of the State of Georgia"

ⓛ Copies of proposed rule sent to presiding officer of each house for assigning to appropriate standing committee

② Consideration of proposed rule by standing committee in each house

③ Committee takes no action to block rule

Committee objects to rule

④ If agency adopts rule despite committee objection, resolution to veto rule may be introduced in house whose committee objects

Resolution to veto fails in one or both houses, and rule is upheld

⑤ If resolution passes both houses by less than 2/3 of total members, it goes to the governor

If resolution passes both houses by at least 2/3 of total members, it does not go to governor

Governor vetoes resolution, and rule is upheld

Governor does not veto resolution

⑥ Rule is void as of next day

is, in office.[73] After the members of the House have voted to pass the "articles of impeachment" against a particular official, the Senate is vested with the sole power of trying the case.[74]

When sitting for the purpose of trying impeachments, the members of the Senate are on oath or affirmation, and are presided over by the chief justice of the Georgia Supreme Court. If the chief justice should be disqualified, the presiding justice conducts the trial. Should the presiding justice be disqualified, the Senate selects for its presiding officer another supreme court justice.[75]

To convict a defendant in an impeachment case, two-thirds of the total membership of the Senate must vote to do so.[76] Judgments of the Senate in such cases can extend no further than removal from office and disqualification from holding and enjoying any office of honor, trust, or profit within this state. However, the convicted official is still liable and subject to indictment, trial, judgment, and punishment by the appropriate courts of the state.[77]

LIMITATIONS ON POWERS

It would seem appropriate to consider some of the limitations and restrictions placed upon the powers exercised by the General Assembly. The limitations vary widely in nature and importance, and only some of the more general ones will be mentioned here.

General limitation. The General Assembly cannot validly pass any act that is in violation of the Georgia or United States constitutions.[78] It can enact no law that curtails or restrains the liberty of speech or of the press.[79] The social status of citizens can never be the subject of legislation.[80]

The legislature is prohibited from passing any bill of attainder, ex post facto law, retroactive law, or law impairing the obligation of contract. It is forbidden to make any irrevocable grant of special privileges or immunities.[81]

Monopolies. Contracts or agreements which tend to lessen competition or encourage monopoly are expressly illegal in Georgia, and the legislature is forbidden to authorize them.[82]

Taxation. The power of the General Assembly is limited in that it cannot irrevocably give, grant, limit, or restrain the right of taxation except as provided by the constitution.[83]

Donations and gratuities. Except as specifically authorized in the constitution, lawmakers are prohibited from (1) making any donation or granting any gratuity, (2) forgiving any debt owed the state, or (3) granting extra compensation to any public officer, agent, or contractor after a contract has been signed or a service rendered.[84] Several exceptions to this rule allowed by the constitution include educational scholarships[85] and indemnification of law enforcement officers, prison guards, emergency medical technicians, and public school teachers, administrators, and employees who are killed or permanently disabled in the line of duty.[86]

Appropriations. The General Assembly may not appropriate funds for any fiscal year that exceed the current surplus plus anticipated revenue.[87] In other words, deficit budgets are prohibited by the constitution. The appropriation of money to aid any church, sect, or denomination, or any sectarian institution, is also prohibited.[88]

Separation of powers. In addition to these types of limitations, the General Assembly is constrained by the separation of powers clause in the constitution from encroaching on the functions of the executive and judicial branches, as well as voluntarily yielding legislative powers to these branches. Thus, not only is the legislature prohibited from assuming or exercising executive powers, but its members may not sit on state boards entrusted with executive functions.[89]

Similarly, the General Assembly may not dictate to the judiciary how to write its opinions or what form the decisions must take,[90] nor may it alter judgments of such courts.[91] The legislature cannot circumscribe the power of the supreme court by adopting rules and regulations governing the bar and practice of law in the state.[92]

Binding future legislatures. Another important limitation on the General Assembly is that one legislature cannot bind or tie the hands of its successors, or impose upon them conditions with reference to subjects upon which they have an equal power to legislate.[93] However, an act of one legislature—such as setting salaries—will be binding upon future legislatures, unless they choose to repeal or amend it. The important point is that no one statute can preclude or bind future statutes on the same subject. Similarly, one legislature has no power to declare the intent of a prior General Assembly in enacting a law, as this would be a legislative attempt to construe a law—a judicial function under Georgia's constitution.[94]

Powers of cities and counties. In a variety of designated areas—such as police and fire protection, garbage and solid waste collection, public health facilities and services, parks and recreational programs, water treatment and distribution, public housing, and public transportation—

the General Assembly, by general legislation, may regulate, restrict, or limit the exercise of powers by local governments. But it cannot withdraw such powers.[95]

Other. Additional limitations on the General Assembly are discussed in the following chapter, particularly those that relate to requirements for legislation.

NOTES

1. GA. CONST. art. 1, §2, ¶3.
2. *See* 16 *American Jurisprudence* 2d, §211, p. 450.
3. Parks v. State, 212 Ga. 433, 93 S.E.2d 663 (1956); Fortson v. Weeks, 232 Ga. 472, 208 S.E.2d 68 (1974); Mosely v. Sentence Review Board, 631 S.E.2d 704 (2006).
4. McCutcheon v. Smith, 199 Ga. 685, 35 S.E.2d 144 (1945); Parks v. State, 212 Ga. 433, 93 S.E.2d 663 (1956); Etkind v. Suarez, 271 Ga. 352, 519 S.E.2d 210 (1999). *See also* Galer v. Board of Regents, 239 Ga. 268, 236 S.E.2d 617 (1977).
5. Beall v. Beall, 8 Ga. 210 (1850); Mayor & Council of Americus v. Perry, 114 Ga. 871, 40 S.E. 1004 (1902); Department of Transportation v. Atlanta, 260 Ga. 699, 398 S.E.2d 567 (1990).
6. Myers v. U.S., 272 U.S. 52 (1926). As Georgia's high court noted on one occasion, "While, in theory, the other departments, judicial and executive, may be coordinate, yet it is a fact authenticated by history, that the people attach themselves to the Legislature as the fountain of power, whose right it is to direct the action and enlarge or limit the powers exercised by the others. [Walker v. Whitehead, 43 Ga. 538 (1871)]"
7. Southern Railway v. Melton, 133 Ga. 277, 65 S.E. 665 (1909); Stephens v. State, 207 Ga. App. 645, 428 S.E.2d 661 (1993); Wolcott v. State, 278 Ga. 664, 604 S.E.2d 478 (2004).
8. Wayman v. Southard, 23 U.S. 1 (1825); Adams v. Georgia Department of Corrections, 274 Ga. 461, 553 S.E.2d (2001); Harbuck v. State, 631 S.E.2d 351 (2006).
9. *Black's Law Dictionary* (8th ed., 2004) suggests the executive function relates to management, control, and supervision of programs or activities, with accompanying authority to outline duties and direct the work of subordinate employees. According to this same source, "executive agencies" are those departments in government whose activities are subject to statute and whose contracts are subject to judicial review (p. 610).
10. Springer v. Philippine Islands, 277 U.S. 189 (1928); Rich v. State, 237 Ga. 291, 227 S.E.2d 761 (1976). Framers of Georgia's Constitution of 1945 were aware of this problem but unable to resolve precisely what constitutes the executive branch. See Albert B. Saye, ed., *Records of the Commission of 1943–44 to Revise the Constitution of Georgia*, vol. I, p. 197 (1946).
11. Greer v. State, 233 Ga. 667, 212 S.E.2d 836 (1975); Murphy v. State, 233 Ga. 681, 212 S.E.2d 839 (1975).
12. Greer v. State, 233 Ga. 667, 212 S.E.2d 836 (1975).
13. A list of joint legislative oversight committees currently authorized by statute can be found in Chapter 4 notes 47 and 117.
14. Caldwell v. Bateman, 252 Ga. 144, 312 S.E.2d 320 (1984).
15. Rich v. State, 237 Ga. 291, 227 S.E.2d (1976).
16. Ibid.
17. Greer v. State, 233 Ga. 667, 212 S.E.2d 836 (1975); Department of Transportation v. City of Atlanta, 260 Ga. 699, 398 S.E.2d 567 (1990); Rich v. State, 237 Ga. 291, 227 S.E.2d 761 (1976).

18. GA. CONST. art. 3, §1, ¶1.

19. According to the court, "The nondelegation doctrine is rooted in the principle of separation of powers, in that the integrity of our tripartite system of government mandates that the General Assembly not divest itself of the legislative power granted to it by Art. 3, Sec. 1, Par. 1, of our Constitution, see *generally*, Mistretta v. United States, 488 U.S. 361, 109 S. Ct. 647, 654, 102 L.Ed. 2d. 714 (1989)." Department of Transportation v. Atlanta, 260 Ga. 699, 398 S.E.2d 567 (1990); Harbuck v. State, 631 S.E.2d 351 (2006).

20. Georgia Railroad v. Smith, 70 Ga. 694 (1883); Southern Railway v. Melton, 133 Ga. 277, 65 S.E. 665 (1909); Moseley v. Garrett, 182 Ga. 810, 187 S.E. 20 (1936); Long v. State, 202 Ga. 235, 42 S.E.2d 729 (1947); Phillips v. Atlanta, 210 Ga. 72, 77 S.E.2d 723 (1953); Harrison Company v. Code Revision Commission, 244 Ga. 325, 260 S.E.2d 30 (1979).

21. Bohannon v. Duncan, 185 Ga. 840, 196 S.E. 897 (1938). Somewhat related to this principle—though dealing with the broader issue of delegation of *governmental* power—is a supreme court ruling that the legislature cannot delegate the power to appoint members of a public agency or board to a private organization. *See* Rogers v. Medical Association of Ga., 244 Ga. 151, 259 S.E.2d 85 (1979); *Atlanta Journal* v. Hill, 257 Ga. 398, 359 S.E.2d 913 (1987).

22. Sundberg v. State, 234 Ga. 482, 216 S.E.2d 332 (1975); Johnston v. State, 227 Ga. 387, 181 S.E.2d 42 (1971); Department of Transportation v. Atlanta, 260 Ga. 699, 398 S.E.2d 567 (1990); HCA Health Services of Georgia v. Roach, 265 Ga. 501, 458 S.E.2d 118 (1995).

23. Sundberg v. State, 234 Ga. 482, 216 S.E.2d 332 (1975).

24. Abbot v. Commissioners, 160 Ga. 657, 129 S.E. 381 (1925); Campbell v. Farmer, 223 Ga. 605, 157 S.E.2d 276 (1967); Scoggins v. Whitfield Finance Co., 242 Ga. 416, 249 S.E.2d 222 (1978); Department of Transportation v. Del-Cook Timber Co., 248 Ga. 734, 285 S.E.2d 913 (1982). For a discussion of delegation of legislative power to local governments in Georgia, *see* R. Perry Sentell, Jr., "Delegation in Georgia Local Government Law," 7 *Georgia State Bar Journal* 9 (August 1970).

25. Bohannon v. Duncan, 185 Ga. 840, 843, 196 S.E. 897, 899 (1938). *See also* Department of Transportation v. Atlanta, 260 Ga. 699, 398 S.E.2d 567 (1990).

26. Southern Railway v. Melton, 133 Ga. 277, 65 S.E. 665 (1909); Russell v. Venable, 216 Ga. 137, 115 S.E.2d 103 (1960); Scoggins v. Whitfield Finance Co., 242 Ga. 416, 249 S.E.2d 222 (1978); Department of Transportation v. Atlanta, 260 Ga. 699, 398 S.E.2d 567 (1990).

27. *The Book of the States, 2006*, Vol. 38 (Lexington, Ky.: Council of State Governments, 2006), Table 6.10, p. 307.

28. Ibid.

29. GA. CONST. art. VII, §2, ¶2(a)(1).

30. GA. CONST. art. VII, §2, ¶2(a)(2); art. VII, §2, ¶3(a); art. IX, §3, ¶2.

31. Hines v. Etheridge, 173 Ga. 870, 872, 162 S.E. 113, 115 (1931); Phillips v. Atlanta, 210 Ga. 72, 77 S.E.2d 723 (1953).

32. Ga. Laws 1935, p. 327.

33. Mayor and Council of Brunswick v. Finney, 54 Ga. 317, 324 (1875); Reynolds v. State, 181 Ga. 547, 182 S.E. 917 (1935); Holcombe v. Georgia Milk Producers Confederation, 188 Ga. 358, 3 S.E.2d 705 (1939).

34. 1993 Op. Att'y Gen. 93-5.

35. Ga. Laws 2003, p. 26.

36. GA. CONST. art. 3, §6, ¶1.

37. Nicholas v. Hovenor, 42 Ga. 514 (1870); Plumb v. Christie, 103 Ga. 686, 30 S.E. 759 (1898); Green v. Harper, 177 Ga. 680, 170 S.E. 872 (1933); Petty v. Hospital Authority

of Douglas County, 233 Ga. 109, 210 S.E.2d 317 (1974); Sears v. State, 232 Ga. 547, 208 S.E. 93 (1974).

38. GA. CONST. art. 7, §3, ¶1.

39. GA. CONST. art. 3, §9, ¶2.

40. GA. CONST. art. 6, §1, ¶1; art. 6, §3, ¶1; art. 6, §6, ¶3.

41. GA. CONST. art. 6, §1, ¶7.

42. GA. CONST. art. 5, §3, ¶3.

43. GA. CONST. art. 3, §6, ¶2(a)(2).

44. GA. CONST. art. 8, §7, ¶1.

45. GA. CONST. art. 2, §2, ¶4.

46. GA. CONST. art. 3, §8, ¶1.

47. GA. CONST. art. 1, §2, ¶9.

48. *See, for example,* GA. CONST. art. 9, §§1–6; art. 7, §§1–2; art. 8, §5.

49. GA. CONST. art. 10, §1.

50. GA. CONST. art. 7, §4, ¶3.

51. O.C.G.A. Title 45.

52. O.C.G.A. §28-1-12.

53. O.C.G.A. §50-6-1.

54. GA. CONST. art. 4, §4, ¶1; O.C.G.A. §32-2-20.

55. O.C.G.A. §45-12-54. *See also* 1966 Op. Att'y Gen. 66-231 for elaboration on confirming authority of Senate. Sec. 45-12-54 appears inconsistent with §45-12-53, which was passed two years earlier and states: "No appointment by the governor shall be subject to confirmation by the Senate unless the statute under which such appointment is made requires confirmation or confirmation is otherwise required by law."

56. Richmond County v. Jackson, 234 Ga. 717, 218 S.E.2d 11 (1975); Glynn County v. Waters, 268 Ga. 500, 491 S.E.2d 370 (1997).

57. GA. CONST. art. 5, §2, ¶9.

58. GA. CONST. art. 2, §2, ¶4.

59. O.C.G.A. §45-6-6.

60. O.C.G.A. §50-14-1.

61. O.C.G.A. §45-15-19.

62. O.C.G.A. §45-15-17.

63. O.C.G.A. §50-6-4.

64. O.C.G.A. §50-6-23.

65. O.C.G.A. §50-6-7.

66. GA. CONST. art. 5, §2, ¶6.

67. O.C.G.A. §45-12-39.

68. O.C.G.A. §45-12-177.

69. O.C.G.A. §28-5-5.

70. O.C.G.A. §50-13-4.

71. GA. CONST. art. 3, §7.

72. *Black's Law Dictionary* (8th ed., 2004), p. 768.

73. GA. CONST. art. 3, §7, ¶1.

74. GA. CONST. art. 3, §7, ¶2.

75. Ibid.

76. Ibid.

77. GA. CONST. art. 3, §7, ¶3.

78. Ga. Const. art. 1, §2, ¶5.

79. Ga. Const. art. 1, §1, ¶5.

80. Ga. Const. art. 1, §1, ¶25; art. 3, §6, ¶4(c).

81. Ga. Const. art. 1, §1, ¶10.

82. Ga. Const. art. 3, §6, ¶5(c). *See, e.g.*, Harrison Co. v. Code Revision Comm., 244 Ga. 325, 260 S.E.2d 30 (1979).

83. Ga. Const. art. 7, §1, ¶1.

84. Ga. Const. art. 3, §6, ¶6.

85. Ga. Const. art. 8, §7, ¶1.

86. Ga. Const. art. 3, §6, ¶6.

87. Ga. Const. art. 3, §9, ¶4(b).

88. Ga. Const. art. 1, §2, ¶7.

89. Greer v. State, 233 Ga. 667, 212 S.E.2d 836 (1975); Murphy v. State, 233 Ga. 681, 212 S.E.2d 839 (1975).

90. Taylor v. Columbia County Planning Commission, 232 Ga. 155, 205 S.E.2d 287 (1974); Southeastern Plumbing Supply Company v. Lee, 232 Ga. 626, 208 S.E.2d 449 (1974).

91. Jenkins v. Jenkins, 233 Ga. 902, 214 S.E.2d 368 (1975); Northside Manor v. Vann, 219 Ga. 298, 133 S.E.2d 32 (1963).

92. Sams v. Olah, 225 Ga. 497, 169 S.E.2d 790 (1969); Attwell v. Nichols, 466 F. Supp. 206 (1979); Grecaa, Inc. v. Omni Title Services, Inc., 277 Ga. 312, 588 S.E.2d 709 (2003).

93. State Highway Dept. v. Hatcher, 218 Ga. 299, 127 S.E.2d 803 (1962); Shaw v. Mayor & Council of Macon, 21 Ga. 280 (1857).

94. Undercofler v. Swint, 111 Ga. App. 117, 140 S.E.2d 894 (1965); Road Builders, Inc. of Tennessee v. Hawes, 228 Ga. 608, 187 S.E.2d 287 (1972); J.M.I.C. Life Insurance Company v. Toole, 2006 WL, July 10, 2006.

95. Ga. Const. art. 9, §2, ¶3(c).

CHAPTER 6

BILLS AND RESOLUTIONS

Before considering the procedure for introduction and passage of legislation, lawmakers should be aware of the various classifications of legislation. Knowledge of these is necessary in order to understand some of the legal and procedural matters associated with the legislative process.

TYPES OF LEGISLATION

All legislation introduced in the Georgia General Assembly is classified as either a "bill" or a "resolution." The word "bill" refers to proposed legislation, from the draft as introduced in one of the houses, through the various committee and floor stages, until finally enacted into law. A "resolution" is similar to a bill but may or may not have the force of law, depending on the subject matter and intent of the legislature. Although resolutions represent a formal expression of legislative opinion on a given subject, they may be used for other purposes, as noted later.

One important distinction between the two types of legislation is that bills are used to propose changes or additions to existing statutes, while resolutions are not. There are a few exceptions. For instance, annual appropriations measures—usually not considered to be statutes—are introduced as bills. Also, proposed constitutional amendments, which may affect or even override existing statutes, are introduced as resolutions.

A bill becomes what is known as an "act," "law," or "statute" when it passes both houses in identical form and is signed by the governor, becomes law without the governor's signature, or is passed over the governor's veto. Though these three terms tend to be used interchangeably, there is a slight distinction among them, depending on the context in which each is used.

"Statute" refers to formal enactments of the legislature of a more permanent nature (as distinguished from legislation of a temporary character, e.g., appropriation acts). "Statute" also is used to designate *written* law, as distinguished from unwritten law. "Law" is a general term, often used to refer not only to formal legislative enactments, but also to include the whole body of rules enacted by government, including constitutional provisions, judicial interpretation, etc. An "act" is any bill that has passed both houses in identical form and has been signed by the governor (or has become law without that signature or has been repassed after a governor's veto).

OFFICIAL CODE OF GEORGIA ANNOTATED

A "code" is a compilation of all statutes currently in force within a political jurisdiction (regardless of when enacted) and is the most important single source for finding existing statutory law on any subject. A code typically is divided into major subject areas (e.g., education, elections, health) called "titles." Titles are further subdivided into component "chapters," which, in turn, are further divided into the code's basic entry, "the section." It is the section that contains the actual language of the law (see Fig. 2).

In 1977, the General Assembly created a Code Revision Committee to initiate work on a new code for Georgia (the last official code having been adopted in 1933). The committee began reorganizing Georgia's general statutes, making grammatical and typographical changes, omitting obsolete sections, deleting material that had previously been repealed by implication, and resolving conflicts within existing laws. The next year, the legislature contracted with the Michie Company, a legal publishing firm, to work with the state in preparing a new official code. During a special session in 1981, the General Assembly adopted the results of this effort—the Official Code of Georgia Annotated (O.C.G.A.)—marking the first comprehensive and official code for Georgia in nearly 50 years. It became effective November 1, 1982, simultaneously repealing all prior codes and most general laws.

The resulting 44-volume code includes all general statutes (organized into 53 titles), a 2-volume index to these statutes, the U.S. and Georgia constitutions, and a 1-volume index to local acts. (Local acts have not been codified, but citations are given to the location in

FIGURE 2. Official Code of Georgia Annotated

12-8-79. Effect of other laws on permits issued under article and rules and regulations.

Subject to the provisions of the Constitution of Georgia, no other law of this state and no action, ordinance, regulation, or law of any county, municipality, or other political subdivision shall operate to prevent the location or operation of a hazardous waste facility holding a valid hazardous waste facility permit issued under this article and the rules and regulations promulgated hereunder, provided that nothing in this Code section shall prevent any county, municipality, or other political subdivision from challenging a facility's compliance with this article or any rule or regulation, order, or permit provision or condition adopted or issued under this article. (Ga. L. 1979, p. 1127, § 21; Ga. L. 1992, p. 2234, § 5.)

Law reviews. — For survey article on constitutional law, see 34 Mercer L. Rev. 53 (1982). For survey article on environment, natural resources, and land use, see 34 Mercer L. Rev. 145 (1982). For survey article on real property, see 34 Mercer L. Rev. 255 (1982).

JUDICIAL DECISIONS

Preemption feature of O.C.G.A. Art. 3, Ch. 8, T. 12 operates only in regard to facility already holding valid permit. Earth Mgt., Inc. v. Heard County, 248 Ga. 442, 283 S.E.2d 455 (1981).

12-8-80. Applicability of article.

Reserved.

Editor's notes. — The former Code section was repealed by Ga. L. 1992, p. 2234, § 5, effective July 1, 1992, and was based on Ga. L. 1979, p. 1127, § 3.

12-8-81. Civil penalties; procedures for imposing penalties.

(a) Any person violating any provision of this article, the rules or regulations effective under this article, or any permit condition or limitation established pursuant to this article or any person negligently or intentionally failing or refusing to comply with any final or emergency order of the director issued as provided in this article shall be liable for a civil penalty not to exceed $25,000.00 per day. Each day during which the violation or failure or refusal to comply continues shall be a separate violation.

(b) Whenever the director has reason to believe that any person has violated any provision of this article, any rule or regulation effective under this article, or any permit condition or has negligently or intentionally failed or refused to comply with any final order or emergency order of the director, he may upon written request cause a hearing to be conducted before a hearing officer appointed by the board. Upon finding that such the annual session laws where each act may be found.) Georgia and federal court decisions construing Georgia statutes and the Georgia and U.S. Constitution have been annotated along with summaries of attorney general opinions and research references to notes or articles in legal encyclopedias and journals.

GENERAL LEGISLATION

Bills considered by the General Assembly are classified as either (1) general or (2) local or special in their application.

General laws are those enacted by the General Assembly that have statewide application. (Fig. 3 presents an example of a general act.) A law may be categorized as general by virtue of its uniform territorial application (e.g., a law affecting all counties), its uniform subject matter application (e.g., a law affecting observance of holidays), or a combination of both.

Georgia's constitution provides that all general laws will have uniform operation throughout the state, and no local or special law may be passed in subject areas covered by a general law.[1] One exception is that the General Assembly may, by general law, authorize local governments to enact local ordinances and resolutions based on their police powers, as long as they do not conflict with general laws.[2]

Georgia courts, however, have held that the constitutional prescription that a general law will have uniform operation throughout the state does not mean that it necessarily applies to every citizen of the state, or even produces a uniform effect on every person or entity subject to the act.[3] The Fourteenth Amendment's "equal protection" clause does not prohibit the General Assembly from drawing lines that treat one class of individuals or entities differently from others, as long as

1. the legislative purpose is legitimate and the classification has a reasonable relation to furthering that purpose;
2. the classification is rational and not arbitrary nor invidious;
3. the classification employed furnishes a legitimate ground of differentiation; and
4. the law will operate uniformly on all persons or classes who will be subject to its application.[4]

Any general law currently in force may be amended or repealed by any future legislature. As noted previously, no legislature may bind future bodies with respect to statutory law.

135

FIGURE 3. General Act

MOTOR VEHICLES – WINDOW TINTING; MEDICAL EXEMPTION ATTESTED TO BY OPTOMETRIST.

No. 761 (Senate Bill No. 570).

AN ACT

To amend Code Section 40-8-73.1 of the Official Code of Georgia Annotated, relating to affixing of materials which reduce light transmission or increase light reflectance through windows or windshields of motor vehicles, so as to authorize a person who is a certified optometrist to provide an attestation in support of a medical exemption for restrictions to limitations on reducing light transmission or increasing light reflectance on windows of motor vehicles; to provide for related matters; to provide an effective date; to repeal conflicting laws; and for other purposes.

BE IT ENACTED BY THE GENERAL ASSEMBLY OF GEORGIA:

SECTION 1.

Code Section 40-8-73.1 of the Official Code of Georgia Annotated, relating to affixing of materials which reduce light transmission or increase light reflectance through windows or windshields of motor vehicles, is amended by striking subsection (d) and inserting a new subsection (d) to read as follows:

"(d) The Department of Public Safety may, upon application from a person required for medical reasons to be shielded from the direct rays of the sun and only if such application is supported by written attestation of such fact from a person licensed to practice medicine under Chapter 34 of Title 43 or a person certified as an optometrist under Chapter 30 of Title 43, issue an exemption from the provisions of this Code section for any motor vehicle owned by such person or in which such person is a habitual passenger. The exemption shall be issued with such conditions and limitations as may be prescribed by the Department of Public Safety."

SECTION 2.

This Act shall become effective on July 1, 2006.

SECTION 3.

All laws and parts of laws in conflict with this Act are repealed.

Approved May 3, 2006.

To change an existing law, a new statute is enacted that specifically cites the code section to be amended or stricken and then specifies the new language to be inserted in its place. Georgia courts acknowledge—but discourage—a second way to change general law—repeals by implication.[5] This occurs when legislators enact a new law that contains provisions inconsistent with statutes currently in force but that include no specific directions in the new act relative to amending or repealing existing law in conflict. If a court challenge is filed, and there appears to be no way to reconcile both new and existing law, a judge may be forced to rule that lawmakers repealed the former law by implication.

General laws inconsistent with federal or state constitutions or federal statutes may be ruled inoperative by state or federal judges. However, formal amendment or repeal of such laws must be enacted by the General Assembly before such action is officially incorporated into the state code.

Population Acts

Because of the constitutional prohibition against passing a local law in a subject area covered by general law, lawmakers historically relied on a device known as the "population act" to allow their city or county to get around provisions of existing general law (see Fig. 4).

As used until July 1, 1983, the population act was a hybrid variety of general law. It was drafted to affect only localities falling within certain population brackets according to a definite census as specified in the act (e.g., a law providing that property titles may be recorded on microfilm in any county of the state having a population of not less than 185,000 or more than 190,000 according to the 1970 or any future census). Typically, only one city or county in the state fell within the brackets selected by the bill's drafter, resulting in what was technically a "general law" but clearly one of local application.

Criticism that population acts were eroding the constitutional supremacy of general law by allowing the exemption of cities and counties from uniform state policy led framers of the Constitution of 1983 to restrict their use by providing, "No population bill, as the General Assembly shall define by general law, shall be passed."[6] In 1983, the legislature enacted a law defining population bills. Subsequently, effective January 1, 1989, an amendment was adopted that expanded the definition in order to further restrict their passage. The amended law states that a population bill is one that uses a classification by population as a means for determining the applicability of a

FIGURE 4. Population Act

COUNTY TREASURER – COUNTIES WITH POPULATIONS OF
NOT MORE THAN 191,000 AND NOT LESS THAN 188,000
ACCORDING TO 1990 CENSUS; COUNTIES WITH
POPULATIONS OF NOT MORE THAN 205,000 AND NOT
LESS THAN 195,000 ACCORDING TO 2000 CENSUS.

No. 857 (House Bill No. 1436).

AN ACT

To amend an Act to abolish the office of County Treasurer in any county with a
population of not more than 165,000 and not less than 150,000, according to the
1970 Federal decennial census, or any future federal census, and to provide the
procedure whereby the County Treasurer in any county with a population of not
more than 165,000 and not less than 150,000, according to said census, shall be
eligible to become County Treasurer Emeritus, approved April 24, 1975 (Ga. L.
1975, p. 4529), so as to revise and change the population and census application;
to provide for effective dates; to provide for automatic repeal of certain provisions;
to repeal conflicting laws; and for other purposes.

BE IT ENACTED BY THE GENERAL ASSEMBLY OF GEORGIA:

SECTION 1.
An Act to abolish the office of County Treasurer in any county with a population
of not more than 165,000 and not less than 150,000, according to the 1970 Federal
decennial census, or any future federal census, and to provide the procedure
whereby the County Treasurer in any county with a population of not more than
165,000 and not less than 150,000, according to said census, shall be eligible to
become County Treasurer Emeritus, approved April 24, 1975 (Ga. L. 1975, p.
4529), is amended by striking Sections 1 and 2 and inserting in their place new
Sections 1 and 2 to read as follows:

"SECTION 1.
The office of County Treasurer in any County with a population of not more than
191,000 and not less than 188,000, according to the 1990 Federal decennial
census or any future Federal census, is hereby abolished.

SECTION 2.
Any County Treasurer of any county with a population of not more than 191,000
and not less than 188,000, according to the 1990 Federal decennial census, or any
future Federal census, who shall be serving in the capacity of County Treasurer
at the time said office is abolished by this Act, and who shall have at least ten
years of service as County Treasurer of said County and shall have obtained the
age of 65 years, shall be eligible to become County Treasurer Emeritus by

bill or law to any political subdivision or groups of political subdivisions. A political subdivision is defined as any county, municipality, county school district, independent school district, judicial circuit, militia district, or any other geographical area less than the entire area of the state. The general law defines the following bills as *not* being population bills:

1. A bill applicable to one specified type of political subdivision and containing a combination of population classifications that includes the population of and affects all political subdivisions of the type specified, including but not limited to statewide minimum salary bills for county officers.

2. A bill classifying political subdivisions having less than a specified population and affecting three or more such political subdivisions. This does not affect the legality of any bills classifying political subdivisions having less than a specified population enacted prior to or becoming effective on July 1, 1988.

3. A bill classifying political subdivisions having more than a specified population and affecting three or more such political subdivisions. The legality of any bills classifying political subdivisions having more than a specified population enacted prior to or becoming effective on July 1, 1988, is not affected. Neither are amendments to those bills affected.

4. A bill classifying political subdivisions on the basis of the population of standard metropolitan statistical areas and affecting three or more such political subdivisions. The legality of any bills classifying on the basis of population of standard metropolitan statistical areas enacted prior to or becoming effective on July 1, 1988, is not affected.

5. A bill amending a population act for purposes of changing the population classification defined by general law in order for it to remain applicable to the political subdivisions it affected immediately prior to the time the most recent census figures applied to those political subdivisions.

6. A bill repealing a population law.[7]

In order to be permissible under the foregoing exceptions, a bill must fit within only one of the exceptions; and any bill that uses two or more of the foregoing classification devices is a prohibited population bill.[8]

REPRESENTATIVE GOVERNMENT AT WORK

Georgia's most notable contribution to constitutional requirements for legislation can be traced to the Yazoo Land Fraud of
1795. That year, the General Assembly passed a bill practically
giving away Georgia's western lands. This was possible because
the bill's introductory summary—called a "title"—made no mention of the
land deal. As a result, the new Georgia Constitution of 1798 and every state
constitution since has contained a prohibition on passing a bill containing
provisions not mentioned in the title. Georgia was the first state to enact
a constitutional provision governing the title and the content of bills, and
many other state constitutions now include a similar provision.

Despite the six exceptions, the General Assembly in 1997 further
restricted the use of population as a classification basis in legislation.
Specifically, the legislature prohibited any measure that used classification by population to determine the bill's applicability to any political
subdivision or groups of subdivisions with respect to

1. the salary of any official or employee of a city, county, or other
   political subdivision (excluding statewide minimum salary bills
   for county officers otherwise authorized by law); and
2. the property, affairs, or operation of the governing authority
   of a city or county, including such matters as annexation, de-
   annexation, incorporation, and dissolution.

Moreover, such legislation was prohibited even if the bill's purpose
fell within exemptions 1–4 in the "Population Acts" section of this
chapter.[9]

Clearly, the Constitution of 1983 authorized the legislature to
curtail the passage of population acts. This was accomplished when
population bills were first defined. Their passage was further restricted when the original law was amended several years later.
Thus, the legislature has made it increasingly difficult to pass a population bill.

LOCAL OR SPECIAL LEGISLATION

Local or special legislation is generally defined as that which applies
to special or particular places or persons, as distinguished from legislation relating to classes of persons or subjects.[10] Although similar

in many ways, there are differences as well between local and special legislation.

A local act is a legislative measure that applies to a specific city, county, or special district named in the act. Such acts are commonly used to create cities, change city boundaries, alter forms of local government, create local authorities or special districts, and make other changes that apply only to the political subdivision named in the act. Special procedures are spelled out by the state constitution and code for consideration of local legislation in the General Assembly, such as requirements for advertising in local newspapers before introduction.

Another type of nongeneral legislation is the special act. At one time, these were fairly common in Georgia and were used to provide special benefits or privileges to private individuals or companies named in the act. For instance, private acts were used early in the state's history to grant divorces. Later, special acts incorporated railroads, banks, and other companies; provided relief from judgments and tax penalties; and authorized individuals to peddle without obtaining a state license. Today, it is rare for the General Assembly to utilize special legislation, but the Georgia Supreme Court has upheld its right to do so if (1) it has not previously legislated in the area by general law, and (2) the classification of those affected is reasonable and does not violate standards of equal protection.[11] An additional qualification is that the state constitution forbids passage of any special act relating to the rights or status of private persons.[12]

Local acts not inconsistent with the state or federal constitutions or with federal law have the force of statutory law. However, a provision in the Georgia Constitution stipulates that no local or special law can be enacted in any case for which provision has been made by an existing general law.[13] A review of the extensive number of appellate court decisions applying to this section cited in the annotations to this provision in the Official Code of Georgia Annotated suggests that the courts have had little reluctance to enforce this constitutional mandate.

The court's attitude has been that if a general act has been passed relative to a given subject matter, no local law can later be enacted that would repeal some portion of the general law.[14] Moreover, a local act can neither expand nor contract the meaning of a general statute, even if passed in the guise of an amendment to the general law.[15] Also disallowed are purported general acts that apply to all counties or cities in the state but then exclude one city or county by name.[16]

When no general act has preempted an area for legislation, a local act is permissible. Should a general act later be passed covering a subject area already touched by one or more local acts, the local act will be allowed to stand unless the language of the general law makes it clear that the legislature contemplated or intended a repeal or unless provisions of the two acts are clearly repugnant and irreconcilable.[17] Where both can stand, they should be construed accordingly, but where there is inconsistency, the general statute repeals the local act.[18]

As discussed in Chapter 5, many local acts (such as those involving annexation) incorporate referendum requirements, where voters of the city, county, or area to be affected decide whether that act will become effective.

The use of local legislation to lengthen, shorten, or abolish the term of office of a local official during the time for which he or she has been elected is prohibited unless the legislation is approved in a referendum by the people of the jurisdiction affected.[19]

Historically the majority of bills enacted by the Georgia General Assembly have been local in nature. However, as Table 6 shows, general bills now tend to be passed more than local bills. The number of general bills passed is not necessarily increasing; rather, the recent trend has been a small overall decline in local bills.

ENACTMENT OF LOCAL BILLS IN THE GENERAL ASSEMBLY

The large number of local acts in the General Assembly is generally accounted for by the limited amount and utilization of "home rule" authority by cities and counties.[20] "Home rule" refers to the ability of local governments to frame, adopt, and amend their own charters, powers, and laws. Because local governments are created by the state—and do not possess sovereignty as such—major changes often have to go before the legislature, rather than local governing authorities. (Fig. 5 presents an example of a local act.)

Introduction of Local Legislation

The constitution authorizes the General Assembly to enact procedures for considering local legislation. In addition, rules of the House and Senate prescribe special requirements for committe consideration of local legislation.

TABLE 6. Enactment of Local and General Bills in the General Assembly

Year	Total Bills Introduced[a]	Total Bills Passed[a]	Bills Passed General	Bills Passed Local	Local Acts as % of Total Bills Passed
1970	1,002	634	246	388	61.2
1971	1,447	830	270	560	67.5
1972	1,339	779	321	458	58.8
1973	1,662	800	319	481	60.1
1974	1,171	677	289	388	57.3
1975	1,636	780	357	423	54.2
1976	1,928	709	360	349	49.2
1977	1,593	767	320	447	58.5
1978	1,898	760	391	369	48.6
1979	1,393	677	292	385	56.9
1980	1,817	766	419	347	45.3
1981	1,598	839	353	486	57.9
1982	1,891	753	358	395	52.4
1983	1,199	583	310	273	46.8
1984	1,658	783	385	398	50.8
1985	1,429	774	344	430	55.5
1986	1,893	913	381	532	58.2
1987	1,574	808	352	456	56.4
1988	1,781	693	427	266	38.3
1989	1,542	714	404	310	43.4
1990	2,133	769	435	334	43.4
1991	1,556	608	374	234	38.5
1992	2,429	870	507	363	41.7
1993	1,559	632	327	305	48.3
1994	2,157	654	354	300	45.9
1995	1,575	520	298	222	42.6
1996	2,514	563	338	225	39.9
1997	1,515	511	298	213	41.6
1998	2,117	524	306	218	41.6
1999	1,386	461	219	242	52.4
2000	1,836	503	333	170	33.7
2001	1,290	396	205	191	48.2
2002	2,014	621	256	365	58.7
2003	1,437	414	199	215	51.9
2004	2,038	394	208	186	47.2
2005	1,304	408	227	181	44.3
2006	1,937	509	275	229	44.9

[a]General and local.

Figure 5. Local Act

CITY OF ALPHARETTA – HOMESTEAD EXEMPTION;
CITY TAXES; REFERENDUM.

No. 490 (House Bill No. 1341).

AN ACT

To amend an Act to provide for an additional $10,000.00 homestead exemption from certain City of Alpharetta ad valorem taxes for municipal purposes, approved April 23, 1999 (Ga. L. 1999, p. 4836), as amended, so as to increase the exemption amount; to provide for a referendum, effective dates, and automatic repeal under certain circumstances; to repeal conflicting laws; and for other purposes.

BE IT ENACTED BY THE GENERAL ASSEMBLY OF GEORGIA:

SECTION 1.

An Act to provide for an additional $10,000.00 homestead exemption from certain City of Alpharetta ad valorem taxes for municipal purposes, approved April 23, 1999 (Ga. L. 1999, p. 4836), as amended, is amended by striking subsection (b) of Section 1 and inserting in lieu thereof a new subsection (b) to read as follows:

"(b) Each resident of the City of Alpharetta is granted a $30,000.00 exemption on that person's homestead from all City of Alpharetta ad valorem taxes for municipal purposes. The value of the homestead in excess of any exemption granted therefor shall remain subject to ad valorem taxation."

SECTION 2.

The exemption granted by this Act shall apply to all taxable years beginning on or after January 1, 2007.

SECTION 3.

Unless prohibited by the federal Voting Rights Act of 1965, as amended, the election superintendent of the City of Alpharetta shall call and conduct an election as provided in this section for the purpose of submitting this Act to the electors of the City of Alpharetta for approval or rejection. The election superintendent shall conduct that election on the date of the state-wide general primary in July, 2006, and shall issue the call and conduct that election as provided by general law. The superintendent shall cause the date and purpose of the election to be published once a week for two weeks immediately preceding the date thereof in the official organ of Fulton County. The ballot shall have written or printed thereon the words:

"YES ( ) Shall the Act be approved which increases the homestead exemption from all City of Alpharetta ad valorem taxes for municipal purposes
NO ( ) for residents of the City of Alpharetta from $20,000.00 to $30,000.00?"

Notice of Intention

According to the constitution, the General Assembly must provide by law for advertising a notice of intention to introduce a local act. Before the bill is introduced in the legislature, such notice must be advertised once in the newspaper in which the sheriff's advertisements for the affected locality are published. It cannot be advertised more than 60 days prior to the convening date of the session at which it will be introduced. When the advertisement has been published prior to the convening date, the bill may be introduced at any time during that session. If, however, the advertisement is published during the session, the bill may not be introduced before Monday of the calendar week following the week in which the advertisement was published. A copy of the advertised notice and an affidavit stating that the notice has been published as provided must be attached to the bill and become a part of the bill. The affidavit is made by the author of the bill.[21]

No local bill amending a municipal charter or the enabling act for the governing authority of any county or consolidated government may become law unless a copy of the notice of intention to introduce local legislation as required by law is mailed, faxed, or otherwise provided to the governing authority of any county, municipality, or consolidated government that is the subject of the bill. The notice must be provided during the calendar week when the notice is published or during the seven days immediately following the date of the publication of such notice. The copy of the notice provided to the governing authority may be an actual or photostatic copy of the notice. An affidavit prepared by the author of the bill stating that notice has been provided to the governing authority must be attached to the bill.[22]

In the past, the Georgia Supreme Court has rather strictly interpreted this requirement. For example, the court has invalidated local laws on the sole ground that, during the process of their enactment, the enrolled bills did not embody a copy of the publication notice accompanied by the publisher's certification or the author's affidavit.[23] Further, it has held that the author of the local act be solely responsible for ensuring that the enrolled bill contains the notice and certification of publication, regardless of the fact that their omission may have been due to the fault or neglect of the clerk.[24]

On the other hand, the court has been rather liberal on the actual content of the notice. For example, it ruled that no more information need be included than that in the title of the bill, and that a rather broadly worded notice was sufficient.[25]

Readings

The constitution requires that a local act be read at least once—by title—before being voted upon.[26] A House member may ask for unanimous consent that a local bill or resolution be taken up out of the normal order of business for its reading and passage, but this must be done within the first 30 minutes after the confirmation of the journal. In the Senate, the president cannot recognize any senator for the purpose of asking unanimous consent to vote on the passage of any local bill or resolution.[27]

Committee and Floor Consideration

Most local bills that have the support of a majority of the representatives and senators whose districts encompass any city or county affected by the local act are passed in each house without opposition under the tradition of "local courtesy." The idea behind local courtesy is that when a legislative delegation from a city or county agrees on the need for a legislative enactment to affect that city or county only, the other house members will defer to the judgment of the delegation and support the bill. Of course, other legislators expect the same courtesy for their local bills. It should be noted, however, that local courtesy is a custom in the General Assembly and is not provided for by the rules of either house. Hence, it cannot be enforced should legislators decide to challenge a local act.

House rules allow the legislative delegation from a city or county to set its own majority requirement (e.g., simple, two-thirds, three-fourths) of members who must sign the bill before it will be favorably reported from the Committee on State Planning and Community Affairs. If a delegation has not agreed upon the matter of majority requirement, then all representatives whose districts are wholly or partially located within the affected local government must sign the bill.[28] However, House rules also provide that if the committee staff determines that the local bill meets the technical requirements (e.g., advertising before introduction) and has been signed by the requisite number of members of the local delegation, the legislation is reported favorably as a matter of course and without the necessity of any action by the committee.[29]

In the Senate, local bills may be assigned to the State and Local Government Operations Committee, or any other committee as local legislation or general operation. If assigned as local legislation, and the committee reports it favorably, the bill is placed on the Senate Local Consent Calendar.

If a local bill is assigned to the State and Local Government Operations Committee, it must be signed by a majority of the senators representing the affected local government before receiving a favorable report. If the local delegation is equally divided, the committee may report the local bill with a favorable or unfavorable recommendation.[30]

When the time arrives for floor consideration for local bills, both houses permit a number of them to be voted on at once. Uncontested bills are placed on a local consent calendar and are voted on as a group.

RESOLUTIONS

A resolution is another device that formally expresses the actions of either house or both houses concurrently. Resolutions are either (1) *simple* (requiring passage by only one house) or (2) *joint* (requiring passage by both houses). A joint resolution is identified by the phrase, "Be it resolved by the General Assembly."

Simple Resolutions

Simple resolutions are typically of several types. These are

1. privileged resolutions that express sympathy, appreciation, recognition, congratulations, or commendation;
2. resolutions expressing the opinion of the body on a particular issue;
3. resolutions authorizing creation of special study committees;
4. resolutions inviting some individual to speak to that body;
5. housekeeping resolutions authorizing appointment, employment, and compensation of aides and staff for officials and committees of that body for the biennium;
6. resolutions adopting or amending the rules of that house; and
7. resolutions formally notifying the other house of the convening of that body.

Simple resolutions do not have the effect of law and are typically read only once before adoption by the particular house. Privileged resolutions that commend, congratulate, extend condolences, or are of a similar nature are not referred to committee; House rules, however, provide that other privileged resolutions be assigned to committee, and the speaker determines whether the resolution is referred to committee.[31] House members can introduce up to 10 privileged resolutions per session but must pay the full cost for additional resolutions.[32]

Also, members can have the clerk mail not more than two copies of each privileged resolution but must pay for the mailing of any additional copies.[33] Although initial adoption of the rules of procedure for each house at a session's beginning requires only a majority of the members, any subsequent resolutions that propose changes in the rules must be assigned to the Rules Committee of that house and be adopted by two-thirds of the members voting if the two-thirds amounts to a majority of the members elected to that house.[34] While practice varies between the two houses, certain other simple resolutions are customarily referred to committee, including those to establish interim study committees and many of those expressing an opinion held by a house.

Housekeeping Resolutions

Of special note is the housekeeping resolution, as it is commonly termed, adopted by each house at the beginning of every biennium (see Fig. 6). This resolution is introduced the first day of the session, without reference to committee and without the concurrence of the other house. It details and prescribes the number of aides, assistants, secretaries, and other legislative staff to be appointed for that house, its officers, party leaders, and committees, along with specifying the compensation for these staff members.

Typically, the housekeeping resolution provides authorization for (1) the presiding officer to appoint interim legislative study committees and prescribe the time during which they may function; (2) the presiding officer to designate standing committees or subcommittees to function during the interim between sessions; (3) designated legislative officers to keep their offices open and retain the staff and personnel deemed necessary during any period of adjournment during or following a session, and further entitling these officers to function as a *committee of one* for each day spent on official business; and (4) legislators to serve as a *committee of one* for a limited number of days in the interim. Unless subsequently amended, provisions of a housekeeping resolution apply to a house throughout the two-year life of the legislature.

Joint Resolutions

Joint resolutions, sometimes termed concurrent resolutions, require adoption by both houses and, depending on the intent of the legislature and the procedure used in passage, may or may not have the effect of law. Unlike the practice in Congress and some other states,

148

FIGURE 6. Housekeeping Resolution

05   LC 14 8971

Senate Resolution 5

By: Senators Johnson of the 1st, Stephens of the 27th and Balfour of the 9th

A RESOLUTION

1   Relative to officials, employees, and committees in the Senate; and for other purposes.

2   BE IT RESOLVED BY THE SENATE that the following provisions shall be in effect during

3   the 2005 regular session and thereafter until otherwise provided for by resolution of the

4   Senate:

5   **PART I**

6   **SECTION 1-1.**

7   Subject to the availability of funds appropriated or otherwise available for the Senate, the

8   Senate Committee on Administrative Affairs is authorized to employ on behalf of the Senate:

9   a postmaster or postmistress, assistant doorkeepers, a director of pages, pages, aides,

10 secretaries, stenographers, typists, clerks, court reporters, consultants, and other necessary

11 personnel; and the Senate Committee on Administrative Affairs is authorized to provide for

12 a Senate Research Office, a Senate Budget Office, and a Senate Information Office,

13 including a Senate Photographer, and to employ personnel for said offices. The numbers and

14 compensation of personnel so employed pursuant to this section shall be fixed by the Senate

15 Committee on Administrative Affairs within the limitations of funds appropriated or

16 otherwise available for the operation of the Senate. Personnel employed pursuant to this

17 section may be employed on a permanent or temporary basis and on a part-time or full-time

18 basis, as may be determined by the Senate Committee on Administrative Affairs. The

19 assignment and duties of personnel employed pursuant to this section shall be as determined

20 by the Senate Committee on Administrative Affairs; and any such personnel may be assigned

21 to Senate officers, committees, and committee officers as deemed appropriate by the Senate

22 Committee on Administrative Affairs, including assignment of aides to the President of the

23 Senate, the President Pro Tempore, the Majority Leader, and the Minority Leader.

24

no distinction is made between a joint and a concurrent resolution by Georgia law or legislative rules of either house. Thus the two terms can be—and are—used interchangeably.

The decision to employ the format of a joint resolution rather than a bill is dictated in some instances by custom or by the inclination of the author. The General Assembly is required to use a joint resolution when proposing constitutional amendments;[35] awarding compensation;[36] authorizing land conveyances, leases, and easements of state-owned land;[37] and taking certain other actions.[38]

Additionally, joint resolutions are used to

1. name or rename state parks, buildings, memorial highways, roads, bridges, or other public entities (in the Senate, these are termed "commemorative resolutions");
2. create joint legislative overview committees, joint interim study committees, and other special agencies;
3. ratify executive orders of the governor that temporarily suspend collection of certain taxes;* and
4. authorize the Department of Revenue to write off uncollectable sales and use tax accounts.

Since these kinds of joint resolutions have the effect of law, they must be assigned to a standing committee and receive three readings in both houses before passage.[39] Once adopted by the two houses, they are submitted to the governor and given an act number if signed by the governor or if enacted without his or her signature. As with bills, joint resolutions that will have the force of law may be vetoed by the governor; resolutions that propose constitutional amendments do not require the governor's signature, however, and, in any event, cannot be vetoed.[40]

Joint resolutions are also used for other purposes, such as (1) expressing the sympathy, appreciation, or recognition of both houses; (2) expressing an opinion shared by the two houses; (3) notifying the governor that the General Assembly has convened; (4) providing for a

---

*Pursuant to O.C.G.A. §45-12-22, the governor is authorized to suspend the collection of all or part of any taxes due the state, but only until the next meeting of the General Assembly, at which session the action is reviewed by the legislature and either ratified or rejected. The vehicle by which such ratification occurs is a joint resolution embodying the governor's executive order along with formal ratification, approval, and confirmation of that order. Because this action touches on the raising of revenue, the joint resolution must be introduced in the House.

joint session of the General Assembly; and (5) setting dates for formal adjournments of the General Assembly during a session. For these purposes, the joint resolution generally does not carry the weight of law, and thus assignment to committee, three readings, and submission to the governor are not necessary. In actual practice, some of these joint resolutions are assigned to committee in one or both houses; others are not. Some receive only one reading, while others receive three readings before adoption.

As with a bill, a joint resolution may be introduced in either house unless it pertains to raising revenue or appropriating money—in which case it must originate in the House.[41]

Compensation Resolutions

Compensation resolutions are used to allow the General Assembly to compensate citizens who, through no fault of their own, have been injured or have suffered damages because of negligence or certain other actions by state officials and employees and who have no other recourse to recover for damages (see Fig. 7).

Under the Georgia Constitution, the state is immune from being sued except for cases involving a breach of written contract by the state and cases where the state has specifically waived its immunity within the Georgia Tort Claims Act.[42] Otherwise, Georgia state government is not subject to suit for negligent or other tortious acts by its personnel. Georgia courts have held that the injured party must seek redress for such wrongs from the legislature, not from the courts.[43] Furthermore, payment of compensation in these cases is "purely a matter of legislative grace based upon a strong moral obligation and equitable duty and not upon the assumption of legal liability.[44]

To assist the General Assembly in the adoption of compensation resolutions, a Claims Advisory Board has been established, consisting of the secretary of state and the commissioners of human resources, corrections, and transportation.[45] This board receives notice of claims against the state, conducts investigations, holds hearings, prepares statements of its findings, and presents its recommendations regarding the merits of each case and such compensation as should be awarded the injured party. Its policy has been to recommend reimbursement for actual and substantiated out-of-pocket expenses only. Such recommendations, however, are advisory only and are not binding on the legislature.[46]

In 1982, the General Assembly acted to reduce the need for compensation resolutions by providing a procedure for small claims to

FIGURE 7. Compensation Resolution

House Resolution 108 (AS PASSED HOUSE AND SENATE)

By: Representatives Benfield of the 85th, Watson of the 91st, Talton of the 145th, Crawford of the 127th, Henson of the 87th, and others

A RESOLUTION

1   Compensating Mr. Clarence Harrison; and for other purposes.

2   WHEREAS, in the early morning hours of October 25, 1986, a woman was attacked as she
3   walked to a bus stop in downtown Decatur, Georgia. The woman was grabbed from behind,
4   struck on the head, and dragged to an unknown location where she was sexually assaulted.
5   The woman was subsequently dragged to two other unknown locations and again sexually
6   assaulted and her wrist watch was stolen; and

7   WHEREAS, physical evidence was collected from the victim, including the clothing that she
8   was wearing and other evidence that was capable of showing DNA; and

9   WHEREAS, in June of 1987, Mr. Harrison was tried for rape, kidnapping, and robbery in
10   DeKalb County, Georgia. Mr. Harrison maintained his innocence from his arrest on
11   November 5, 1986, and throughout his trial, but the victim identified Mr. Harrison from a
12   photographic line-up and a witness who lived in the neighborhood where the attack occurred
13   identified Mr. Harrison as a man who had come to her door on the evening of the attack and
14   circumstances suggested to her that he was the assailant; and

15   WHEREAS, Mr. Harrison was convicted and on June 26, 1987, he was sentenced to life in
16   prison for rape and 20 years each for kidnapping and robbery to run consecutive to the life
17   sentence; and

18   WHEREAS, in September 1998, Mr. Harrison sought DNA testing but the laboratory
19   conducting the analysis was unable to produce results due to previous testing of the evidence;
20   and

21   WHEREAS, despite being told that all of the evidence in his case had been destroyed, Mr.
22   Harrison continued to try to prove his innocence. In 2004, with the consent of the DeKalb
23   County District Attorney and Mr. Harrison's attorney, further DNA testing, which was not

be settled without going before the legislature. As a result, claims of $500 or less must be submitted to the Claims Advisory Board.[47]

In addition, the board can make recommendations to the legislature concerning payment of compensation, under certain conditions, to innocent persons who sustain injury or property damage and to the dependents of innocent persons killed while attempting to aid prevention of a crime against another person or to aid a law officer at his or her request.[48]

Any resolution seeking compensation or reimbursement from the state of Georgia or any of its agencies for a person injured or property damaged must be introduced in the House of Representatives within the first 10 days of a regular session.[49] However, before the preceding November 15, a notice of the claim *must* have been filed with the Claims Advisory Board. Should the event giving rise to the claim not occur until after November 5, the notice must then be filed with the board within 10 days after the occurrence.[50] Additionally, in the case of claims for compensation for damages resulting from attempts to prevent crimes, notice of the claim must have been filed with the board within 18 months of the personal injury or death. The incident or offense resulting in the injury or death must have been reported to a law enforcement officer within 5 days of its occurrence, or if the incident or offense could not reasonably have been reported within that period, within 5 days of the time when a report could reasonably have been made.[51]

After a claim has been filed, the board must then specify in writing to the claimant what information it must have for investigatory purposes, including accident reports, affidavits, statements, or receipts. All such information must be provided to the board before any action of the legislature on the claim.[52]

Thereafter, any member of the House of Representatives may introduce a compensation resolution in that body. The speaker is required to refer it to the Appropriations Committee, and the clerk is required to send a certified copy to the chair of the Claims Advisory Board. The board investigates the claim, holding a hearing if necessary, and then meets to take final action. The board must transmit its statement to the chair of the Appropriations Committee by the 30th day of the session. The representative who introduced the resolution is also notified of the board's actions and, if dissatisfied, can demand a hearing if one was not previously held. Although the board's recommendations are advisory and not binding, the Appropriations Committee and the House of Representatives usually accept the board's recommendations.[53]

GENERAL REQUIREMENTS FOR LEGISLATION

In January 1795, the most controversial law in Georgia's history—the infamous "Yazoo Act"—was enacted under this caption:

> An Act supplementary to an Act, entitled an Act for appropriating a part of the unlocated territory of this State, for the payment of the late State troops, and for other purposes therein mentioned, declaring the right of this State to the unappropriated territory thereof, for the protection of the frontiers, and for other purposes.[54]

Under the patriotic language of this summary title, the body of the act proceeded to sell the greater part of the territory now comprising Alabama and Mississippi to four land companies for the incredible sum of $490,000, with most legislators being given shares in one or more of the companies. A new legislature immediately repealed this action, and the Yazoo Land Fraud precipitated a constitutional requirement for enacting legislation: no law can be passed that contains matter different from that expressed in the title.[55] A second constitutional prohibition—that no law can be passed that refers to more than one subject matter—is also frequently attributed to the Yazoo scandal, although in fact it was not included until the Constitution of 1861.[56]

Legislators should be cautioned that these two prohibitions regarding multiple subject matter and the title have constituted the bases for numerous contests regarding the validity of various statutes passed by the General Assembly, and that the Georgia Supreme Court has ruled these requirements to be mandatory and not merely directory.[57]

Multiple-Subject-Matter Prohibition

The constitutional requirement against multiple subject matter is designed to prevent "omnibus" bills that combine many unrelated provisions, none of which could succeed upon its own merits, with the intent of combining the votes of advocates of each.[58]

The "subject of an act" is regarded as the thing or matter forming the groundwork of the act and is not synonymous with "provision."[59] The courts tend to give a broad meaning to the term "subject matter" so as to allow the legislature to include in one act all matters having a logical or natural connection.[60] Whether an act violates the multiple-subject-matter prohibition depends on whether all the bill's provisions seek to accomplish a single objective.[61] The multiple subject rules relating to legislation and constitutional amendments are analogous, and the test to be applied is the same.[62]

To contain multiple subject matter, then, an act must embrace two or more dissimilar and discordant subjects that in no reasonable way can be considered as having any logical connection with or to each other.[63] Examples of laws held invalid because of multiple subject matter include an act that attempted to amend the charters of two separate and distinct municipal corporations[64] and an act to authorize the construction of telephone lines in the state while providing criminal penalties for divulging any private messages by any persons connected with telephone companies.[65]

On the other hand, the court has upheld an act levying excise taxes against malt beverages and wine;[66] an act removing the clerk of superior court and tax commissioner of one county from the fee system;[67] the Executive Reorganization Act of 1972, which affected numerous different agencies in the executive branch;[68] and an act amending different sections and chapters of the Official Code of Georgia Annotated.[69]

Subject Matter Noted in a Bill's Title

Required by the constitution, a "title" (formerly also called a "caption") is the formal introduction that summarizes the substantive provisions of a bill. It prefaces the main body of a bill and always precedes the phrase "Be It Enacted by the General Assembly of Georgia." (Fig. 8 presents an example of a title of a bill.)

Georgia's Constitution of 1798 was the first state constitution to formally dictate that the body of an act cannot contain matter not mentioned in the title of that act.[70] The title is not only a safeguard against covert and surprise legislation, but also a practical device to notify legislators and the public of the scope and content of proposed legislation. Additionally, the title is used for the three readings of general bills in each house, unless the presiding officer or a majority of the members who will vote on the bill order that the bill be read in its entirety on the third reading.[71]

Examples of contested laws held invalid because of discrepancies between the title and body include a statute, the title of which enumerated particular land lots, while its body attempted to deal with other lots;[72] a statute, the title of which referred only to civil cases, with provisions purporting to apply to criminal cases as well;[73] and a statute whose title provided for campaign financing disclosures for certain state offices but whose body included all county and municipal elected officials.[74]

FIGURE 8. Title of Bill

06   LC 34 0746

House Bill 1598

By: Representative Fleming of the 117th

A BILL TO BE ENTITLED

Title

AN ACT

1   To amend Article 1 of Chapter 4 of Title 32 of the Official Code of Georgia Annotated,

2   relating to general provisions concerning state, county, and municipal road systems, so as to

3   not require the Department of Transportation to require turn lanes based on daily turning

4   volume; to provide for related matters; to provide for an effective date; to repeal conflicting

5   laws; and for other purposes.

6   BE IT ENACTED BY THE GENERAL ASSEMBLY OF GEORGIA:

7   **SECTION 1.**

8   Article 1 of Chapter 4 of Title 32 of the Official Code of Georgia Annotated, relating to

9   general provisions concerning state, county, and municipal road systems, is amended by

10   inserting a new Code section immediately following Code Section 32-4-3, relating to naming

11   of state roads, bridges, or interchanges, to read as follows:

12   "32-4-4.

13   (a) Right turn deceleration lanes shall not be required to be constructed on public roads at

14   no cost to the Department of Transportation if the daily right turning volume meets the

15   following criteria:

16   (1) On two-lane public roads:

17   (A) The speed limit is 40 miles per hour or less and the daily right turning volume is

18   300 or more; or

19   (B) The speed limit is over 40 miles per hour and the daily right turning volume is 150

20   or more; or

21   (2) On public roads with more than two lanes:

22   (A) The speed limit is 40 miles per hour or less and the daily right turning volume is

23   300 or more;

24   (B) The speed limit is between 40 miles per hour and 55 miles per hour and the daily

25   right turning volume is 150 or more; or

In the majority of cases, the court appears to have been fairly liberal in its interpretations and has stated that the constitution does not require that the substance of the entire act be set forth in the title, that every detail stated in the body be mentioned in the title, or that the title contain a synopsis of the law. Rather, a title need only indicate the general object and subject matter to be dealt with and be broad enough to protect people against covert or surprise legislation.[75]

At an early date, legislators initiated the practice of adding the words "and for other purposes" at the end of a bill's title, in hopes that this broad phrase might sufficiently cover provisions in the act that the title might not otherwise specify. And in some early cases, the court upheld portions of an act not indicated in the title by virtue of this general clause. For example, a statute, the title of which referred only to licensing the sale of intoxicating liquors but that possessed provisions making the sale of such liquors without a license a misdemeanor, was held invalid.[76] However, similar statutes were later sustained by the court on the sole grounds that their titles contained the phrase "and for other purposes."[77]

Obviously, there are limits on using the phrase in a bill's title. But the general attitude of the court has been that provisions that are germane to general subject matter embraced in the title and designed to carry into effect the purposes for which the act was passed may be constitutionally included in the body of an act, though not referred to in the title except by "and for other purposes."[78]

If a bill or resolution contains matter different from that expressed in the title or contains provisions in conflict with the title, only that part containing such material will be declared void unless this material is so integral to the whole act that it is not severable.[79] The question has also arisen as to whether a statute is unconstitutional because its title mentioned more items than were covered in its body. The Georgia Supreme Court has held this type of statute valid.[80]

An examination of court cases involving statutes with either multiple subject matter or matter in the body not mentioned in the title suggests that most occur not because of surreptitious strategy but because of committee or floor amendments. Material may be added to or deleted from a bill during the legislative deliberations, and, through simple oversight, the title is not changed to reflect it. At this stage, it is principally the responsibility of a bill's author to consider whether proposed changes are germane to the bill's subject matter and, following all amendments, whether the bill's title accurately reflects provisions within the measure.

Amending and Repealing Statutes

Another constitutional provision for ensuring that legislators understand legislation upon which they must act is the declaration "no law or section of the Code shall be amended or repealed by mere reference to its title or to the number of the section of the Code; but the amending or repealing Act shall distinctly describe the law or Code to be amended or repealed as well as the alteration to be made."[81] Refusing to abolish the concept of repeal by implication, the Georgia Supreme Court has repeatedly held that this provision applies only in instances in which an amending or repealing statute purports to *expressly* repeal or amend a former statute.[82]

Such an approach by the court has the rather peculiar effect of rendering the requirement inapplicable in those confusing instances that it could have remedied, i.e., in cases where the amending act does not expressly refer to an earlier statute that it will modify.

Even where express repeal is attempted, however, this requirement of the constitution has apparently received a rather liberal interpretation. For example, the requirement has been held satisfied in which the amending act included in its title only the title of the statute to be amended.[83] The court also has sustained an amending statute after considering its title and it as a whole, although the amended statute was not specifically mentioned. In the latter case, the court said of the constitutional requirement, "One, if not the only, object of this provision is to put everyone, legislators and the public who might be affected, on guard as to all matters connected with the subject matter."[84]

Repeals by Implication

When the legislature enacts a measure that conflicts with but does not expressly repeal or amend existing law, the courts generally presume that (1) it acted with full knowledge of existing law; (2) the new act must be construed in relation to other statutes of which it will become a part; and (3) statutes relating to the same subject must be harmonized wherever possible.[85] Although they express disfavor with the practice, the courts will acknowledge an implicit repeal of former law where such statutes cannot be harmonized if (1) a later statute is so irreconcilable with an earlier statute that the two cannot stand together and (2) the later statute is manifestly intended to cover the same subject matter and to operate as a substitute for the earlier statute.[86]

In instances of conflict among statutes, the courts regard the latest expression of the General Assembly on a subject as controlling.[87] This rule applies to not only acts passed at different sessions but those passed at the same session; the act that the governor signs last will control.[88] The same principle applies if two provisions within a single act conflict. The provision last in position stands, as it is presumed to be the last expression of legislative will.[89]

The attitude of the court makes it important for a legislator to consider, when proposing a bill, whether there is an existing statute that should be expressly repealed in the new act.

Legislative Intent and Judicial Interpretation

Members of the General Assembly are constantly urged, when drafting legislation, to use precise and unambiguous language that makes their intention clearly understandable.[90] Toward this end, the attention of the legislator is directed to the many commonly used words and phrases with statutory or judicial definition, such as "may," "shall," "reasonable," "adequate," "as soon as possible," and "anything in this act to the contrary not-withstanding."[91] Even if the language should be awkward or unusual, the legislative intent manifested by a statute must be determined and enforced as law. This avoids the occurrence of absurd results not intended by the legislature. Grammatical errors may not be used as the basis for invalidating an act. A transposition of words and clauses or interposition of punctuation may be undertaken by judges when the sentence or clause is without meaning as it stands.[92]

"Judicial construction" refers to the process whereby courts analyze, construe, interpret, define, and explain a statute (either in whole or part)—both alone and in conjunction with other laws and court decisions—as well as determine the validity or invalidity of statutes. A general rule for avoiding judicial construction of legislative enactments is that the use of plain and unequivocal language precludes any *necessity* for judicial interpretation.[93] If the language used in drafting a statute is clear and not susceptible to two interpretations, the courts cannot construe the act according to the supposed intention of the legislature but must let the act speak for itself.[94] Furthermore, if a statute is unambiguous, its wisdom of expediency is of no legitimate concern to the judiciary.[95]

However, should interpretation of the meaning or validity of any statute become necessary—due to ambiguous wording, vagueness, uncertain legislative intent, conflict with other laws, questionable constitutionality, or for other reasons—Georgia law imposes upon the courts sole responsibility for construction of statutes.[96] It should be noted that this responsibility lies with the judge or judges and is not a matter for determination by a jury.[97]

The Official Code of Georgia Annotated stipulates that when construing statutory enactments, the courts must look diligently for the intention of the General Assembly in passing them, "keeping in view, at all times, the old law, the evil, and the remedy."[98] Therefore, a basic rule of construction used by the courts is to carry legislative intent and purpose into effect if that intent is ascertainable and within constitutional limits.[99] Such intent should come from the language of the statute, hence the need for plain and unequivocal language.

On innumerable occasions, the courts have ruled that legislative intent must prevail over literal meaning of words, if the two appear in conflict. Unfortunately, despite the general rule that plain and unequivocal language will preclude any need for judicial interpretation, exceptions occur in which an act uses words whose meanings are generally accepted, yet literal application of them would defeat the purpose of the legislation. In these instances, the responsibility of the court is to first ascertain legislative intent in enacting a law. The court must then give the statute that construction that will effect this purpose, even if it is necessary to disregard some words within the statute.[100]

Where judicial construction is necessary to determine legislative intent, the court is not limited in the sources it may use for enlightenment.[101] For instance, it may inquire into the history of an act,[102] the surrounding facts and circumstances that influenced its passage,[103] or objective evidence gathered from polls or studies.[104] Events occurring during the progress of a statute's enactment, as disclosed by the official House and Senate journals, may be reviewed in seeking to find the intent of the legislature.[105]

Georgia courts have held that the testimony of members of the legislature—even the bill's author—is inadmissible to show legislative intent.[106] While conceding that the opinions of members of the General Assembly might be valuable and constructive in interpreting an act and discovering legislative intent, the courts have nevertheless viewed such sources as both improper and impractical. There is not only the probability that legislators would differ as to what the act meant but also the possibility that they had varying reasons for voting for the bill in its final form.[107] Allowing such testimony, it is suggested, would be tantamount to allowing members of the legislative branch to perform a judicial function. Rather than inquire into what was in the minds of the authors of a law, the courts have said that proper judicial inquiry is into what the legislature intended when it enacted a statute.[108] Similarly, the U.S. Supreme Court ruled that the trial court's presumption—that the Georgia General Assembly, in enacting a statute, knew the facts relative to the needs and problems of the tobacco market—cannot be overthrown by the testimony of individual legislators.[109]

While testimony of a legislator is inadmissible for showing legislative intent (although occasionally it has been allowed regarding the history of a law's passage), expressions of legislative opinion through resolutions may be looked at by the courts in determining intent for passing a certain act,[110] as may subsequent acts of the General Assembly on the same subject. However, the court has viewed a resolution expressing legislative opinion as an unconstitutional attempt to perform the court's judicial function of construing the meaning or intent of a statute.[111]

Not uncommonly, an enactment of the General Assembly will contain a legislative declaration of fact, purpose, or intent as a justification for the act, as well as a statement such as, "This Act, being for the welfare of the State and its inhabitants, shall be liberally construed to effect the purposes hereof."

In some cases, the courts have taken judicial notice of such expressions of intent, even on occasion noting, "When looking to the intent of a statute, the most significant provisions for this court are those wherein the statute itself defines its intent."[112]

In other cases, however, Georgia courts have ruled that the effect of such provisions on court interpretation of legislative intent is advisory only.[113] For instance, although the General Assembly stated that one particular statute was an exercise of the state's "police powers," the courts held that the validity of this declaration was a question for the judiciary.[114] The court also disregarded the express provision within an act that an authority created by it would exercise "governmental functions," holding that the General Assembly cannot preclude the court by a legislative interpretation of its own act.[115]

The courts may turn to officials of those executive agencies that are involved in administering a particular law in question when attempting to determine legislative intent. Although the interpretation given a statute by these officials may be considered persuasive by the court, the ultimate responsibility for construction and interpretation rests with the judiciary.[116]

Constitutionality of Statutes

The constitution of Georgia provides that "legislative acts in violation of this Constitution, or the Constitution of the United States are void, and the judiciary shall so declare them."[117] The courts, however, generally entertain a strong presumption that a statute is constitutional, assuming that the General Assembly was conscious of constitutional questions at the time of enactment.[118] Also, courts presume that the legislature is aware of all applicable state and federal law when it enacts legislation.[119] Thus, legislative enactments are presumed to be constitutional by the courts, with the burden of proof placed on those who would suggest otherwise.[120] Furthermore, a long-established principle of judicial interpretation is that the authority of the courts to declare acts of the legislature void should be exercised with great caution and restraint and should not be resorted to except in clear and urgent cases.[121]

For the courts to consider a constitutional challenge to a statute or provision, the attack must be levied by a person whose interests or rights are affected by the statute.[122] Georgia courts will not rule on the constitutionality of a law in the abstract. To attack the validity of a law, a petitioner must (1) be within the class of persons whose rights are adversely affected by the statute or (2) have suffered harm or stand to suffer harm by the mere presence of the statute upon the books. The courts require strict adherence to the rule that any attack on the constitutionality of an act, in whole or part, be stated in clear, definite, and specific terms, noting with fair precision (1) the statute or parts of a statute that are being challenged; (2) the provision of the constitution that is presumably violated; and (3) the basis of claiming the statute offends the constitution.[123] These requirements are to ensure that appellate courts can determine precisely how the trial court ruled on the challenge to the act's constitutionality. Also, questions of constitutionality must be raised in the lower trial court (usually the superior court) and specifically passed on by the trial judge. Appellate courts in Georgia will not rule on constitutional attacks against a statute that are raised for the first time in an appeal from a lower court ruling.[124]

Even if a challenge is properly raised, courts will avoid passing on a statute's constitutionality when the case can be disposed of on other grounds.[125] Similarly, if two constructions of an act are possible—one that will uphold its constitutionality and one that will not—an act must be construed by the courts as constitutional.[126]

Enrolled Bill Rule

Further evidence of the judiciary's restraint in declaring legislative acts unconstitutional is its adherence to what is known as the "enrolled bill rule." A duly enrolled act, authenticated by the presiding officer of each house of the General Assembly, approved by the governor, and deposited with the secretary of state as an existing law, will be conclusively presumed by the courts to have been enacted in accordance with constitutional requirements, and no evidence to the contrary will be considered.[127] The only exception to this rule appears to involve local legislation, which can be struck down if proof of notice of proper advertising before introduction is not attached to the enrolled copy.[128]

Neither legislative journals nor other extrinsic evidence may be used in court to impeach the validity of a bill on the basis that it was not enacted according to constitutional requirements, such as being read on three separate days or having been approved by a majority of the membership. Georgia's high court has also refused to void a bill because of charges that a house failed to follow its internal rules of procedure in approving a bill.[129]

Georgia courts follow the enrolled bill rule because of (1) the respect due a coequal and independent branch of government and (2) recognition of the great confusion that would follow if courts were permitted or called upon to conduct an independent inquiry as to whether constitutional requirements were complied with on each bill approved by the General Assembly.[130]

Severability of Unconstitutional or Invalid Provisions within Acts

A statute, unconstitutional or invalid in part, is not necessarily void in its entirety. The courts will dismiss an attack that an entire statute is unconstitutional when some portions of it can be found to be constitutional.[131] Although an entire act may be adjudged unconstitutional, there are certain instances in which the court will partially invalidate an act, striking those provisions that offend the constitution or are otherwise invalid while upholding the remaining provision of the act.

The courts are generally guided by the following questions in determining whether a challenged statute must be totally or partially invalidated:

1. Are the nonoffending provisions separable from the offending?
2. If so, can they be given separate legal effect, and are they sufficient to accomplish the legislative scheme and purpose?
3. Does it appear that the General Assembly intended the law to stand or fall as a whole?[132]

If the court finds that the violative sections, provisions, sentences, or phrases of a legislative act can be severed without destroying the general legislative scheme, and that the legislature did not intend for the act to stand or fall as a whole, then the court will strike only the offending provisions, leaving the remainder of the act intact.[133] If, on the other hand, the objectionable portions are so connected with the general legislative scheme that they are indispensable, then the whole statute must fall.[134]

To illustrate, the state supreme court ruled in similar cases involving legislative membership in agencies within the executive branch that such membership violated the constitutional separation of powers provision. In one instance, since it was possible to remove legislative membership from the board and still leave enough members to constitute a quorum and to accomplish the purpose of the legislation, the entire act was not declared unconstitutional.[135] In the other instance, however, the court ruled that the language of the statute and special voting requirements showed that the intent of the General Assembly had been to create a balance on the commission between the executive and legislative branches. Since the primary legislative intent could not be carried out without legislative representation, the court ruled that the entire act must fall.[136]

The supreme court has also ruled that where the General Assembly has passed companion acts with each part of one general legislative scheme, if one is judged unconstitutional, the companion act, though itself not violative of the constitution, must also be considered ineffective.[137]

Because of the willingness of courts to uphold portions of laws that contain unconstitutional provisions under conditions previously cited, legislative bill drafters in recent decades increasingly added "severability clauses" within bills. These clauses declared that if any section, sentence, or provision of an act should be ruled invalid or unconstitutional by the courts, it was the intent of the legislature that the remaining sections, sentences, and provisions remain in full force and effect.

Though severability clauses were not considered binding on the courts in determining whether nonoffending provisions within an act were truly separable from the offending provisions, they did place the General Assembly on record as not intending the law to stand or fall as a whole. On a number of occasions, the courts have taken judicial notice of such legislative intentions.[138]

When the Official Code of Georgia Annotated was adopted in 1982, the need for separate severability clauses in each piece of legislation was eliminated by the inclusion in the code of a general severability section. Now, unless an act contains an express provision to the contrary, the legislature's intention is considered to be that the sections and provisions of an act are separable.[139]

SPECIAL REQUIREMENTS FOR LEGISLATION

In addition to the general requirements for legislation discussed in the preceding sections, several types of legislation must meet specific requirements for introduction in the General Assembly.

Appropriation Acts

Probably the General Assembly's single most important function each session is to authorize funding for all agencies and programs of state government. Although appropriation acts are passed in the same way as legislative statutes, there are distinct differences. For one thing, statutes continue in effect until repealed, amended, or overruled as unconstitutional. Appropriation acts, however, are valid only during the fiscal year for which enacted. A second difference is that, unlike statutes, appropriation acts are not incorporated into the Official Code of Georgia Annotated. A third distinction—one long argued by Georgia's attorney general—is that while appropriation acts authorize agencies to spend up to the maximum stated amount for purposes authorized by general law, they (1) do not mandate these expenditures, (2) cannot authorize agencies to take actions not already permitted by general law, and (3) cannot alter any agency powers derived from general law.[140]

What type of quasi-statutory language can be included within an appropriation act? Lawmakers commonly include extensive statements of intent on how a particular agency's appropriation can be spent, plus instructions to agencies and officials on what they can and cannot do.[141] The constitutionality of the practice (or the legal consequences of not following these instructions) has not been before Georgia's appellate courts. Nor have the courts ruled on the governor's use of the line-item veto to strike down instructions in appropriation acts. It is the attorney general's role to render an official opinion, at the request of an executive agency head, when legislative instructions in an appropriation act appear to conflict with that agency's discretionary power previously authorized by general law.[142]

Although also granting certain exceptions, Georgia's constitution mandates that no funds can be withdrawn from the state treasury except as appropriated by law.[143] However, this does not mean that every function or activity of a state agency must be specifically mentioned in the appropriation act. At one extreme, the legislature can appropriate a single lump sum to an agency, giving the agency broad discretion on how to spend its appropriation. At the other extreme, lawmakers can choose to control almost every aspect of agency spending through a detailed "line-item budget." Prior to 1974, Georgia's General Assembly appropriated lump sums to agencies, specifying only a few categories (such as personnel and operating expenses). Lawmakers shifted to a line-item budget in 1974 after one agency used internal funds to implement a new program that had been turned down by the House Appropriations Committee.[144]

State agencies carry out programs initiated by the state legislature, and most are involved in implementing federally supported programs. State agencies sometimes find they can qualify for federal grants and contracts that were not anticipated at the time the state appropriation act was considered by the legislature. To allow state agencies to take advantage of these federal funds, Georgia's constitution provides that all additional or unanticipated federal funds "are hereby continually appropriated for the purposes authorized and directed by the federal government in making the grant."[145]

As noted earlier, Georgia's constitution requires that all bills for raising revenue or appropriating money originate in the House of Representatives.[146] This provision, however, does not completely deprive the Senate of a role with respect to fiscal measures. The Georgia Supreme Court has sustained a revenue-raising measure that, though originally introduced in the House, actually came from the Senate in the form of a substitute measure. The court's rationale was that under general rules of parliamentary procedure, a substitute is merely an amendment—and thus permissible under Georgia's constitution.[147]

Among other requirements, open-ended appropriations are not allowed; each agency's allotment must be for a specific sum of money.[148] Unless specific exception is made in the constitution, no appropriation can allocate the proceeds of any tax or revenue source to a particular agency or program.[149] Although a few dedicated revenue sources (e.g., lottery net proceeds must go to education, motor fuel taxes must go to roads and bridges, federal grants must be used for the purpose authorized by the federal government) are recognized by the constitution, the overall scheme is that all other state revenues are to be deposited in the state treasury, with the governor then free to budget and the General Assembly free to appropriate based on the respective needs of state agencies and programs.

With the exception of the general appropriations bill, "all other appropriations shall be made by separate bills, each embracing but one subject."[150] When an appropriation measure is being voted on, the constitution requires that a roll call vote be taken in each house.[151]

According to Georgia's constitution, "The General Assembly shall annually appropriate those state and federal funds necessary to operate all the various departments and agencies."[152] As noted earlier, no money can be drawn from the state treasury unless appropriated by law.[153] Every appropriation must expire at the end of the fiscal year for which it was enacted.[154] In the absence of an appropriation act, there seems to be no legal way for state agencies to spend money—with the exception of taxes earmarked in the constitution for specific purposes (currently only the motor fuel tax), mandatory appropriations required by the constitution, contractual obligations authorized by the constitution, federal grants, and lottery proceeds used to pay lottery prizes and operating expenses—all of which continue with or without an appropriation act.[155] For other state programs, however, it is not clear what would happen if the General Assembly failed to pass an appropriation act for the next fiscal year. The governor would call a special session, but if the two houses were still unable to agree on a new budget, nonessential state services likely would shut down on July 1. This eventuality has never happened in Georgia.

General Appropriations Act

Each year, the General Assembly enacts a single, omnibus spending bill for state government known as the "general appropriations act." According to the state constitution, this act "shall embrace nothing except appropriations fixed by previous laws; the ordinary expenses of the executive, legislative, and judicial departments of the government; payment of the public debt and interest thereon; and for support of the public institutions and educational interests of the state."[156]

The general appropriations act (see Fig. 9) authorizes all funding for the state's fiscal year, which begins July 1 and ends the following June 30. (The fiscal year is identified in terms of the ending year— FY 07 begins July 1, 2006, and concludes June 30, 2007.) Appropriated funds not spent or contractually obligated by an agency by the end of the fiscal year lapse and return to the state's general fund as surplus.[157] Several trust funds provided for in the constitution are exempt from this requirement and can carry forth unspent funds into the next fiscal year.[158] Unspent lottery proceeds lapse to a special lottery education account in the state treasury.[159]

Georgia's constitution provides that the General Assembly cannot appropriate more money for a fiscal year than the total of (1) anticipated revenues and (2) any surplus or reserves carried over from the previous fiscal year.[160] The constitution also allows the legislature to appropriate money borrowed through issuance of general obligation and guaranteed revenue debt, so long as the annual debt service (i.e., interest and repayment of principle) does not exceed 10 percent of the net revenue receipts for the previous fiscal year.[161] There is also a limit of 1 percent on guaranteed revenue debt incurred for water and sewer facilities. (Actually, in recent years, interest on the state debt has been averaging 5 to 6 percent of the previous year's net treasury receipts.)

In Georgia, the budgetary process leading to a general appropriations act is a year-round process involving both executive and legislative branches. During the fall, the governor meets with state agency heads to give them a chance to explain their budget request for the coming fiscal year. Prior to the legislative session, department heads are also to explain and argue for their budget requests before the appropriations committees of the House and Senate. Inevitably, agencies request more money than will be available. Deciding which requests to fund and to what degree, within the policies and priorities of the governor, becomes an important tool for the state's chief executive.

Neither the governor nor the Office of Planning and Budget (OPB), a full-time agency that exists within the governor's office, has any authority to review or change budget requests for the legislative and judicial branches. The chief justice of the Georgia Supreme Court and the chief judge of the Georgia Court of Appeals submit their estimates of funding needed for the next fiscal year for inclusion in the governor's budget report. Budget estimates for each house of the General Assembly are prepared separately by the respective houses.[162]

The constitution requires the governor to present an annual budget message, a detailed report on the financial condition of the state, and the draft of a general appropriations act for the next fiscal year to the General Assembly within five days of its convening each year.[163] The governor's proposed budget cannot exceed the state's anticipated revenue, but projecting that revenue with fair precision is an extremely complex task. Under Georgia's constitution, the governor is to make that estimate. It has long been practice for the chief

168

FIGURE 9. General Appropriations Act

Section 37: Public Safety, Department of

4067	**Total Funds**	**$121,273,100**
4068	**Federal and Other Funds**	**$14,559,906**
4069	Federal Funds Not specifically Identified	$8,328,935
4070	Agency Funds	$1,634,073
4071	Other Funds	$4,596,898
4072	**State Funds**	**$103,561,759**
4073	State General Funds	$103,561,759
4074	**Intra-State Government Transfers**	**$3,151,435**
4075	Other Intra-State Government Payments	$3,151,435

Administration

To work cooperatively with all levels of government to provide a safe environment for residents and visitors to our state.

4076	Total Funds	$9,274,504
4077	State Funds	$9,274,504
4078	State General Funds	$9,274,504

The above amounts include the following adjustments, additions, and deletions to the previous appropriation act:

		State Funds	Total Funds
4079	Amount from prior Appropriation Act (HB 85)	$9,816,239	$9,816,239
4080	Annualize the cost of the FY2006 salary adjustment.	$45,740	$45,740
4081	Provide for a salary increase in FY 2007 of up to 4% effective January 1, 2007.	$60,976	$60,976
4082	Increase funds to reflect an adjustment in the employer share of the State Health Benefit Plan premiums from 14.20% to 16.713%.	$88,616	$88,616
4083	Increase funds to reflect an adjustment in the Workers' Compensation premiums.	$16,111	$16,111
4084	Transfer 1 position and $30,000 in personal services from the Georgia Department of Revenue.	$30,000	$30,000
4085	Reduce personal services in the Administration program.	($373,178)	($373,178)
4086	Realign program budgets to meet projected expenditures.	($410,000)	($410,000)
4087	Amount appropriated in this Act	$9,274,504	$9,274,504

Aviation

To provide air support to the Georgia State Patrol and other state, federal and local agencies improving public safety for the citizens of Georgia.

4088	Total Funds	$2,365,895
4089	State Funds	$2,365,895
4090	State General Funds	$2,365,895

The above amounts include the following adjustments, additions, and deletions to the previous appropriation act:

		State Funds	Total Funds
4091	Amount from prior Appropriation Act (HB 85)	$2,307,130	$2,307,130
4092	Annualize the cost of the FY2006 salary adjustment.	$11,804	$11,804
4093	Provide for a salary increase in FY 2007 of up to 4% effective January 1, 2007.	$17,282	$17,282
4094	Increase funds to reflect an adjustment in the employer share of the State Health Benefit Plan premiums from 14.20% to 16.713%.	$25,113	$25,113
4095	Increase funds to reflect an adjustment in the Workers' Compensation premiums.	$4,566	$4,566
4096	Amount appropriated in this Act	$2,365,895	$2,365,895

Capitol Police Services

To protect life and property, prevent and detect criminal acts, and enforce traffic regulations throughout the Capitol.

4097	Total Funds	$3,151,435
4098	Intra-State Government Transfers	$3,151,435
4099	Other Intra-State Government Payments	$3,151,435

executive to rely on an economist experienced in economic forecasting to project a range of expected revenue. The governor, using those figures, generally makes a conservative to mid-range estimate. That figure becomes the official revenue estimate, which Georgia's proposed budget cannot exceed (plus any surplus or reserve funds in the state treasury available for appropriation).

The governor's proposed state budget does not set aside funds for miscellaneous expenditures or new programs that may be proposed at that year's legislative session. Nor is money set aside for the General Assembly to allocate to programs of special interest to lawmakers. Rather, the governor's general appropriations bill allocates every dollar of the official revenue estimate for specified purposes as identified in the bill.* Funds for any new or expanded programs can only be found by taking them from funds the governor has recommended for other programs or by raising the official revenue estimate—a power that only the governor has.[164]

Special mention should be made of one category of expenditure within the general appropriations act: the governor's "emergency fund." Each year, an appropriation is made to the governor for "emergency needs of the state agencies, which needs were not ascertainable at the time of the submission of the budget report to the General Assembly or at the time of the enactment of the general appropriations act."[165] (For FY 2007, the appropriation was $3,469,576.) An agency head requesting money from this fund must make a request in writing to the governor, who has full discretion in fulfilling the request. The only restriction on use of the emergency fund specifically mentioned by state law is that no money can be allotted to a purpose that creates a continuing obligation for the state.[166] Georgia's attorney general, however, has ruled that the money must be used for previously unbudgeted emergency needs, the recipient must be a state agency or budget unit, and the funding cannot create a continuing state obligation.[167] These restrictions preclude use of the governor's emergency fund for extending a municipal water main, building a radio beacon at a city airport, and paying the fees of city and county police officers to attend the police academy.[168]

---

*Contingency and set-asides may be provided if the governor sets the budget estimate below the total of anticipated revenues and, in the budget message to the General Assembly, publicly acknowledges a discrepancy between the explicit and implicit revenue estimates. Thus, funds for boosting reserves may be assured even though all of the budget estimate is allocated. Alternately, funds supporting tax cuts may be removed from expected total revenues to derive the budget estimate.

The General Assembly is also involved in the appropriation process through the House Budget Office (HBO) and the Senate Budget
and Evaluation Office (SBEO), known prior to 2007 as the Senate
Budget Office. The staffs of these two offices work year-round to give
legislators an independent source of budget information, including a
"continuation budget" for lawmakers to compare with the governor's
estimates of a continuation budget.* In past years, the House and
Senate Appropriations Committees have held joint hearings, giving
legislators an opportunity to hear directly from most agency heads
about their budget needs and to question OPB officials about the
governor's recommendations. More recently, these hearings have been
scaled back to focus on the large agencies that make up the greatest
portion of the state's budget. The HBO and SBEO alternately coordinate duties for holding joint appropriations committee hearings.

When the Senate leadership created the SBEO in 2003, it wanted
the new office to provide analysis and evaluation of state programs
in addition to assistance with production of the Senate versions of
both appropriations measures. During its first two years, the SBEO
developed the capacity to produce a program budget that took the
line item figures from the House version and allocated the funds to
specific programs within state agencies. Still, the final appropriations
bills through FY 2005 were in the familiar line item format. For
FY 2006, the House bill included information on agency programs
in boxes embedded within the bill. Only the line item appropriations
for programs, however, were enacted into law. The boxes containing
program descriptions and detail are for information purposes only
and explain how the program total is determined. In the section of
H.B. 1027—the general appropriations act for FY 2007 shown in
Fig. 10—the total appropriation for the Department of Early Care and
Learning is $422,657,470. The line item for the Child Care Services
program is $7,665,219, including $4,056,199 in state funds.

The SBEO style bill is shown in Fig. 11. In this example from
FY 2006, the Department of Economic Development is appropriated
a budget of $29,671,123 (which primarily consists of state funds). The
first of many programs listed for this agency are Business Recruitment
and Expansion and Departmental Administration. The budgets for
these programs are shown as detail under the agency total budget.

---

*A continuation budget is one that factors in cost-of-living increases, anticipated changes
in federal grants, and other expected changes and then attempts to show what it would
cost for each agency to continue its current programs and services in the next fiscal year
at the same level as in the current fiscal year.

The goal of the SBEO is to introduce performance measurements for each program that would be reported to the General Assembly. Targets for the performance measures could be included in either the appropriations bills as information items or in another document.

The appropriations bills that result from the deliberations of the General Assembly are produced by either the HBO or the SBEO.

FIGURE 10. House Budget Office Bill

Section 21: Early Care and Learning, Department of

1701	**Total Funds**	**$422,657,470**
1702	**Federal and Other Funds**	**$116,647,824**
1703	Federal Funds Not Specifically Identified	$116,492,824
1705	Other Funds	$155,000
1706	**State Funds**	**306,009,646**
1707	Lottery Funds	$301,953,447
1708	State General Funds	$4,056,199
1709	**Intra-State Government Transfers**	**$0**

Child Care Services

To guide and assist child care learning facilities to provide safe, healthy, quality child care so that children exerience optimum opportunities for learning and growth.

1711	Total Funds	$7,665,219
1712	Federal and Other Funds	$3,609,020
1713	Federal Funds Not Specifically Indentified	$3,454,020
1714	Other Funds	$155,000
1715	State Funds	$4,056,199
1716	State General Funds	$4,056,199

The above amounts include the following adjustments, additions, and deletions to the previous appropriation act:

		State Funds	Total Funds
1717	Amount from prior Appropriation Act (HB85)	$4,030,671	$7,620,926
1718	Annualize the cost of the FY 2006 salary adjustment.	$35,981	$54,746
1719	Provide for a salary increase in FY 2007 of up to 4% effective January 1, 2007.	$60,640	$60,640
1720	Increase funds to reflect an adjustment in the employer share of the State Health Benefit Plan premiums from 14.20% to 16.713%.	$58,141	$58,141
1721	Increase funds to reflect an adjustment in the Workers' Compensation premiums.	$14,706	$14,706
1722	Eliminate contract in the Child Care Services program.	($165,000)	($165,000)
1723	Provide funds in per diem and fees ($5,460) and travel ($15,600) in the Child Care Services program for a new Board of Directors for the Department of Early Care and Learning.	$21,060	$21,060
1724	Reflect $3,435,255 in base budget funds in Child Care Development Block Grant from Department of Human Resources.	$0	$0
1725	Amount appropriated in this Act	$4,056,199	$7,665,219

Under the current arrangements, the HBO produces the general appropriations act for odd-numbered fiscal years and the subsequent corresponding amended general appropriations act. The SBEO produces the general appropriations act for even-numbered fiscal years, plus the corresponding amended general appropriations act. These arrangements, and even the structure of the staff agencies themselves, continue by agreement between the House and Senate leadership and the Legislative Services Committee. Because there is no statutory provision for either budget office, the arrangements could be changed at any time under a new agreement or by statute.

State law requires the general appropriations bill to be assigned to the House Appropriations Committee. In the event the committee makes changes to the bill, neither the Committee of the Whole nor the full house can consider the bill until at least 24 hours after a copy of the bill as amended has been placed on the desk of each member.[169]

During the course of a session, numerous changes will be made to the governor's budget by the House and Senate. Each house will

FIGURE 11. Senate Budget and Evaluation Office Bill

Section 21: Economic Development, Department of	
Total Funds	**$29,671,123**
Non State Funds	**$20,244**
Agency Funds	$20,244
State Funds	**$29,650,879**
State General Funds	$29,650,879
Intra-State Government Transfers	**$0**

BUSINESS RECRUITMENT AND EXPANSION

The purpose is to provide assistance to local communities and to the state to recruit, retain, and expand businesses in Georgia.

474	Total Funds	$6,783,664
475	State Funds	$6,783,664
476	State General Funds	$6,783,664

DEPARTMENTAL ADMINISTRATION

The purpose is to influence, affect, and enhance economic development in Georgia and provide information to people and companies to promote the state.

477	Total Funds	$6,213,661
478	State Funds	$6,213,661
479	State General Funds	$6,213,661

come up with a version of the budget that reflects important priorities of that body's leadership. Invariably, each house will refuse to yield on certain budget items, so the appropriations act usually is reconciled in a conference committee. The final budget approved by the legislature tends to contain most of the governor's recommendations, in part because so many expenditures in the budget (such as education, Medicaid, and welfare) are mandated by state and federal law, leaving little funding discretion to the governor or General Assembly.

Once the legislature enacts a new state budget, the governor has extensive authority in its implementation, with broad powers and responsibilities over how state agencies spend their funds. Many observers of state government consider the budgetary power as the governor's single most important power. To help with this responsibility, the OPB conducts year-round studies of the programs and budget requests of every agency in the executive branch. But ultimately it is the governor who makes the final decisions about what will go in the general appropriations bill submitted to the legislature.

Amended General Appropriations Act

The general appropriations act for the next fiscal year typically is adopted late in the legislative session—usually in March or April—prior to the July 1 beginning date of that fiscal year. While economists have sophisticated forecasting models to project how the economy will perform, they must rely to some degree on guesswork. If actual revenue is more than anticipated or, more seriously, if it is less than expected, the governor and the General Assembly will have to make some adjustments, necessitating amendment of a general appropriations act.

Another important reason for making midyear corrections to the budget is that the Quality Basic Education Act requires that adjustments be made in state spending for education based on public school enrollment figures that only become known after the beginning of the fiscal year.

To deal with these situations, state law requires that there be a reserve of state funds known as the "revenue shortfall reserve." The amount of surplus in state funds existing at the end of each fiscal year is reserved and added to the revenue shortfall reserve, and such funds carry over from fiscal year to fiscal year without reverting to the general fund at the end of each fiscal year. Money in the revenue shortfall reserve is maintained, accumulated, appropriated, and disbursed only as provided by the law creating the fund.[170]

For each fiscal year, the General Assembly may appropriate from the revenue shortfall reserve up to 1 percent of the net revenue collections of the preceding year for funding K–12 needs, and the governor may release for appropriation by the General Assembly a stated amount from the funds in the reserve that are in excess of 4 percent of the net revenue of the preceding fiscal year.[171]

At the end of each fiscal year, an amount is released from the revenue shortfall reserve to the general fund to cover any deficit in which total state expenditures and contractual obligations exceed net revenues and other appropriated amounts. However, the revenue shortfall reserve cannot exceed 10 percent of the previous year's net revenue from any fiscal year.[172]

Another way to deal with revenue shortfalls is for the governor to order OPB to cut back quarterly allotments to state agencies to bring spending into line with revenue. Or, at the extreme, the governor can call the legislature back into special session to pass an amended general appropriations act that cuts state spending to the level of a new revenue estimate.

At each legislative session, the governor submits two budgets to lawmakers. The first budget priority is to amend the current general appropriations act to cover the final months of that fiscal year. Only after that is done do lawmakers turn their attention to a budget for the next fiscal year.

Historically, the amended general appropriations act has also been called the "supplemental appropriation act" because of the common practice in good revenue years of having additional money to appropriate for the final half of the fiscal year. However, Georgia's constitution has a specific set of rules for "supplementary appropriations," and the more accurate term for the annual mid-fiscal-year budget adjustment is "amended general appropriations act."

Supplementary Appropriation Acts

Georgia's constitution provides for a second type of appropriation act: the "supplementary appropriation act."[173] This is used to provide additional funding to a particular agency to finish out the fiscal year. The constitution sets certain restrictions on supplementary appropriations. For example, all "shall be made by separate bill, each embracing but one subject." Although this caveat would seem to require a separate act for each agency, the General Assembly on occasion has used a single supplementary appropriation act to change the appropriations of a number of state agencies.[174] In any event, the appropriation change is only for the remainder of that fiscal year.[175]

No supplementary appropriation act can be passed until the general appropriations act has been passed by the legislature and approved by the governor and unless (1) there is an unappropriated surplus in the state treasury or (2) the revenue necessary to fund such appropriation has been provided for by a tax enacted for that purpose and collected into the general fund of the state treasury.[176]

Revenue, Expenditure, and Compensation Bills

Any bill changing the compensation or allowances of any elected or appointed state official or agency head must be introduced in the General Assembly during the first 10 days of a session.[177] Any bill that would significantly impact the anticipated revenues or expenditure levels of any state agency or any cities or counties must be introduced during the first 20 days of a session.[178]

The sponsor of any bill affecting anticipated revenue or expenditure levels of state agencies must request a fiscal note from the OPB and Department of Audits and Accounts by November 1 preceding the session, and a member-elect must make the request for a fiscal note by December 1 preceding the session.[179] (This requirement can be waived by a majority of the members of the committee to which the bill is assigned.) The fiscal note must outline the fiscal effect of the proposed bill, including, if possible,

1. a reliable estimate in dollars of the anticipated change in revenue or expenditures under the bill and
2. a statement as to the immediate and, if determinable, long-range effect of the measure.[180]

If, after investigation, it is impossible to make a dollar estimate of the impact of the proposed measure, the fiscal note must explain why it is not possible. In this event, the note must give an example based on a specific situation or reflecting the average group of persons possibly affected by the bill so as to indicate the likely cost of the bill.[181]

No comment or opinion can be included in the fiscal note regarding the merits of the measure for which the statement is prepared, although technical or mechanical defects may be noted. Additionally, if there is a difference of opinion between the state auditor and the director of the OPB, the fiscal note—which is jointly prepared—must point out the areas of difference.[182]

Fiscal notes for revenue bills must be attached to the bill and read in each house at the bill's third reading. Additionally, each General Assembly member must be furnished with a copy of the note before the bill can come up for a vote.[183]

With respect to bills changing the compensation of state officials, the state auditor is directed to prepare and furnish a fiscal note for each bill, unless no state funds are used, in whole or part, in an official's salary. These fiscal notes must show the compensation and allowances of an officer, any longevity increments, and any personal expense allowances (other than mileage and travel), as well as provide a statement of the proposed increase in compensation and allowances and the total cost of such changes. Copies of these fiscal notes must be distributed to each legislator before a vote can be taken on a compensation measure.[184]

Retirement Bills

The Public Retirement Systems Standards Law defines minimum funding standards for state and local public retirement systems, establishes legislative procedures to control the passage of bills amending or creating public retirement systems, and requires that enacted bills be concurrently funded.[185] The law was passed in 1983 to comply with the requirements of the constitution that the legislature must define pension funding standards in order to ensure the actuarial soundness of such systems.[186]

Before amendments granting a benefit increase in any legislatively controlled retirement system can be made, the law requires the administrator of the system to certify to the governor and General Assembly that the system meets the minimum funding standards prescribed by the law. Any bill passed amending a system that is not certified may not become law and will be null and void and stand repealed in its entirety on the first day of July following its enactment.[187]

Retirement legislation must be identified by the state auditor as being fiscal or nonfiscal. Nonfiscal retirement bills make no financial changes in a retirement system. They must be introduced within the first 20 days of any regular legislative session and bear written certification from the state auditor of their nonfiscal status. The state auditor must certify the nonfiscal/fiscal status of all amendments; a nonfiscal retirement bill cannot proceed in the legislative process if it is amended in any way causing it to have a fiscal impact.[188]

A more rigorous procedure applies to retirement bills that have a fiscal impact. They can only be introduced during the first year of the term of office of General Assembly members and can only be passed during the second year of the legislative biennium. The period between introduction of the bill and final consideration by the General Assembly is to permit study and perfection through joint meetings of the standing retirement committees of both houses (if necessary) and to allow enough time for a required actuarial investigation to be made through the state auditor's office. All reports and summaries must be attached to printed copies of the bill. The only allowable amendments to the bill after an actuarial investigation has been made are those certified to be nonfiscal.[189]

A fiscal retirement bill, if enacted, can only become effective as law if it is concurrently funded. If the enacted bill is not funded, it will be null and void and stand repealed in its entirety on the first day of July following its enactment.[190]

Special Requirements in the House

In addition to the distinctions noted earlier between general and local acts, the Georgia House of Representatives has adopted a special rule that directs that any bill relating to or affecting the political partisanship of any elected office, state revenues, general taxation, parimutuel wagering, alcoholic beverages, water resources, hazardous wastes, or nonpartisan election of county officials cannot be treated as local or special legislation in the House. Rather, any measure touching on such subjects must be treated as general legislation.[191] No similar rule exists in the Senate.

NOTES

1. GA. CONST. art. 3, §6, ¶4(a).
2. Ibid.
3. City of Calhoun v. N. Ga. Elec. Membership Corp., 233 Ga. 759, 213 S.E.2d 596 (1975); Employers Mut. Liability Ins. Co. v. Carson, 100 Ga. App. 409, 111 S.E.2d 918 (1960).
4. Blackmon v. Monroe, 233 Ga. 656, 212 S.E.2d 827 (1975); Black v. Blanchard, 227 Ga. 167, 179 S.E.2d 228 (1971); Cragg v. State, 224 Ga. 196, 160 S.E.2d 817 (1968). *See also* Gravely v. Bacon, 263 Ga. 203, 429 S.E.2d 663 (1993). *But see* Franklin v. Hill, 264 Ga. 302, 444 S.E.2d 778 (1994).
5. Gilbert v. Richardson, 211 Ga. App 795, 440 S.E.2d 684 (1994); Kyles v. State, 254 Ga. 49, 326 S.E.2d 216 (1985); Cotton States Mut. Ins. Co. v. DeKalb County, 251 Ga. 309, 304 S.E.2d 386 (1983).
6. GA. CONST. art. 3, §6, ¶4(b).
7. OFFICIAL CODE OF GEORGIA ANNOTATED (O.C.G.A.) §28-1-15.
8. Ibid.
9. Ibid.
10. *Black's Law Dictionary* (8th ed., 2004), p. 918.
11. Lasseter v. Ga. Public Service Comm., 253 Ga. 227, 319 S.E.2d 824 (1984).
12. GA. CONST. art. 1, §1, ¶25; art. 3, §6, ¶4(c).
13. GA. CONST. art. 3, §6, ¶4(a).
14. Mathis v. Jones, 84 Ga. 804, 11 S.E. 1018 (1890). *See also* extensive citations to appellate court decisions in annotations to GA. CONST. art. 3, §6, ¶4(a) in O.C.G.A.

15. City of Atlanta v. Hudgins, 193 Ga. 618, 19 S.E.2d 508 (1942); Franklin County v. Fieidale Farms Corp., 270 Ga. 272, 507 S.E.2d 460 (1998).

16. Lorentz & Ritter v. Alexander, 87 Ga. 444, 13 S.E. 632 (1891); City of Cochran v. Lanfair, 139 Ga. 249, 77 S.E. 93 (1912).

17. Crosby v. Dixie Metal Co., 124 Ga. App. 169, 183 S.E.2d 59 (1971); White Oak Acres, Inc. v. Campbell, 113 Ga. App. 833, 149 S.E.2d 870 (1966); Johnson v. Caldwell, 229 Ga. 548, 192 S.E.2d 900 (1972).

18. Nash v. National Preferred Life Ins. Co., 222 Ga. 14, 148 S.E.2d 402 (1966); Parrish v. Mayor and Aldermen of Savannah, 185 Ga. 828, 196 S.E. 721 (1938).

19. O.C.G.A. §1-3-11.

20. For a list of home rule powers that have been granted to local governments, *see* GA. CONST. art. 9, §2 and O.C.G.A. ch. 36-35.

21. GA. CONST. art. 3, §5, ¶9; O.C.G.A. §28-1-14.

22. O.C.G.A. §28-1-14(b).

23. Smith v. McMichael, 203 Ga. 74, 45 S.E.2d 431 (1947); Smith v. City Council of Augusta, 203 Ga. 511, 47 S.E.2d 582 (1948); City of Mountainview v. Clayton County, 242 Ga. 163, 249 S.E.2d 541 (1978).

24. Smith v. McMichael, 203 Ga. 74, 45 S.E.2d 431 (1947), Smith v. Abercrombie, 235 Ga. 741, 221 S.E.2d 802 (1975).

25. Walker Electric Co. v. Walton, 203 Ga. 246, 46 S.E.2d 184 (1948); Swiney v. City of Forest Park, 211 Ga. 154, 84 S.E.2d 573 (1954); Walls v. Board of Education of Chatham County, 242 Ga. 566, 250 S.E.2d 408 (1978).

26. GA. CONST. art. 3, §5, ¶8.

27. Senate Rule 4-2.10(c); House Rule 148.1.

28. House Rule 18.1.

29. House Rule 18.2.

30. Senate Rule 3-2.2.

31. House Rule 54.3.

32. House Rule 162.

33. House Rule 161.

34. Senate Rule 10-1.3; House Rule 37.

35. GA. CONST. art. 10, §1, ¶2.

36. O.C.G.A. §§28-5-80, 28-5-105.

37. O.C.G.A. §§50-16-34(12), 50-16-39(d).

38. *See, e.g.,* O.C.G.A. §§28-10-3, 50-8-4(f).

39. GA. CONST. art. 3, §5, ¶7.

40. GA. CONST. art. 5, §2, ¶4; art. 10, §1, ¶5.

41. GA. CONST. art. 3, §5, ¶2; Senate Rules 206, 208.

42. GA. CONST. art 1, §2, ¶9; O.C.G.A. §§50-21-1, 50-21-20 et seq.; *See* Gilbert v. Richardson, 211 Ga. App. 795, 440 S.E.2d 684 (1994); Donaldson v. Department of Transportation, 212 Ga. App. 240, 441 S.E.2d 473 (1994).

43. Trice v. Wilson, 113 Ga. App. 715, 149 S.E.2d 530 (1966); Crowder v. Department of State Parks, 228 Ga. 436, 185 S.E.2d 908 (1971).

44. Trice v. Wilson, 113 Ga. App. 715, 149 S.E.2d 530 (1966); Sikes v. Candler County, 247 Ga. 115, 274 S.E.2d 464 (1981).

45. O.C.G.A. §28-5-60.

46. O.C.G.A. §28-5-83.

47. O.C.G.A. §28-5-85.

48. O.C.G.A. §§28-5-100 through 28-5-108.

49. O.C.G.A. §28-5-80(a).

50. Ibid.

51. O.C.G.A. §28-5-106.

52. O.C.G.A. §28-5-80(b).

53. O.C.G.A. §28-5-82.

54. Walter McElreath, *A Treatise on the Constitution of Georgia* (Atlanta: The Harrison Co., 1912), p. 90.

55. Ibid., pp. 93, 106; GA. CONST. art. 3, §5, ¶3; Cady v. Jardine, 185 Ga. 9, 193 S.E.2d 869 (1937); Camp v. MARTA, 229 Ga. 35, 189 S.E.2d 56 (1972); Mead Corporation v. Collins, 258 Ga. 239, 367 S.E.2d 790 (1988); Lutz v. Furan, 262 Ga. 819, 427 S.E.2d 248 (1993); Perdue v. O'Kelley, 632 S.E.2d 110 (2006).

56. Ibid.

57. GA. CONST. art. 3, §5, ¶3; Protho v. Orr, 12 Ga. 36 (1852); McCaffrey v. State, 193 Ga. 827, 189 S.E. 825 (1937); Black v. Jones, 190 Ga. 95, 8 S.E.2d 385 (1940).

58. Camp v. MARTA, 229 Ga. 35, 189 S.E.2d 56 (1972); Central of Ga. R. Co. v. State, 104 Ga. 831, 846, 31 S.E. 531 (1898); American Booksellers Ass'n v. Webb, 254 Ga. 399, 329 S.E.2d 495 (1985).

59. Crews v. Cook, 220 Ga. 479, 139 S.E.2d 490 (1964); Capitol Distributing Co. v. Redwine, 206 Ga. 477, 57 S.E.2d 578 (1950); Bembry v. State, 250 Ga. 237, 297 S.E.2d 36 (1982); Lutz v. Foran, 262 Ga. 819, 427 S.E.2d 248 (1993).

60. Hines v. Etheridge, 173 Ga. 870, 162 S.E. 113 (1931); American Booksellers Ass'n v. Webb, 254 Ga. 399, 329 S.E.2d 495 (1985).

61. Wall v. Board of Elections, 242 Ga. 566, 250 S.E.2d 408 (1978); Lutz v. Foran, 262 Ga. 819, 427 S.E.2d 248 (1993).

62. Perdue v. O'Kelley, 632 S.E.2d 110 (2006).

63. Wall v. Board of Elections, 242 Ga. 566, 250 S.E.2d 408 (1978); Lutz v. Foran, 262 Ga. 819, 427 S.E.2d 248 (1993).

64. Schneider v. City of Folkston, 207 Ga. 434, 62 S.E.2d 177 (1950), *affirmed* by City of Chamblee v. Village of North Atlanta, 217 Ga. 517, 123 S.E.2d 663 (1962).

65. W. U. Tel. Co. v. Cooledge, 86 Ga. 104, 12 S.E. 264 (1890).

66. Capitol Dist. Co. v. Redwine, 206 Ga. 477, 57 S.E.2d 578 (1950).

67. Gainer v. Ellis, 226 Ga. 79, 172 S.E.2d 608 (1970).

68. Carter v. Burson, 230 Ga. 511, 198 S.E.2d 151 (1973).

69. American Booksellers Ass'n v. Webb, 254 Ga. 399, 329 S.E.2d 495 (1985).

70. McElreath, *A Treatise on the Constitution of Georgia*, p. 93; GA. CONST. art. 3, §5, ¶3; Cady v. Jardine, 185 Ga. 9, 10, 193 S.E. 869 (1937).

71. GA. CONST. art. 3, §5, ¶7.

72. Bray v. City of East Point, 203 Ga. 315, 46 S.E.2d 257 (1948).

73. Cade v. State, 207 Ga. 135, 60 S.E.2d 763 (1950).

74. Fortson v. Weeks, 232 Ga. 472, 208 S.E.2d 68 (1974).

75. Bray v. City of East Point, 203 Ga. 315, 46 S.E.2d 257 (1948); Rich v. State, 237 Ga. 291, 227 S.E.2d 761 (1976); Frazer v. City of Albany, 245 Ga. 399, 265 S.E.2d 581 (1980); Board of Public Education of City of Savannah v. Hair, 276 Ga. 575, 581 S.E.2d 28 (2003).

76. Sasser v. State, 99 Ga. 54, 25 S.E. 619 (1896).

77. Burns v. State, 104 Ga. 544, 30 S.E. 815 (1898); Mikell v. Mikell, 219 Ga. 550, 134 S.E.2d 630 (1964).

78. Devier v. State, 247 Ga. 635, 277 S.E.2d 729 (1981); Milhollen v. State, 221 Ga. 165, 143 S.E.2d 730 (1965); Mikell v. Mikell, 219 Ga. 550, 134 S.E.2d 630 (1964); Collins

v. State, 206 Ga. 95, 55 S.E.2d 599 (1949); Black v. Jones, 190 Ga. 95, 8 S.E.2d 385 (1946); Cady v. Jardine, 185 Ga. 9, 193 S.E. 869 (1937).

79. City of Savannah v. State, 4 Ga. 26 (1848). *See also* Greer v. State, 233 Ga. 667, 212 S.E.2d 836 (1975); Sams v. Olah, 225 Ga. 497, 169 S.E.2d 790 (1969); Fortson v. Weeks, 232 Ga. 472, 208 S.E.2d 68 (1974).

80. Hill v. Perkins, 218 Ga. 354, 127 S.E.2d 309 (1962). *See also* Fortson v. Weeks, 232 Ga. 472, 208 S.E.2d 68 (1974).

81. GA. CONST. art. 3, §5, ¶4.

82. Edalgo v. Southern Ry., 129 Ga. 258, 58 S.E. 846 (1907); Town of McIntyre v. Scott, 191 Ga. 473, 12 S.E.2d 883 (1941); Fortson v. Fortson, 200 Ga. 116, 35 S.E.2d 896 (1945).

83. Tison v. City of Doerun, 155 Ga. 367, 116 S.E. 615 (1923).

84. Ragans v. Ragans, 200 Ga. 890, 892, 39 S.E.2d 162, 164 (1946).

85. Ellis v. Johnson, 263 Ga. 514, 435 S.E.2d 923 (1993); Poteat v. Butler, 231 Ga. 187, 200 S.E.2d 741 (1973); West v. Forehand, 128 Ga. App. 124, 195 S.E.2d 777 (1973); Plantation Pipe Line Co. v. City of Bremen, 227 Ga. 1, 178 S.E.2d 868 (1970); Buice v. Dixon, 223 Ga. 645, 157 S.E.2d 481 (1967).

86. Kyles v. State, 254 Ga. 49, 326 S.E.2d 216 (1985); Jones v. Hartford Acc. & Indem. Co., 132 Ga. App. 130, 207 S.E.2d 613 (1974); Board of Public Education and Orphanage for Bibb County v. Zimmerman, 231 Ga. 562, 203 S.E.2d 178 (1974).

87. Tomblin v. S. S. Kresge Co., 132 Ga. App. 212, 207 S.E.2d 693 (1974); George C. Const. Co. v. Langford Const. Co., 182 Ga. App. 258, 355 S.E.2d 756 (1987).

88. County of Butts v. Straham, 151 Ga. 417, 419, 107 S.E. 163 (1921); Keener v. Mac-Dougall, 232 Ga. 273, 206 S.E.2d 519 (1974).

89. Stansell v. Fowler, 113 Ga. App. 377, 147 S.E.2d 793 (1966); Tyler v. Huiet, 199 Ga. 845, 36 S.E.2d 358 (1945). However, Georgia courts are obligated to reconcile apparent conflicts between different sections of the same statute to make them consistent with one another, if possible. *See* Undercofler v. Capitol Auto Co., 111 Ga. App. 709, 143 S.E.2d 206 (1965).

90. Board of Tax Assessors v. Catledge, 173 Ga. 656, 160 S.E. 909 (1931); Sawnee Electric Membership Corporation v. Georgia Public Service Commission, 273 Ga. 702, 544 S.E.2d 158 (2001). For an interesting judicial observation on the language of statutes, *see* concurring opinion, Fortson v. Weeks, 232 Ga. 472, 208 S.E.2d 68 (1974).

91. *See* O.C.G.A. §§1-3-1, 1-3-3.

92. Groover v. Johnston, 277 Ga. App. 12, 625 S.E.2d 406 (2005); Reynolds v. State, 209 Ga. App. 628, 434 S.E.2d 166 (1993); Mansfield v. Pannell, 261 Ga. 243, 404 S.E.2d 104 (1991); Fortson v. Weeks, 232 Ga. 472, 208 S.E.2d 68 (1974); City of Jesup v. Bennett, 226 Ga. 606, 176 S.E.2d 81 (1970).

93. State v. Simmons, 270 Ga. App. 301, 605 S.E.2d 846 (2003); Six Flags Over Georgia v. Kull, 276 Ga. 210, 576 S.E.2d 880 (2003); Seaboard Coast Line R. Co. v. Blackmon, 129 Ga. App. 342, 199 S.E.2d 581 (1973); City of Jesup v. Bennett, 226 Ga. 606, 176 S.E.2d 81 (1970); Stone Mountain Memorial Association v. Herrington, 225 Ga. 746, 171 S.E.2d 521 (1969).

94. Lunda Construction Co. v. Clayton County, 201 Ga. App. 106, 410 S.E.2d 446 (1991); Hollowell v. Jove, 247 Ga. 678, 279 S.E.2d 430 (1981); Graham v. McKesson Information Solutions, 279 Ga. App. 364, 631 S.E.2d 424 (2006); In re LJ, 279 Ga. App. 237, 630 S.E.2d 771 (2006).

95. City of Calhoun v. N. Ga. Elec. Membership Corp. 233 Ga. 759, 213 S.E.2d 596 (1975); Blackmon v. DeKalb Pipeline Co., Inc., 127 Ga. App. 395, 193 S.E.2d 635 (1972).

96. Modern Homes Const. Co. v. Burke, 219 Ga. 710, 135 S.E.2d 383 (1964); Etkind v. Suarez, 271 Ga. 352, 519 S.E.2d 210 (1999). *See also* Douglas County v. Abercrombie,

226 Ga. 39, 172 S.E.2d 419 (1970); Thompson v. Talmadge, 201 Ga. 867, 41 S.E.2d 883 (1947).

97. Curlee v. Mock Enterprises Inc., 173 Ga. App. 594, 327 S.E.2d 736 (1985); Crosby Aeromarine, Inc. v. Hyde, 115 Ga. App. 836, 156 S.E.2d 106 (1967).

98. O.C.G.A. §1-3-1; Franklin v. Hill, 264 Ga. 302, 444 S.E.2d 778 (1994); Curlee v. Mock Enterprises, Inc., 173 Ga. App. 594, 327 S.E.2d 736 (1985); Wall v. Youmans, 223 Ga. 191, 154 S.E.2d 191 (1967); Seaboard Coast Line R. Co. v. Blackmon, 129 Ga. App. 342, 199 S.E.2d 581 (1973).

99. State Bar of Georgia v. Haas, 133 Ga. App. 311, 211 S.E.2d 161 (1974); Poteat v. Butler, 231 Ga. 187, 200 S.E.2d 741 (1973); Plantation Pipe Line Co. v. City of Bremen, 227 Ga. 1, 178 S.E.2d 868 (1970). *See also* 1971 Ops. Att'y Gen. 71-21, 71-23.

100. Greene County v. North Shores Resort at Lake Oconee, 238 Ga. App. 236, 517 S.E.2d 553 (1999); Jones v. City of College Park, 223 Ga. 778, 158 S.E.2d 384 (1967); State v. Livingston, 222 Ga. 441, 150 S.E.2d 648 (1966); Southern Ry. Co. v. Brooks, 112 Ga. App. 324, 145 S.E.2d 76 (1965).

101. Maddox v. Schrader, 268 Ga. 661, 492 S.E.2d 521 (1997); Moore v. Robinson, 206 Ga. 27, 55 S.E.2d 711 (1949).

102. Georgia Mental Health Institute v. Brady, 263 Ga. 591, 436 S.E.2d 219 (1993); International Minerals & Chemical Corp. v. Bledsoe, 126 Ga. App. 243, 190 S.E.2d 572 (1972); Wilen Mfg. Co. v. Standard Products Co., 409 F. 2d 56 (5th Cir. 1969); Sharpe v. Lowe, 214 Ga. 513, 106 S.E.2d 28 (1958).

103. Chanin v. Bibb County and Blackmon v. Chanin, 234 Ga. 282, 216 S.E.2d 250 (1975); Barton v. Atkinson, 228 Ga. 733, 187 S.E.2d 835 (1972).

104. Fleming v. Zant, 259 Ga. 687, 386 S.E.2d 339 (1989).

105. Sharpe v. Lowe, 214 Ga. 513, 106 S.E.2d 28 (1958); Stanley v. Sims, 185 Ga. 518, 195 S.E. 439 (1938).

106. Southern Railway Co. v. A. O. Smith, 134 Ga. App. 219, 213 S.E.2d 903 (1975); McLarty v. Board of Regents, 231 Ga. 22, 200 S.E.2d 117 (1973). *But see* Johnson v. Miller, WL 506780 (S.D. Ga., 1994) in which Georgia legislators were allowed to testify as to intent in federal court.

107. McLarty v. Board of Regents, Transcript of Proceedings, Clarke County [Georgia] Superior Court (March 10, 1973), p. 60.

108. City of Calhoun v. N. Ga. Electric Membership Corp., 233 Ga. 759, 213 S.E.2d 596 (1975); Ga. Railroad & Banking Co. v. Wright, 125 Ga. 589, 54 S.E. 52 (1906).

109. Townsend v. Yeomans, 301 U.S. 441 (1937).

110. Schrenko v. DeKalb County School District, 276 Ga. 786, 582 S.E.2d 109 (2003); Carter v. Oxford, 102 Ga. App. 762, 118 S.E.2d 216 (1960); *affirmed* 216 Ga. 821, 120 S.E.2d 298 (1961); Price v. State, 76 Ga. App. 108, 45 S.E.2d 84 (1947); Wingfield v. Kutres, 136 Ga. 345, 71 S.E. 474 (1911). The court, however, has ruled that one legislature has no power to declare intent of a prior General Assembly in enacting a law, since that would be a legislative attempt to perform a judicial function by construing a law. Road Builders, Inc. of Tenn. v. Hawes, 228 Ga. 608, 187 S.E.2d 287 (1972).

111. Martin v. Baldwin, 215 Ga. 293, 110 S.E.2d 344 (1959).

112. Fender v. Fender, 249 Ga. 765, 294 S.E.2d 472 (1982); Freeman v. W.O.W. Life Ins. Society, 200 Ga. 1, 36 S.E.2d 81 (1945). *See also* Calhoun v. McLendon, 42 Ga. 405 (1871); Pearle Optical of Monroeville, Inc. v. Ga. State Board of Examiners in Optometry, 219 Ga. 364, 133 S.E.2d 374 (1963); City of Calhoun v. N. Ga. Elec. Membership Corp., 233 Ga. 759, 213 S.E.2d 596 (1975).

113. Thompson v. Eastern Air Lines, 200 Ga. 216, 36 S.E.2d 675 (1946); Georgia Penitentiary Co. No. 2 v. Nelms, 65 Ga. 67 (1880).

114. Smith v. City of Atlanta, 161 Ga. 769, 132 S.E. 66 (1925). However, *see* Pye v. State Highway Dept., 226 Ga. 389, 175 S.E.2d 510 (1970); Rives v. Atlanta Newspapers, Inc., 220 Ga. 485, 139 S.E.2d 395 (1964).

115. Sheffield v. State School Building Authority, 208 Ga. 575, 68 S.E.2d 590 (1952).
116. Mousetrap of Atlanta, Inc. v. Blackmon, 129 Ga. App. 805, 201 S.E.2d 330 (1973); Mason v. Service Loan & Finance Co., 128 Ga. App. 828, 198 S.E.2d 391 (1973); Belton v. Columbus Finance & Thrift Co., 127 Ga. App. 770, 195 S.E.2d 195 (1972); Woodford v. Kinney Shoe Corp., 369 F. Supp. 911 (N.D. Ga. 1973).
117. Ga. Const. art. 1, §2, ¶5.
118. Luther v. State, 255 Ga. 706, 342 S.E.2d 316 (1986); Kirton v. Biggers, 232 Ga. 223, 206 S.E.2d 33 (1974); Buice v. Dixon, 223 Ga. 645, 157 S.E.2d 481 (1967); Mayes v. Daniel, 186 Ga. 345, 198 S.E. 535 (1938). Furthermore, the court will not attribute to members of the General Assembly a purpose to circumvent provisions of the state constitution. McLucas v. State Bridge Bldg. Authority, 210 Ga. 1, 77 S.E.2d 531 (1953).
119. Battallia v. Columbus, 199 Ga. App. 897, 406 S.E.2d 290 (1991).
120. Adams v. Ray, 215 Ga. 656, 113 S.E.2d 100 (1960); State Farm Insurance Company v. Five Transportation Company, 246 Ga. 447, 271 S.E.2d 844 (1980).
121. City of Calhoun v. N. Ga. Elec. Membership Corp., 233 Ga. 759, 213 S.E.2d 596 (1975); Kirton v. Biggers, 232 Ga. 223, 206 S.E.2d 33 (1974); Black v. Blanchard, 227 Ga. 167, 179 S.E.2d 228 (1971). Nevertheless, when a statute is clearly in violation of the constitution, the supreme court has a duty to so determine, irrespective of the consequences. Calhoun County v. Early County, 205 Ga. 169, 52 S.E.2d 854 (1949).
122. Payne v. Bradford, 231 Ga. 487, 202 S.E.2d 422 (1973); Bryant v. Prior Tire Co., 230 Ga. 137, 196 S.E.2d 14 (1973); Northeast Factor & Discount Co., Inc. v. Jackson, 223 Ga. 709, 711, 157 S.E.2d 731 (1967); Wilson Foundation v. Bell, 223 Ga. 588, 157 S.E.2d 287 (1967).
123. Marchman & Marchman v. Atlanta, 250 Ga. 64, 295 S.E.2d 311 (1982); Taylor v. Moultrie Tobacco Sales Board, Inc., 227 Ga. 384, 180 S.E.2d 737 (1971); Ledford v. J. M. Muse Corp., 224 Ga. 617, 163 S.E.2d 815 (1968).
124. O'Kelley v. State, 210 Ga. App. 686, 436 S.E.2d 760 (1993); Walker v. Hall, 226 Ga. 68, 172 S.E.2d 411 (1970); Roberts v. Roberts, 226 Ga. 203, 173 S.E.2d 675 (1970); Shelton v. Housing Authority, 122 Ga. App. 535, 177 S.E.2d 832 (1970).
125. Grantham v. Grantham, 269 Ga. 413, 499 S.E.2d 67 (1998); Farmer v. State, 228 Ga. 225, 184 S.E.2d 647 (1971); Cross v. State, 225 Ga. 760, 171 S.E.2d 507 (1969).
126. Board of Education for City of Savannah v. Hair, 276 Ga. 575, 581 S.E.2d 28 (2003); Lasseter v. Ga. Public Service Commission, 253 Ga. 227, 319 S.E.2d 824 (1984).
127. Battallia v. Columbus, 199 Ga. App. 897, 406 S.E.2d 290 (1991); Wilson v. Ledbetter, 194 Ga. App. 32, 389 S.E.2d 771 (1989); Collins v. Woodham, 257 Ga. 643, 361 S.E.2d 800 (1987); Atlantic Coast Line Railroad v. State, 135 Ga. 545, 69 S.E. 725 (1910); Capitol Distributing Co. v. Redwine, 206 Ga. 477, 57 S.E.2d 578 (1980).
128. Richmond County v. Pierce, 234 Ga. 274, 215 S.E.2d 665 (1975); Smith v. McMichael, 203 Ga. 74, 45 S.E.2d 431 (1974).
129. Thompson v. Talmadge, 201 Ga. 867, 41 S.E.2d 883 (1947).
130. Williams v. MacFeely, 186 Ga. 145, 197 S.E. 225 (1938).
131. Cunningham v. State, 260 Ga. 827, 400 S.E.2d 916 (1991).
132. Moseley v. State, 176 Ga. 889, 169 S.E. 97 (1933); U.S. v. Raines, 362 U.S. 17 (1959); City Council v. Mangley, 243 Ga. 358, 254 S.E.2d 315 (1979); State v. Jackson, 269 Ga. 308, 496 S.E.2d 912 (1998).
133. Geng v. State, 276 Ga. 428, 578 S.E.2d 115 (2003); Collins v. Woodham, 257 Ga. 643, 362 S.E.2d 61 (1987); Martin v. Ellis, 242 Ga. 340, 249 S.E.2d 23 (1978).
134. Georgia Franchise Practices Commission v. Massey-Ferguson, 244 Ga. 800, 262 S.E.2d 106 (1979); Murphy v. State, 233 Ga. 681, 212 S.E.2d 839 (1975); Greer v. State, 233 Ga. 667, 212 S.E.2d 836 (1975); Fortson v. Weeks, 232 Ga. 472, 208 S.E.2d

68 (1974); Sams v. Olah, 225 Ga. 497, 169 S.E.2d 790 (1969); State v. Jackson, 269 Ga. 308, 496 S.E.2d 912 (1998).

135. Greer v. State, 233 Ga. 667, 212 S.E.2d 836 (1975).

136. Murphy v. State, 233 Ga. 681, 212 S.E.2d 839 (1975).

137. Gay v. Laurens County, 213 Ga. 518, 100 S.E.2d 271 (1957).

138. Rutledge v. Gaylord's, Inc., 233 Ga. 694, 213 S.E.2d 626 (1975); Chanin v. Bibb County, 234 Ga. 282, 216 S.E.2d 250 (1975); Martin v. Ellis, 242 Ga. 340, 249 S.E.2d 23 (1978).

139. O.C.G.A. §1-1-3.

140. 1967 Op. Att'y Gen. 67-189; 1973 Op. Att'y Gen. 73-80; 1977 Op. Att'y Gen. 77-87; 1979 Op. Att'y Gen. 79-46; 1980 Op. Att'y Gen. 80-118; 1984 Op. Att'y Gen. 84-19; 1991 Op. Att'y Gen. 91-26.

141. For example, in the 1994 general appropriation act, language was included stating that it was the General Assembly's intent that the State Forestry Commission keep a particular nursery open and that the agency continue publishing a magazine and another publication (Sec. 59), that the Department of Public Safety buy full-size pursuit vehicles (Sec. 66), and that a technical school's satellite facility be located on the campus of a particular college (Sec. 70). In addition, numerous agencies were directed to institute new policies or to take (or not to take) certain actions. *See* Ga. Laws 1994, p. 1506.

142. 1989 Op. Att'y Gen. 89-28; 1991 Op. Att'y Gen. 91-26.

143. GA. CONST. art. 3, §9, ¶1. Exceptions are found in GA. CONST. art. 1, §2, ¶8 (c); art. 3, §9, ¶4 (a); art. 3, §9, ¶6 (b); art. 7, §4, ¶3 (2) (A).

144. To see how the pre- and post-1974 budgets compare, *see* Ga. Laws 1973, p. 1353, and Ga. Laws 1974, p. 1508.

145. GA. CONST. art. 3, §9, ¶2(b).

146. GA. CONST. art. 3, §5, ¶2.

147. Mayes v. Daniel, 186 Ga. 345, 198 S.E. 535 (1938).

148. GA. CONST. art. 3, §9, ¶6(a).

149. Ibid. *See* endnote GA. CONST. art. 3, §5, ¶6 for exceptions allowed by the constitution.

150. GA. CONST. art. 3, §9, ¶3.

151. GA. CONST. art. 3, §5, ¶6.

152. GA. CONST. art. 3, §9, ¶2(b).

153. GA. CONST. art. 3, §9, ¶1.

154. GA. CONST. art. 3, §9, ¶4(a).

155. GA. CONST. art 1, §2, ¶8(c); art. 3, §9, ¶4(a); art. 3, §9, ¶6(b); art. 7, §4, ¶3(2)(A).

156. GA. CONST. art. 3, §9, ¶3.

157. GA. CONST. art. 3, §9, ¶4(c).

158. *See* GA. CONST. art. 3, §9, ¶6(f) et seq., for a list of the trust funds.

159. O.C.G.A. §50-27-13.

160. GA. CONST. art. 3, §9, ¶4(b).

161. *See* GA. CONST. art. 7, §4, for constitutional provisions governing state debt.

162. O.C.G.A. §45-12-78(b).

163. GA. CONST. art. 3, §9, ¶2; O.C.G.A. §§45-12-74, 45-12-75.

164. 1979 Op. Att'y Gen. 79-18.

165. O.C.G.A. §45-12-77.

166. Ibid.

167. 1979 Op. Att'y Gen. 79-70.

168. 1969 Op. Att'y Gen. 69-51; 1967 Op. Att'y Gen. 67-322; 1965–66 Op. Att'y Gen. 66-18.

169. O.C.G.A. §28-5-4.

170. O.C.G.A. §45-12-93.

171. Ibid.

172. Ibid.

173. GA. CONST. art. 3, §9, ¶5.

174. *See, e.g.,* Ga. Laws 1988, p. 68.

175. GA. CONST. art. 3, §9, ¶4.

176. GA. CONST. art. 3, §9, ¶5.

177. O.C.G.A. §28-5-1.

178. O.C.G.A. §28-5-42(a).

179. Ibid.

180. O.C.G.A. §28-5-42(g).

181. Ibid.

182. Ibid.

183. O.C.G.A. §28-5-44.

184. O.C.G.A. §28-5-42.

185. O.C.G.A. ch. 47-20.

186. GA. CONST. art. 3, §10, ¶5.

187. O.C.G.A. ch. 47-20.

188. Ibid.

189. Ibid.

190. Ibid.

191. House Rule 50.

CHAPTER 7

THE LAWMAKING PROCESS

Perhaps the best method of depicting the Georgia legislature in action is to follow a bill from the time of its introduction in one of the houses through the various stages that it must pass before it can become a "law." (Fig. 12 illustrates this process.)

SOURCES OF BILLS

A member of either house of the General Assembly can introduce any measure, except that revenue and appropriation bills, compensation resolutions, and resolutions to impeach must be introduced in the House. Only a member can introduce a bill or resolution. The governor, for example, although an important source of legislation, introduces none directly but rather designates a legislator, usually the administration floor leader in one of the houses, to introduce administration measures.

The Georgia legislature permits multiple sponsoring of legislation by members of the same house. Georgia's constitution also allows the General Assembly to provide by statute for joint sponsorship of bills and resolutions by members of both houses.[1] To date, however, this provision has not been implemented.

There are no limits on the number of legislators who may sign a proposal to be introduced, although usually no more than a dozen will be listed by name on the actual bill. When many members cosponsor legislation, the major sponsors are listed by name, followed by the notation "and others." A complete list of sponsors is maintained on file with either the clerk of the House or secretary of the Senate.

186

FIGURE 12. How a Bill Becomes a Law

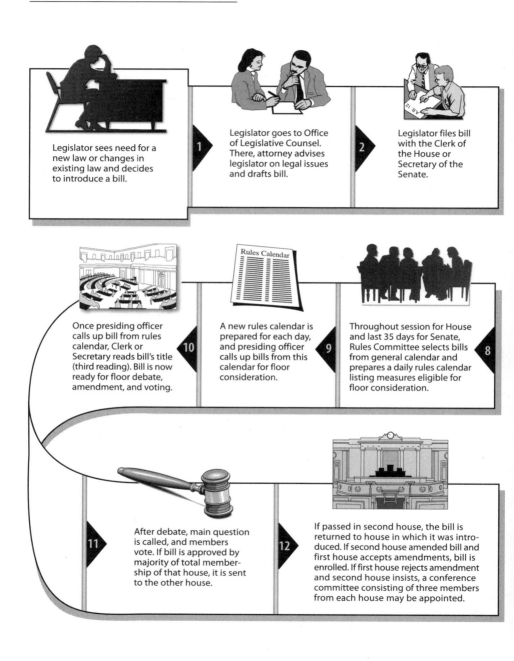

Legislator sees need for a new law or changes in existing law and decides to introduce a bill.

1 Legislator goes to Office of Legislative Counsel. There, attorney advises legislator on legal issues and drafts bill.

2 Legislator files bill with the Clerk of the House or Secretary of the Senate.

10 Once presiding officer calls up bill from rules calendar, Clerk or Secretary reads bill's title (third reading). Bill is now ready for floor debate, amendment, and voting.

9 A new rules calendar is prepared for each day, and presiding officer calls up bills from this calendar for floor consideration.

8 Throughout session for House and last 35 days for Senate, Rules Committee selects bills from general calendar and prepares a daily rules calendar listing measures eligible for floor consideration.

11 After debate, main question is called, and members vote. If bill is approved by majority of total membership of that house, it is sent to the other house.

12 If passed in second house, the bill is returned to house in which it was introduced. If second house amended bill and first house accepts amendments, bill is enrolled. If first house rejects amendment and second house insists, a conference committee consisting of three members from each house may be appointed.

3 On legislative day after filing, bill is formally introduced. In chamber, bill's title is read during period of first readings.

4 Immediately after first reading, presiding officer assigns bill to a standing committee.

5 In the House only, on next legislative day, Clerk reads bill's title (second reading) in chamber, although actual bill is now in committee. In Senate, second reading comes after bill is reported favorably from committee.

7 Clerk or Secretary prepares a daily general calendar of bills favorably reported from committee. For first five days of session (only in Senate), presiding officer calls up bills from this calendar for floor action.

6 Bill is considered by committee. Amendments can be added or bill rewritten as a committee substitute. Bills may be reported out favorably or unfavorably, but most die in committee.

13 If the conference committee agrees to a compromise and each house accepts compromise, the bill is enrolled and sent to the governor (if requested). Otherwise, all enrolled bills sent to governor following adjournment *sine die*.

14 Governor has 40 days after adjournment *sine die* to sign bill, do nothing (in which case, the bill becomes law), or veto the bill. Veto can be overridden by two-thirds vote of each house.

15 Acts and other laws enacted at the session are printed in the *Georgia Laws*. Also, act is incorporated into the Official Code of Georgia Annotated.

Act becomes effective the following July 1, unless a different effective date is provided in act.

THE LEGISLATIVE COUNSEL (RIGHT) ADVISES LEGISLATORS ON
LEGAL MATTERS, PARTICULARLY DRAFTING BILLS AND RESOLUTIONS.

DRAFTING BILLS

Although only a legislator can introduce a bill or resolution, it is
not mandatory that he or she actually draft the text of the measure;
however, some do. Often, private citizens, attorneys, special committees, and interest groups will draw up a proposal and seek a legislator
willing to introduce it. Similarly, the governor, state agencies, and
local governments may assign attorneys or legal specialists to draft a
measure and seek a legislator to sponsor it.

Before introduction, however, all proposals for bills and substantive joint resolutions are taken by sponsoring legislators to the Office
of Legislative Counsel for drafting, redrafting, or at least review.
By law, retirement bills *must* be taken to this office before being
introduced.[2] This office is staffed by attorneys skilled in legislative
matters and bill drafting and offers these services to any legislator.
The office has a computerized statutory retrieval system that includes the code as well as the constitution. It is used along with the
bill-drafting system, so related statutes can be recalled when a bill is
drafted. A request by a legislator for drafting or review of a bill and

REPRESENTATIVE GOVERNMENT AT WORK

Georgia's long-standing constitutional requirement that each bill must be read three times on three different days in each house before voting can take place originated long ago in England's House of Commons. Today, the full text of each bill is no longer read, but each bill's title must be read aloud on three different days in each house. The main purpose of the original procedure was to slow down consideration of bills as a check against surprise or hasty legislative action.

any conversations between the legislator and the counsel's office are treated as privileged information and are not subject to the state's open records requirements.[3]

The Office of Legislative Counsel attempts to make sure proposed legislation does not violate state and federal constitutions. If after reviewing a particular measure the counsel's office believes it to be of doubtful constitutionality, the author or sponsor of the bill is so informed; however, the decision as to whether to introduce the proposed measure in the General Assembly is left entirely with the sponsor.

PREFILING BILLS

A bill or resolution can only be introduced officially during a legislative session. In 1994, however, the General Assembly enacted legislation allowing the prefiling of measures so that informal deliberation by legislative committee can begin before the session.

According to the legislation, any representative or senator "who will be eligible to consider the measure when introduced" can prefile legislation.[4] (Presumably this includes representatives-elect and senators-elect, although the legislation does not indicate whether newly elected members who have not yet been sworn in are included.) The proposed measure is first taken to the Office of Legislative Counsel, which prepares it in a form to indicate its prefiled status, and then to the clerk of the House or secretary of the Senate (depending on the author's house). There, the measure is given an identification number, which, at the clerk or secretary's discretion, may correspond to the number that measure will be assigned when and if officially introduced during the session.

Copies of each prefiled bill or resolution are sent to the presiding officer of that house, who then assigns the measure to a standing committee for consideration. (This preliminary committee assignment does not bind the speaker or president's choice of committee assignments if and when the prefiled measure is officially introduced.) The committee can then consider the prefiled bill, but it can take no official action until the bill is actually introduced and assigned to committee during the session. House rules, however, allow the speaker to authorize a committee to take official action during the interim between sessions.[5]

INTRODUCING A BILL

To introduce a measure during a session, a legislator will pick up the official copy of the bill or resolution that has been prepared by the Office of Legislative Counsel. That copy is then filed with the clerk or secretary, who assigns the bill a number and enters appropriate information about the bill in the records of that office.

A copy of the bill may also be physically carried to the clerk or secretary at the front of either chamber. There is no formally designated "hopper" into which bills are placed for introduction, although

PRINTED COPIES OF NEW BILLS ARE
DISTRIBUTED TO MEMBERS EACH MORNING.

the phrase "putting a bill in the hopper" is sometimes used to refer to the bill-introduction process.

The original copy of the bill is for the exclusive use of the Senate or House and the committee to which the measure will be referred.

Deadlines for Bill Introduction

A bill introduced in the Senate must have been filed in the secretary's office before 4:00 p.m. of the previous legislative day.[6] The House requires only that a bill be filed with the clerk no later than one hour after adjournment for introduction on the next day.[7] These rules allow time for the bill to be entered into the computerized bill-drafting system and multiple copies made for distribution to members before the measure is read to the body and referred to committee.

Since logjams of bills tend to build up in legislative bodies as sessions approach adjournment, most state legislatures now impose specific deadlines for bills to be introduced during a session.[8] (Table 7 lists deadlines for specific bill introductions in Georgia.) Typically, they have provisions whereby members can introduce a measure under special circumstances beyond these deadlines, such as by securing unanimous consent or a certain vote of the whole body, usually a two-thirds majority.[9]

In the Senate, the deadline for introduction of measures that will have the effect of law is the 30th day of the session, unless a suspension of this rule is approved by two-thirds of the Senate's total members.[10] The House does not have a similar deadline.

TABLE 7. Statutory Deadlines for Bill Introductions

Type of Bill	Deadline for Introduction
Any nonfiscal retirement bill for state, county, or municipal officials or employees[a]	20th day of session
Any retirement bill having a fiscal impact[b]	regular session, first year of biennium (odd years only)
Any bill significantly impacting the anticipated revenue or expenditure of any state agency[c]	20th day of session
Any bill significantly impacting the anticipated revenue or expenditure of cities or counties[d]	20th day of session
Any bill changing the compensation or allowances of any elected or appointed state officials or agency heads[e]	10th day of session
Compensation resolutions[f]	10th day of session

[a] O.C.G.A. §47-20-33. [c] O.C.G.A. §28-5-42(a)(1). [e] O.C.G.A. §28-5-1.
[b] O.C.G.A. §47-20-34. [d] O.C.G.A. §28-5-42(a)(4). [f] O.C.G.A. §28-5-80.

Printing of Bills

The rules of both houses require that all bills and resolutions of general application be printed and a copy distributed to each member prior to consideration.[11]

During consideration of a measure, amendments may be proposed either in committee or on the floor. Committee amendments—including substitutes—must be printed and are incorporated into a subsequent printing of an original bill, generally on another color paper, with a notation that this version has been amended by committee.

Amendments on the floor are handled somewhat differently. All amendments in both houses must be in writing.[12] In some instances, printed copies of amendments are distributed to members on the floor, or amendments can be projected on two large screens at the front of the chamber. However, in either house at any time, a majority of a quorum may suspend action upon any pending bill or resolution of general application until the proposed amendments have been printed and distributed.[13]

Bill Numbering and Identification

Bills and resolutions are numbered separately in the House and Senate in the order submitted to the clerk in the House and the secretary in the Senate. In both houses, bills and resolutions are numbered consecutively throughout the biennium. Thus, the first bill or resolution introduced in a house in the second year of the biennium is given the number immediately following the last bill or resolution of the preceding session.

Following the daily adjournment of each house, the clerk and secretary utilize the computerized bill-drafting system to reprint any measures that have been changed or amended in that day's session. If amendments occur in committee or on the floor or if the committee reports a substitute measure, such changes are incorporated when reprinting the bill or resolution. Even though a bill may be so completely rewritten in committee that it bears little or no resemblance to the measure as originally submitted, the number and author(s) of the bill must remain the same.

A code in the upper right corner of a bill or resolution identifies certain information on that bill for the clerk or secretary, as well as for the legislator (see Fig. 13). For instance, since most measures are drafted or revised by the Office of Legislative Counsel, a code such as "LC 14 2662" is quite common. In this case, "LC" identifies the bill as having been drafted by the legislative counsel; the "14" identifies

FIGURE 13. Identification Numbers, Authors, and Title of Bill

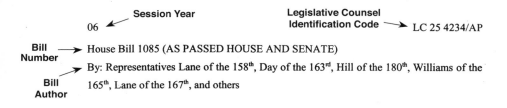

Session Year

Legislative Counsel
Identification Code → LC 25 4234/AP

06 ◄—

Bill Number —► House Bill 1085 (AS PASSED HOUSE AND SENATE)

—► By: Representatives Lane of the 158th, Day of the 163rd, Hill of the 180th, Williams of the

Bill Author 165th, Lane of the 167th, and others

A BILL TO BE ENTITLED

Title ↘ AN ACT

1　To amend Code Section 27-4-130.1 of the Official Code of Georgia Annotated, relating to

2　open seasons, creel and possession limits, and minimum size limits for certain finfish species,

3　so as to change certain provisions relating to tripletail fish; to repeal conflicting laws; and for

4　other purposes.

5　　　　BE IT ENACTED BY THE GENERAL ASSEMBLY OF GEORGIA:

Body ↘

6　　　　　　　　　**SECTION 1.**

7　Code Section 27-4-130.1 of the Official Code of Georgia Annotated, relating to open

►8　seasons, creel and possession limits, and minimum size limits for certain finfish species, is

Line Number 9　amended by striking paragraph (8) of subsection (c) and inserting in lieu thereof the

10　following:

11　　"(8) Tripletail　　　　All year　　　　5 2　　18 inches"

12　　　　　　　　　**SECTION 2.**

13　All laws and parts of laws in conflict with this Act are repealed.

H. B. 1085
- 1 -

the particular staff member who worked on this piece of legislation; and the "2662" identifies that bill for retrieval in the computer system, should reprinting of the bill be required.

If a measure is amended in either house, the code is changed to reflect that version of the original measure that is under consideration. For instance, the code on a bill that has been amended might now be changed to read "SB 439/FA/5." Here, "SB 439" would identify the measure as Senate Bill 439, while "FA" would show that floor amendments were incorporated into this version. The "5" in this example identifies the particular person who prepared the bill (however, this designation is only used on Senate bills).

Among the other abbreviations commonly used, "FS" identifies a measure as a floor substitute; "CA," as a measure that has been amended in committee; and "CS," as a measure that is a committee substitute. These abbreviations may be used together where appropriate; for example, "FSFA" would identify a floor substitute to a floor amendment. A Senate bill amended in the House would be identified as "HFA" (House Floor Amendment) or "HCA" (House Committee Amendment). Finally, the abbreviation "AP" (As Passed) is used to identify a bill or resolution that has been approved by both houses. As noted earlier, however, regardless of what action has taken place in committee or on the floor of either house with regard to a measure, the number of that bill or resolution remains unchanged. The code in the upper right corner merely assists in identifying the version of the bill or resolution under consideration.

Each page of a bill printed by the clerk or secretary has the lines of print numbered consecutively on the left margin, e.g., page 1, line 20, or page 3, line 2. This is for ease of reference when debating a bill in the General Assembly.

DAILY LEGISLATIVE MATERIALS

There are a variety of materials, some updated on a daily basis, that are available to members of the General Assembly and to the public during the session. This information is also available online—on the House and Senate Web sites—although it does not appear in exactly the same format as the printed versions.

1. Calendars—copies of the daily calendar of business for each chamber.
2. First Readers—measures that have been introduced and read only once (by title), with notation of committee referred to.

3. Daily Status Sheet—a single-page listing of floor and committee action taken by one house, along with those measures adopted the previous legislative day by the other house (see Fig. 14).

4. Composite Status Sheet—a multipage consolidated listing of the status of all bills and resolutions introduced that session (or carried over from the previous session in even-numbered years) through the previous legislative day. A computerized bill status reporting system is used to keep track of legislation. This sheet is updated daily and indicates all floor and committee action taken by either house on bills and resolutions, the date of such action, and the action of the governor on those measures that have passed both houses. (Fig. 15 presents an example of a composite status sheet.)

5. Senate Bills and Resolutions—copies of the bills and resolutions to be first considered by the Senate.

6. House Bills and Resolutions—copies of the bills and resolutions to be first considered by the House.

7. Full versions of all legislation, including amendments and substitutes.

8. All votes taken on the electronic voting system.

READING OF BILLS

First-time visitors to the legislative galleries frequently comment about clerks reading bills aloud from the podium at the front of the chamber, especially since members already have printed copies of the bills on their desks. To visitors, it appears that no one is paying attention to the ritual. The requirement for reading bills traces back to British parliamentary procedure before Georgia's founding. The practice continued in Georgia following statehood because illiteracy was common and because typewriters and fast-copy printing equipment had not yet been invented.

Reading bills in the Georgia legislature—or at least their titles—continues today, not only because of long tradition, but because it helps guard against hastily called votes and—most importantly—because it is required by the state constitution.

Today, every general bill and every joint resolution intended to have the effect of general law or to amend the state constitution must be read three times, with each reading on a separate day, before it can be voted upon by each house.[14] The Constitution of 1983 eliminated the requirement that general bills be read in their entirety on third

THE SECRETARY OF THE SENATE (RIGHT) EMPLOYS AN
AIDE TO READ THE TITLES OF BILLS AND RESOLUTIONS.

---

reading—unless the presiding officer or a majority of members voting order a full reading.

The constitution requires local bills and resolutions to be read one time (by title) before a vote and that one full day pass between the reading and the vote. Otherwise, the General Assembly is free to set procedures by statute for considering local legislation—including a greater number of readings.[15] Any additional readings of local bills would be by title only.

First reading. The first reading of all bills and resolutions is by title and occurs the day of introduction (the legislative day following filing with the clerk or secretary). If any legislator wishes to prevent any amendments to a bill as introduced, a motion "to engross" must be made at that bill's first reading. After the measure has been read by title, the presiding officer assigns it to a standing committee. Soon afterward, the clerk and secretary prepare a list for their house titled "First Readers," which cites the bill number, author, title, and committee assignment of each bill and resolution read for the first time that day (see Fig. 16).

THE CLERK OF THE HOUSE READS THE TITLES OF BILLS AND RESOLU-
TIONS FROM THE CLERK'S PODIUM AT THE FRONT OF THE CHAMBER.

Second reading. The second reading, like the first, is by title only. House rules provide that a bill or resolution "requiring three readings prior to its passage" is automatically passed to a second reading on the legislative day following the first reading.[16] This means that a bill is read a second time on the floor of the House while the bill is still in the custody of a committee (unless the committee reported the bill out the same day it received the measure).

In contrast, second reading in the Senate does not occur until the legislative day following the bill's being reported out of committee. One exception is that after the 35th day of the session, second readings occur on the same day a bill is reported from committee.[17]

Third reading. General bills and resolutions have their third reading only after reported from committee, placed on the calendar, and called from the calendar by the presiding officer. Only the title of the bill or resolution need be read at this point, unless the presiding officer or a majority of the members voting direct a full reading of the bill.[18] It is only after a measure's third reading that floor debate, amendment, and voting occur.

198

Figure 14. Daily Status Sheet

HOUSE STATUS NO. 4

THURSDAY, JANUARY 11, 2007

FOURTH LEGISLATIVE DAY

House First Readers

HB	5	MotV	HB	6	JudyNC	HB	15	Judy
HB	24	Judy	HB	40	W&M	HB	41	GF&P
HB	42	NR&E	HB	43	GAff	HB	44	Judy
HB	45	Ins	HB	46	Judy	HB	47	H&HS
HB	48	App	HB	49	MotV	HB	50	JudyNC
HB	51	JudyNC	HB	52	JudyNC	HB	53	Judy
HB	54	NR&E	HB	55	NR&E	HB	56	GAff
HB	57	Rules	HB	58	GAff	HB	59	W&M
HB	60	GAff	HB	61	H&HS	HB	62	GAff
HB	63	HEd	HB	64	JudyNC	HB	65	JudyNC
HB	66	W&M	HB	67	W&M	HR	15	H&HS
HR	16	SI&P						

House Second Readers

HB	2	HB	12	HB	21	HB	26	HB	29	HB	34
HB	35	HB	36	HB	37	HB	38	HB	39	HR	14

House Passed/Adopted

		Yeas	Nays			Yeas	Nays
		----	----			----	----
HR	13	166	0				

House Read and Adopted

HR	20	HR	22	HR	23	HR	24	HR	25	HR	26
HR	27	HR	28	HR	29	HR	31	HR	32	HR	33
HR	34	HR	35	HR	36	HR	37	HR	38	HR	39
HR	40										

House Read and Referred

HR	17	Rules	HR	18	Rules	HR	19	Rules
SR	6	Rules						

HOUSE ADJOURNED UNTIL 1:00 O'CLOCK,
MONDAY, JANUARY 22, 2007

FIGURE 15. Composite Status Sheet

STATE OF GEORGIA - HOUSE OF REPRESENTATIVES

COMPOSITE STATUS   Wednesday, May 10, 2006

Bill	Title	Comm	Ch	Read 1st Time	Read 2nd Time	Favorably Reported	Comm Amend/Sub	Recommitted	Unfavorably Reported	Read 3rd Time	Passed/Adopted	Committee/Floor Amend/Sub	Lost	Notice of Motion to Reconsider	Reconsidered	Postponed	Passed/Adopted	Committee/Floor Amend/Sub	Lost	Amendments/Sub Agreed to	Amendments/Sub Disagreed to	Index on Position	Conf Comm Appointed	Conf Comm Report Adopted	Recede from Position	Position	Sent to Governor	Date Signed by Governor	Act/Veto Number
House Bills																													
377	Chiropractors; revoke license or discipline licensee; add grounds	Regl	H	2/8	2/9	2/25	S	3/31																				
			S																										
379	Employees' Retirement; disability benefits; eligibility provisions	Ret	H	2/9	2/10	3/6	S			3/13	3/13	CS								3/28							4/6	4/19	519
		RET	S	3/14	3/23	3/23	S			3/24	3/24	CS																	
380	McIntosh County; chief magistrate; nonpartisan elections	LLeg	H	2/9	2/10	2/24		2/22		2/17	2/17			2/17	2/17	2/22	2/24									*			
		SLGO	S	2/25																									
383	SHBP; cert vested judges & district attorneys; continue coverage	Ins	H	2/9	2/10			3/24																		*			
			S																										
385	State Bd of Cosmetology; terminate; repeal Chapter 10 of Title 43	Regl	H	2/9	2/10																								
			S																										
386	Conspiracy to commit a crime; change certain penalties	JudyNC	H	2/9	2/10	3/3		3/31																					
			S																										
387	Criminal attempt; change certain penalties	JudyNC	H	2/9	2/10	3/3		3/31																					
			S																										
388	Optional employee benefit plans; cert governmental entities; adm fees	Ins	H	2/9	2/10	3/10		3/31																					
			S																										
391	Retirement; circuit public defender; select Employees' or Judicial System	Ret	H	2/9	2/10	1/11																							
			S																										
393	Income tax credits; telecommuting; employers convert certain work force	W&M	H	2/8	2/9																								
			S																										
395	Special license plates; Purple Heart; certain inscription	MotV	H	2/9	2/10																								
			S																										
398	Criminal solicitation; crime punishable by death or life imprisonment; penalty	JudyNC	H	2/9	2/10	3/3		3/31																					
			S																										
399	Public School Employees Retirement; retire at 60 or 30 years of service	Ret	H	2/9	2/10																								
			S																										
400	Teachers Retirement; postretirement benefit increase; provisions	Ret	H	2/9	2/10	1/25	S			2/13	2/13	CS													*	4/3	5/3	729
		RET	S	3/14	2/22	2/21				3/14	3/14																		
401	Coastal waters & areas; permits or variance apps.; timely decisions	NR&E	H	2/9	2/10																								
			S																										
402	Special license plates; emergency medical services personnel	MotV	H	2/9	2/10																								
			S																										
403	Clerks of superior court and coroners; qualifying; nonpartisan election	GAff	H	2/9	2/10																								
			S																										
405	Ga War Veterans Nursing Home Trust Fund; special license plates; create	MotV	H	2/9	2/10			2/15																		*			
			S																										
417	Hospital Infections Disclosure Act; enact	H&HS	H	2/10	2/14																								
			S																										
419	Misdemeanor traffic offenses; fines to be paid into state treasury	JudyNC	H	2/10	2/14																								
			S																										
421	Student violence against teacher; remain in class at discretion of teacher	Ed	H	2/10	2/14																								
			S																										
422	Dealers in agricultural products; surety bond requirements; amend	A&CA	H	2/10	2/14																								
			S																										
423	Graduation test; students failing science portion; certain eligibility	Ed	H	2/10	2/14																								
			S																										
424	Bianca Walton Anti-Bullying Act; enact	Ed	H	2/10	2/14																								
			S																										
425	Insurers; permit food and refreshments under certain circumstances	Ins	H	2/10	2/14	3/10				3/11	3/11																		
		I&L	S	3/12	3/21	2/9	S	3/29		3/20	3/20	CS								3/22							4/3	4/27	584
426	Georgia Smokefree Air Act of 2005; enact	H&HS	H	2/10	2/14																								
			S																										
427	Insurance; private passenger mot veh; cert state-wide rates & regulations	Ins	H	2/10	2/14																								
			S																										
429	Setoff debt collection; claimant agencies; include public housing authorities	W&M	H	2/14	2/15	3/8	S	3/31		3/13	3/13	CS								3/30					*			
		FIN	S	3/14	3/23	3/22	S			3/28	3/30	CSFA																	
430	"Karon's Law"; enact	H&HS	H	2/14	2/15																								
			S																										
432	Work release programs; felony sentences; provisions	JudyNC	H	2/14	2/15	3/3	S	3/31																					
			S																										
433	Nonpartisan elections; include certain county officers	GAff	H	2/14	2/15																								
			S																										
434	Employees' Ret; temporary full- or part-time; additional creditable service	Ret	H	2/14	2/15																								
			S																										
435	Sales tax exemption; professional hunting guide services	W&M	H	2/14	2/15																								
			S																										
436	Environmental Facilities Authority; rename; amend provisions	W&M	H	2/14	2/15																								
			S																										
439	Free license plates; certain disabled vets; Dept of Veterans Services; duties	MotV	H	2/14	2/15	3/4		3/31																					
			S																										
441	Hunting & fishing; honorary licenses for disabled persons; certification	GF&P	H	2/14	2/15	3/2		3/31																					
			S																										
443	Insurance; insurable interest in life of insured	Ins	H	2/14	2/15																								
			S																										
445	Tax sales; disposition of excess proceeds; amend certain provision	Judy	H	2/15	2/16																								
			S																										
446	Tax sales; excess proceeds; redemption period; amend provisions	Judy	H	2/15	2/16																								
			S																										
447	Tax executions; certain transfers; required notice; amend provisions	Judy	H	2/15	2/16																								
			S																										
448	Tax executions; issuance and transfer; amend provisions	Judy	H	2/15	2/16																								
			S																										
451	Nonprofit youth development organizations; licensing; exemptions	C&Y	H	2/15	2/16			2/17																		*			
			S																										
453	Clerks of courts; documents and records; maintain digital copies	Judy	H	2/15	2/16																								
			S																										
462	Local bds of education; health benefit plan; certain members	Ed	H	2/15	2/16	3/10	S	3/31																					
			S																										
463	Employees' Retirement; group term life; define	Ret	H	2/15	2/16																								
			S																										

FIGURE 16. First Readers

SB 9.   By Senators Rogers of the 21st, Williams of the 19th, Weber of the 40th, Moody of the 56th, Cowsert of the 46th and others:

A BILL to be entitled an Act to amend Article 17 of Chapter 2 of Title 20 of the Official Code of Georgia Annotated, relating to teachers and other school personnel, so as to enact the "Grade Integrity Act of 2007"; to provide that no classroom teacher shall be required, coerced, intimidated, or disciplined in any manner to change the grade of a student; to provide for an ethical violation reportable to the Professional Standards Commission; to provide for statutory construction; to provide for related matters; to repeal conflicting laws; and for other purposes.

Referred to Education and Youth Committee.

SB 22.   By Senator Thomas of the 2nd:

A BILL to be entitled an Act to amend Article 3 of Chapter 5 of Title 42 of the Official Code of Georgia Annotated, relating to conditions of detention, so as to increase the minimum reimbursement rate paid to counties for housing state inmates; to provide for related matters; to provide an effective date; to repeal conflicting laws; and for other purposes.

Referred to Appropriations Committee.

SB 23.   By Senators Douglas of the 17th, Rogers of the 21st, Schaefer of the 50th, Hawkins of the 49th, Staton of the 18th and others:

A BILL to be entitled an Act to amend Article 1 of Chapter 10 of Title 17 of the O.C.G.A., relating to criminal sentencing procedure, so as to provide that in making determinations with respect to probation and suspension of sentences, the court may inquire into and consider the legality of a prisoner's presence in the United States; to amend Article 2 of Chapter 9 of Title 42 of the O.C.G.A., relating to granting of pardons, parole, and other relief in general, so as to provide that the State Board of Pardons and Paroles may inquire into and consider the legality of a prisoner's presence in the United States when making parole decisions; to make a statement of legislative findings and intent with respect to applicability; to provide for related matters; to provide an effective date; to repeal conflicting laws; and for other purposes.

Referred to Judiciary Committee.

SB 24.   By Senators Staton of the 18th, Shafer of the 48th, Chance of the 16th, Carter of the 13th, Rogers of the 21st and others:

A BILL to be entitled an Act to amend Article 6 of Chapter 9 of Title 16 of the Official Code of Georgia Annotated, relating to computer systems security, so as to prohibit persons from using the Internet or electronic mail to induce another to provide identifying information by falsely representing themselves to be a business without the authority or approval of the business; to provide definitions; to provide for penalties and sanctions; to provide for civil actions; to provide for related matters; to repeal conflicting laws; and for other purposes.

Referred to Science and Technology Committee.

SR 4.   By Senators Staton of the 18th, Johnson of the 1st, Shafer of the 48th, Williams of the 19th, Rogers of the 21st and others:

COMMITTEE CONSIDERATION OF BILLS

Assignment of Bills

Before assigning bills and resolutions to committees each day, the speaker of the House and president of the Senate review the title of each newly introduced measure in their respective house and may even study the entire legislation. The determination of the "proper" committee to consider a bill lies with these two officers, excluding bills that, by statute, must be referred to particular committees[19] (e.g., general appropriations bills, compensation resolutions, and retirement bills) and a few other measures. The assignment is usually based on the nature of the measure or its subject matter, though in many cases, there may be several committees that might logically consider a particular bill. Neither House nor Senate rules allow the membership to overrule the speaker or president's committee assignment of a newly introduced bill. However, once a bill is in committee, a motion can be made on the floor to commit the bill to another committee.[20] (Tables 8 and 9 show the workloads of committees during recent legislative sessions.)

Meetings of Standing Committees

Participation in committee deliberations is an understood obligation for all legislators. Although no specific House rule requires attendance, Senate rules provide that failure to attend three consecutive meetings is grounds for removal from the committee unless the senator has been excused from attendance in the Senate or the senator has filed a statement that his or her absence was due to attending a conflicting committee meeting.[21] In Georgia, members of each house serve on several committees, and meeting time conflicts inevitably occur, forcing members to miss some meetings. Senate rules, however, allow a senator who is scheduled to take part in two committee meetings occurring simultaneously to be included in the roll call portion of the minutes of the committee meeting that he or she is unable to attend.[22]

Standing committees can meet during a session or the interim between sessions, although official action (e.g., reporting a bill out of committee) can only take place during a legislative session. Rules of both houses allow standing committees to meet and take official action during a recess or adjournment between the first and final day of session. However, no official action can be taken after adjournment *sine die* until the next session convenes.[23]

TABLE 8. Summary of House Committees' Workload—Regular Sessions, 2001–2006

Committee	Bills and Resolutions					
	2001	2002	2003	2004	2005	2006
Agriculture and Consumer Affairs	15	10	18	11	9	7
Appropriations	24	19	32	15	17	28
Arts and Humanities	—	—	1	0	—	—
Banks and Banking	4	5	7	5	7	11
Children and Youth	4	2	7	4	8	7
Defense and Veterans Affairs	5	6	2	2	6	4
Economic Development and Tourism	—	—	13	9	4	6
Education	44	30	43	42	37	36
Ethics	0	0	0	0	8	2
Game, Fish, and Parks	12	14	7	14	15	13
Governmental Affairs	19	9	7	31	56	36
Health and Ecology	41	24	—	—	—	—
Health and Human Services	—	—	30	36	31	22
Higher Education	9	10	10	20	20	13
Human Relations and Aging	12	3	6	10	9	12
Industry	41	32	—	—	—	—
Industrial Relations	11	7	17	24	11	11
Information and Audits (formerly Journals)	0	0	0	0	0	0
Insurance	29	15	21	18	28	22
Interstate Cooperation	0	0	0	0	12	2
Intragovernmental Coordination	0	0	0	0	4	2
Judiciary	123	62	104	101	75	77
Judiciary, Non-civil	—	—	—	—	76	73
Legislative and Congressional Reapportionment	0	5	3	5	8	5
Motor Vehicles	59	48	67	47	54	39
Natural Resources and Environment	28	19	25	16	15	16
Public Safety	12	10	20	12	12	15
Public Utilities and Telecommunications	—	—	8	14	18	20
Regulated Beverages	4	8	—	—	—	—
Regulated Industries	—	—	19	9	26	16
Retirement	78	5	67	3	75	3
Rules	134	450	133	136	96	97
Special Committee on Civil Justice Reform	—	—	—	—	19	1
Special Committee on MARTA	—	—	—	—	—	1
Science and Technology	—	—	—	—	3	1
Special Judiciary	36	30	52	54	—	—
Special Rules	0	0	0	1	2	13
Local Legislation	189	307	196	162	182	203
State Institutions and Property	6	12	21	18	20	12
State Planning and Community Affairs	34	33	31	19	7	44
Transportation	43	57	77	10	40	86
Ways and Means	158	95	191	114	118	108
TOTAL	1,174	1,327	1,235	962	1,128	1,064

Dash (—) indicates committee not in existence.

TABLE 9. Summary of Senate Committees' Workload—Regular Sessions, 2001–2006

Committee	Bills and Resolutions					
	2001	2001	2003	2004	2005	2006
Agriculture and Consumer Affairs	2	10	2	7	12	7
Appropriations	9	9	7	4	8	25
Banking and Financial Institutions	6	5	4	2	2	4
Children and Youth	—	—	7	3	—	—
Corrections, Correctional Institutions and Property	6	5	—	—	—	—
Defense, Science and Technology	7	7	—	—	—	—
Economic Development	—	—	11	7	5	5
Economic Development, Tourism and Cultural Affairs	4	3	—	—	—	—
Education and Youth	23	12	18	20	22	16
Ethics	10	6	15	5	2	2
Finance	—	—	28	1	8	17
Finance and Public Utilities	37	40	—	—	—	—
Health and Human Services	28	22	24	30	44	22
Higher Education	3	5	5	7	8	16
Insurance and Labor	17	18	19	12	32	25
Interstate Cooperation	0	1	2	0	1	0
Judiciary	56	40	59	44	47	56
Natural Resources and the Environment	13	10	12	26	20	12
Public Safety and Homeland Security	15	9	25	24	44	34
Reapportionment and Redistricting	0	8	5	2	3	1
Regulated Industries and Utilities	—	—	16	9	19	17
Retirement	21	3	14	1	10	1
Rules	17	12	28	23	12	34
Science and Technology	—	—	5	2	13	7
Special Judiciary	8	0	22	5	8	11
State and Local Governmental Operations	57	67	79	48	84	69
State Institutions and Property	—	—	4	5	6	7
Transportation	23	21	30	30	24	19
Veterans and Consumer Affairs	16	9	—	—	—	—
Veterans and Military Affairs	—	—	2	5	2	5
TOTAL	378	322	443	322	436	412

Dash (—) indicates committee not in existence.

Committees generally meet in the morning prior to the convening of a daily session or in the afternoon following adjournment for the day. Notice of the time and place of committee meetings is posted at the offices of the clerk and secretary and on the House and Senate Web sites. Sometimes the meeting must change because of prolonged floor sessions.

In the House, standing committees meet on the call of the chair.[24] Senate rules provide that the secretary of the Senate and the Committee on Administrative Affairs schedule the time and location of Senate committee meetings. Notice is posted by 10 a.m. on the Friday preceding the week of a scheduled meeting. A committee chair can schedule additional meetings if a request in writing is made to the secretary of the Senate at least 24 hours prior to the meeting. A chair can cancel a scheduled meeting in the same manner. If no committee agenda has been posted, the scheduled meeting can be canceled by notifying the secretary of the Senate in writing at least one hour prior to the scheduled meeting.[25] The Rules Committee is exempt from these requirements except when considering bills and resolutions referred to it by the Senate president.[26]

At these meetings, members discuss the various measures that have been assigned to their committee. In the case of a controversial issue, a public hearing may be held to allow all interested persons an opportunity to express their views on the measure before the committee. The committee may also call on executive officials and any other persons to testify before it on the bill or to furnish it with information.

The constitution of Georgia provides that all standing committee meetings be open to the public, although it allows either house to make exception by its rules.[27] Committee meetings are open to the public in both houses, except that House and Senate rules allow a majority of a quorum to exclude the public from meetings of standing committees when discussing real estate acquisition, personnel matters, and charges brought against public officials or employees unless the official or employee requests that the meeting be open to the public.[28]

House rules do not require that minutes of standing committee and subcommittee meetings be taken. However, they do specify that if a meeting that is open to the public is being recorded or transcribed, copies of such recording or transcription must be available to the public upon request and payment of reasonable costs.[29]

In the Senate, the chair of each standing committee and subcommittee is required to arrange to have recorded minutes kept of all meetings that include the time and place of the meeting, attendance of committee members, an accurate record of all votes taken, the number of all bills acted upon, all motions and results, the appearance of any persons other than members, the date and time the committee convened and adjourned, and such additional information as the committee may determine.[30] Testimony before a committee can be recorded at the discretion of the committee; however, any additional paid personnel hired to take testimony must be approved by the Senate Administrative Affairs Committee. Recorded testimony is transcribed or released only at the discretion of the committee or the secretary of the Senate when the Senate is not in session.[31]

Possible Committee Actions

Standing committees in the House and Senate can take three actions on a measure:

1. report the measure back to the full house favorably, with or without amendments (amendments may be so extensive that the bill is designated a "committee substitute");
2. report the measure back unfavorably; or
3. hold the bill without reporting it back.

House committees have one additional option: report the measure back without recommendation.[32]

Both houses require that all committee reports be in writing, and they allow minority members of a committee to make a written report giving the reasons for their dissent.[33] The rules of the House further provide that the committee may order the clerk to print and distribute the majority report to members of the House. If a minority report is written, a majority of the minority of the committee can order the clerk to print and distribute the minority report to members of the House. Whenever practicable, a committee is to include a brief résumé of the bill along with reports.[34]

No committee in either house may deface or interline a measure that has been referred to it. If the committee wishes to recommend an amendment, it must do so on separate paper, noting the section, page, or line to which the amendment relates.[35] For amendments that are proposed by committee, the clerk or secretary is required to have them printed and distributed to each member. Action on any pending bill or resolution of general application may be suspended at any time by a majority of a quorum voting until the substitutes and amendments offered have been printed and distributed.[36]

When favorably reported. In the House, when a measure is favorably reported from committee or reported without recommendation, it is assigned to the Rules Committee for placement on the calendar. In the Senate, a measure that is favorably reported is ready for second reading and assignment to the Rules Committee for calendar consideration.[37]

If a measure has been referred to and reported on by more than one committee or if it has been recommitted to the same committee, the last committee report is the one acted upon by the house.[38]

When unfavorably reported. Although any action by a committee can be overruled by the full membership, and any member can move that the bill be recommitted to another committee, nearly all bills that receive an unfavorable committee report die at this stage.

Only the House has specific rules on challenging an unfavorable committee report. Any member may request that the Rules Committee disagree with the "do not pass" recommendation. Such a request must be made before adjournment of the legislative day following the unfavorable committee report. If the Rules Committee votes to disagree, the measure is placed on the general calendar unless the committee decides to recommit the bill. If the unfavorable committee report is upheld, the bill or resolution is lost.[39] Senate rules provide that should a bill or resolution receive a "do not pass" recommendation in committee, that action is considered an unfavorable report and may not be taken up by the full Senate.[40]

When not reported. The most common committee action on a bill or resolution is simply to hold the bill without taking any formal action. House rules provide that if a measure has been held by a committee for 10 legislative days without being reported, any member may initiate a petition to discharge the bill or resolution. The petition must be signed by two-thirds of the members of the House in a form prescribed by the clerk. When a successful petition is filed with the clerk, the bill or resolution takes its place on the general calendar in the same manner as if favorably reported by a committee.[41]

In the Senate, there is no equivalent procedure for removing a bill from committee and having it sent to the Rules Committee for placement on the calendar. However, both the Senate and House allow any member to introduce a floor motion to withdraw a bill from one committee and send it to another.[42] In both houses, the Rules Committee can recommit any measure being considered for the rules calendar back to the committee that reported it out. Also, the Senate Rules Committee has the option of recommitting the bill to any committee of its choosing; the House Rules Committee has the power to amend a bill that has been reported from committee.[43]

Importance of committee report. Most legislative bodies rely heavily on the work of their committees for a division of labor, which allows close scrutiny of a large number of bills. In the Georgia General Assembly, the committee report is a major determinant in the fate of most bills.

CALENDAR

Even after a committee has favorably reported a bill back to the full house, that bill cannot come before the body until it has been placed on the calendar and called up by the presiding officer. The calendar is a daily listing showing the order in which bills and resolutions that are favorably reported out of committee will receive third reading and legislative consideration on the floor of a house. In the House, uncontested local bills are not placed on the calendar as are general bills but are usually called up and passed on the day following their favorable report from committee. In the Senate, a separate local consent calendar is prepared for these bills.

General calendar. This calendar is prepared daily throughout the entire session by the clerk of the House and the secretary of the Senate for their respective houses. After the first five days in the Senate—and for the entire 40-day session in the House—the general calendar is used by the Rules Committee of each house to prepare the daily rules calendar (see Fig. 17 for an example of a general calendar).[44]

Each house considers the bills introduced by its members first, then the resolutions of its members, then the bills of the other house, and lastly, the resolutions introduced in the other house. The Senate has a policy of placing the bills and resolutions left from the preceding day at the head of the next day's calendar to prevent prolonged delay in their consideration.

Rules calendar. During the entire session in the House and last 35 days in the Senate, the daily legislative agenda on the floor of each house is governed by a rules calendar prepared by each house's Rules Committee (see Fig. 18).[45] The rules calendar is necessary because, except for the first few days of a session, there are always more bills that have been reported out of committee than can be considered on the floor during a single day, so some mechanism is needed to select from all the eligible measures those that are more important or deserving of floor consideration. This subjective and political

FIGURE 17. General Calendar

Section 2
Legislations left in Sections 1, 2 and 3 of General Calendar and defeated legislation that will be reconsidered pursuant to Senate Rule 6-7.4

SENATE GENERAL CALENDAR

THURSDAY, FEBRUARY 16, 2006

TWENTIETH LEGISLATIVE DAY

SB 64   Law Enforcement Motor Vehicles; blue
           lights on roof; repeal requirement (Substitute)(RULES-(17th)

SB 149   School/Extracurricular Activities; written
           notification; withhold permission (Substitute)(ED&Y-(50th)

SB 244   Magistrates Retirement Fund; define terms; create board of
           commissioners; powers (Substitute)(RET-(47th)

SB 248   Rehabilitation Services; delivery to deaf-blind individuals; procedures
           (I&L-(2nd)

SB 249   Adoption; provide original birth certificate; fee/waiting period; provision
           (Amendment)(S JUDY-(2nd)

SB 330   Emergency Medical Provider; include prehospital healthcare/medical
           transportation (H&HS-(54th)

SB 370   License Plate, Special; promote agriculture in Georgia;
           provide for issuance, renewals, fees, donation of revenue (PF) (PS&HS-
           (7th)

SB 396   Crimes; person who is attacked has no duty to retreat;
           provide immunity from prosecution (Substitute)(JUDY-(7th)

SB 427   Public Retirement Systems Investment Authority Law;
           define terms; alternative investments (Substitute)(RET-(32nd)

SB 500   2006 Georgia Accuracy in Elections Act; permanent paper record of
           votes; provide for pilot program/electronic voting (Substitute)(SLGO(G)-
           (27th)

SB 520   Public Safety, Board of; authorize to provide badge/revolver to sworn
           officers; state patrol; change provisions (Amendment)(PS&HS-(1st)

SB 522   Amy's Law; disposition for delinquent acts; change certain provisions
           (Substitute)(JUDY-(30th)

SB 530   Property; liens; change provisions; conditions; value (Substitute)(JUDY-
           (40th)

SR 34   CA: Sales Tax; educational purposes; change certain imposition
           requirements (Substitute)(RULES-(49th)

SR 639   SGT Mike Stokely Memorial Highway; dedicate (PF) (TRANS-(28th)

FIGURE 18. Rules Calendar

SENATE CONVENES AT 10:00 A.M.

SENATE RULES CALENDAR

FRIDAY, JANUARY 26, 2007

NINTH LEGISLATIVE DAY

SB 19 Transportation, Department of; pay costs of removal, relocation, or adjustment of utility facilites necessitated by construction of public roads (TRANS-24th)

SB 24 Computer Security; persons provide identifying information by falsely representing themselves to be a business; definitions; penalties (Substitute)(S&T-18th)

SR 49 Justice, Dept. of U.S.; urged to oppose the proposed unsolicited takeover of Delta Air Lines (ECD-51st)

SB 15 Drivers' Licenses; suspended/revoke; change certain provisions (JUDY-37th)

Respectfully submitted,

Don Balfour

Balfour of the 9th, Chairman
Senate Rules Committee

process must take place each legislative day of the session (with the exclusion of the first five days in the Senate). Generally, the principal author or sponsor of a bill is given at least one opportunity to make a case for his or her bill being placed on the rules calendar. Because of time limits for floor debate and voting, some bills have to be omitted from the calendar, although they are again eligible for placement on the following day. It is possible, however, for a bill that is favorably reported out of committee never to come up for floor consideration if the Rules Committee chooses not to place it on the calendar.

The Rules Committee of each house can meet in the morning prior to convening or in the afternoon or evening following adjournment to set the rules calendar for the next legislative day. In the Senate, the committee makes the decision from the general calendar prepared by the secretary's office. In the House, a Rules Committee Consideration Calendar is prepared from the general calendar, which is prepared by the clerk's office. To place a bill on the consideration calendar, the author or sponsor of the bill that has been reported favorably from committee must submit a request in writing to the Rules Committee. Generally, a consideration calendar will be posted by 5 p.m. for use the next morning in setting the rules calendar. However, legislation may be added at any time at the discretion of the Rules Committee chairman. If a bill on the consideration calendar is not placed on the rules calendar within three days, it is dropped from the consideration calendar.

In addition to deciding which measures will come up and the order in which they will be considered, the House Rules Committee can set time limits for floor debate on any measure. It can also regulate floor amendments for bills on the calendar by imposing one of the following rules:

1. Open Rule: germane amendments may be offered.
2. Modified Open Rule: germane amendments may be offered subject only to an overall time limit on the amendment process and a requirement that the amendments be preprinted and placed upon the desk of members one hour prior to debate.
3. Modified Structured Rule: germane amendments designated by the Rules Committee may be offered. This rule may preclude amendments to a particular portion of the bill, although other parts of the bill may be open to amendment.
4. Structured Rule: no amendments may be offered. However, if a House bill that passed with a structured rule is later amended in the Senate, the author of that bill—with the speaker's

concurrence—may move that the House accept the Senate Amendment.[46]

The House rules calendar indicates which, if any, special rule has been assigned to a bill.

While the rules calendar is in effect in the Senate, all bills and resolutions are called up in the order in which they appear on the calendar. It takes a three-fourths vote (providing the three-fourths constitutes a majority of the Senate) to change the order of bills on the calendar.[47] House rules are silent on changing the rules calendar, but they allow the speaker to call bills from the calendar in any order.[48]

Consent calendars. House rules provide for an Uncontested Resolutions Calander. Eligible measures are resolutions that create study committees and other similar bodies and commemorative resolutions that name or rename roads, streets, highways, parks, bodies of water, bridges, institutions, buildings, structures, and other geographic landmarks. Uncontested resolutions are voted on as a group without debate. However, any member of the House can request that a resolution be removed and placed on the rules calendar.[49]

Although not specifically provided for in House rules, uncontested local bills are placed on the local legislation calendar. All bills on the calendar are voted on as a group, unless a representative asks that a local bill be removed from the calendar, in which case, the challenged local bill is voted on after the bills on the calendar.

Georgia's Senate has two consent calendars. The first is the General Consent Calendar for Commemorative Resolutions. The definition of commemorative resolutions is the same as that for such resolutions in the House, except that Senate rules provide that the landmark to be named or renamed must be located within a single senatorial district. Resolutions to name or rename landmarks within two or more districts are not eligible for the Senate's consent calendar.

The general consent calendar for commemorative resolutions must be placed on each senator's desk at the time of third reading of the resolutions. The title of each resolution is read, and the Senate then votes on all resolutions as a group. If, prior to the vote, any senator objects in writing to any of the commemorative resolutions, that resolution is pulled from the consent calendar and placed at the bottom of that day's rules calendar.[50]

The Senate also has a consent calendar for local bills. At least one hour before the Senate convenes, a local consent calendar is placed on each senator's desk. A single vote is taken on all local bills on the calendar. Before the vote, if three senators (one of whom must be from a district that is directly affected) object in writing to any of the local bills, such bills are pulled from the consent calendar and placed on the calendar for local contested bills.[51] The title of each bill on the local contested calendar is read, and the bill is treated in the same manner for floor consideration as a general bill, except that debate is limited to a total of 10 minutes for each side.[52]

FLOOR CONSIDERATION

Until this point, a bill officially has been before the entire membership of a house on each of the first two readings, but no other floor action has taken place on the bill. Once reported out of committee and placed on the calendar, it is ready for the final stage of the legislative process: floor consideration.

Floor Privileges

Before looking at this stage, it should be noted that the rules of each house limit who may enter the chamber while that house is in session. In the Senate, no one may enter the floor except

1. members and officers of the Senate;
2. members and officers of the House;
3. the governor;
4. the lieutenant governor;
5. staff members of the following offices: secretary of the Senate, clerk of the House, legislative counsel, lieutenant governor, president pro tempore, majority leader, minority leader, Senate Budget and Evaluation Office, Senate Research Office, and Senate Press Office;
6. former senators (except those who are registered as lobbyists or currently employed by the state);
7. senators' secretaries and Senate-paid aides;
8. senators' spouses and families;
9. one intern;
10. Senate photographer and one additional photographer from the Senate Press Office;
11. others as permitted by the president;
12. representatives of the press, radio, television, and other news media in the designated area at the rear of the chamber; and
13. not more than two media photographers and videographers.[53]

Senate rules allow the president to introduce the governor or any member of Georgia's congressional delegation at any time. However, no other person or group may address the Senate except as permitted by the president. Members of the Senate may introduce or recognize persons or groups at any time before third reading and consideration of general bills and resolutions unless the president decides otherwise. Senators can bring persons and groups onto the floor of the Senate for recognition and photographs as permitted by the pesident.[54] Although Senate rules do not specifically mention floor privileges for pages, by necessity they have to be able to deliver messages to senators at their desks.

No person engaged in lobbying or attempting to influence legislation will be admitted onto the floor. During floor consideration of any appropriation bill, the chair of the Senate Appropriations Committee or a majority of members present may invite nonsenators onto the floor to explain or answer questions on that bill.[55]

The House excludes all persons from the floor except

1. members (and their pages) and officers of the House;
2. members and officers of the Senate;
3. the governor;
4. staff members of the Office of Legislative Counsel;
5. representatives of the news media (carrying proper credentials), although no interviews are allowed while the House is in session;
6. photographers and television camera crews;
7. such other persons to whom the speaker may issue a pass and those that the House may allow upon recommendations of its Rules Committee; and
8. spouses and children over 12 years old of House members (although they may not sit at the desk of any member).[56]

Although not specifically mentioned in House rules, floor access also extends to House pages, the House photographer, and House staff (such as employees of the Office of Member Services).

No person who is not a member of the House is permitted to speak unless invited by resolution adopted on or before the previous day. Any person invited to address the House must do so after the conclusion of third reading of bills and resolutions or immediately after the body reconvenes after a recess and prior to the transaction of other business. The speaker can waive this requirement "when warranted by the prominence of the person or the significance of the occasion."[57]

Requests for floor access to nonmembers for the purpose of receiving special recognition must be submitted in writing to a subcommittee of the House Rules Committee at least seven days in advance.[58] However, the speaker at any time can grant special floor access.[59] Excluded specifically from floor access in the House is any person who is lobbying or otherwise attempting to influence legislation.[60]

Floor Debate and Amendment

After a bill or resolution has been called from the calendar and its title read a third time, it is ready for floor consideration. Then members can debate the measure and offer amendments.

To speak for or against a measure, a legislator first must be recognized by the chair. To be recognized, a legislator must notify the speaker prior to the bill being called or during the time the first speaker is in the well.[61] Once recognized, the member comes to the podium at the front of the chamber (known as the "well"). Senators are limited to 30 minutes in the well unless a majority of senators voting extend the time. Time spent answering questions is included in the 30-minute limit.[62] House members are limited to 20 minutes in the well unless the time limit is extended by the speaker or by two-thirds of the members voting on the motion. If the House Rules Committee has set time limits for debate on a particular measure, the speaker determines how much time each member will be allowed.[63]

To ask a question of a legislator in the well, members must be at their own desk in order to be recognized by the chair. Once recognized after raising their hand, members may then ask the chair if the legislator in the well will yield for a question. Usually, the legislator in the well agrees to yield. This procedure is followed for each question, whether from the same legislator or a different legislator. Any member addressing a legislator in the well must phrase his or her remarks in the form of a question.

For the sake of audibility, members have microphones at their desks, which can be switched on by the clerk or secretary's staff after a legislator signals a desire to address the chair or member in the well.

Both houses have strict rules on referring to other members during debate. Senate rules prohibit referring to other senators by name, requiring instead that particular senators be designated by their position on the floor or by the district they represent.[64] House

IN BOTH CHAMBERS, LEGISLATORS SPEAK FOR AND AGAINST MEASURES
FROM A PODIUM AT THE FRONT OF THE CHAMBER KNOWN AS THE WELL.

rules allow referring to another member by "Mr.," "Mrs.," "Miss,"
or "Ms." and his or her last name or by the member's title, position
on the floor, or by the district, city, or county he or she represents.[65]
During debate, neither representatives nor senators can refer to any
private conversation with another member.[66]

Rules of both houses require that a member speaking from the
well confine his or her remarks to the bill or resolution being debated. Also, no member can address the body from the well a second
time until every other member who wishes to speak has been given
an opportunity. Under no circumstances can a member speak more
than twice on any subject.[67] Both houses also have a rule prohibiting a member in the well from making any motion (e.g., to call the
previous question) that would end debate on a measure without first
relinquishing the floor.[68] When addressing the House, no member
can be disrespectful to any other member and must avoid references
to personalities.[69]

At any time during legislative proceedings, a member may direct
a "parliamentary inquiry" or "point of order" to the presiding officer.

This action allows a legislator to ask a question regarding the specific legislative procedure in order to seek a ruling or explanation from the chair. For instance, when a number of amendments are before the body at one time, a member may be unsure of which one is being voted upon or what the effect of one will be on another. Or, a member may have a question about the applicability of the House rules to the proceedings at hand. Rulings of the chair on parliamentary issues can be appealed to the membership. In practice, rulings are very seldom questioned. It should be noted that the parliamentary inquiry is intended to apply to procedural questions on which the chair can rule, and members are generally discouraged from using this device to make substantive arguments to influence members for or against a matter under consideration.

At any time during debate when another member does not have the floor, any member can make a variety of motions (e.g., to postpone, table, or recommit a bill to committee) that would remove from the floor the measure being considered. These motions are discussed in detail in Chapter 7.

To conclude debate, a member may move the previous question, or the presiding officer can inquire if there is any objection to ordering the previous question. If the motion passes, further debate is cut off, except that the chairperson of the standing committee that reported the measure back to the floor is given 20 minutes either to use entirely or to yield to other members for all or any part of this time. Signers of a minority report are allotted 20 minutes, with the same conditions on how time is used. Members who are aligned with the committee majority report always speak last. In actual practice, members rarely use the entire time period allowed by the rules after ordering the previous question.[70]

After the previous question has been ordered, the house then votes on any amendments to the bill or resolution under consideration. After amendments have been addressed, final passage of the measure (otherwise known as the "main question") is voted upon. Both houses follow a similar procedure for this vote. The presiding officer states the following in rapid fashion: "Is there objection to the report of committee, which is favorable to this bill, being adopted? Hearing none, report of committee is adopted. Is there objection to the main question being ordered? Hearing none, the main question is ordered. The question now is on passage of [bill number]. All in favor vote 'aye,' all opposed vote 'nay'—and the clerk [or secretary] will unlock the machine." The "machine" is the electronic voting system used in each house.

VOTING

Voting Requirements

Georgia's constitution requires that in order for a bill to pass, it must receive approval of a majority of the membership of each house. This is referred to as a "constitutional majority." The constitution also requires that the final vote for passage in each house be recorded in the journal of that body.[71]

Additionally, some actions—such as proposed constitutional amendments, overriding a veto, amending legislative rules during a session, and expelling a member—require special majorities (usually two-thirds of either the total membership or of those present).

Many of the procedural votes require only a majority of those present, provided a quorum is present. A Senate rule stipulates that amendments, motions, and procedural matters are to be decided by a majority of a quorum, unless otherwise provided by rules, and that all other resolutions not otherwise provided for require a majority of the membership for approval.[72] If a matter comes up and House rules do not specify the vote required for passage or adoption, then approval by a majority of the membership is required. Excluding bills or resolutions that will become law, the vote also may be by unanimous consent.[73]

Until voting on a bill or resolution begins, a measure may be withdrawn at any stage of the legislative process with the consent of the House or Senate. However, should a bill or resolution be rejected in the final vote in either house, it may not again be proposed during the same session, under the same or any other title, without the consent of two-thirds of the house that rejected it.[74]

Voting Procedures

Subject to constitutional and statutory provisions, as well as the rules of each house, voting in the House and Senate may be by unanimous consent, voice vote (*viva voce*), a show of hands (division), or a roll call (also called a vote by "yeas and nays").

Unanimous consent. This is a procedure for voting or obtaining the permission of the members of a house to allow or dispense with some action (e.g., to dispense with the morning roll call in each house). The presiding officer asks the members if there is objection to the motion or request being voted upon, and if no member voices objection, the vote, motion, or request passes. If objection is raised, then a vote by voice, show of hands, or voting machine is taken.

Viva voce. This is a collective voice vote taken of the members who are present. The vote of the individual legislator is not recorded (unless a *viva voce* roll call has been called), and only the result of the vote—as interpreted by the presiding officer—is announced and recorded. If the presiding officer's interpretation of the result is appealed, a second vote will be taken using the same or another procedure.

Division. This is a vote by show of hands, where only the total number for and against a proposal is recorded. Historically, a division of a house was a call for the members of that house to rise and stand to one side of the chamber or the other to reflect their positions on a question. Now, when the presiding officer calls upon the members in favor of a question "to rise, stand, and be counted," the members reflect their position on the question by raising a hand.

Yeas and nays. In this vote, each member is on record with respect to how he or she voted on a question. Such roll call votes are required in both houses on all proposed constitutional amendments and on all bills appropriating money.[75] Also, when a two-thirds vote of either or both houses is required for the passage of a bill or resolution, the yeas and nays must be taken and entered in the journal. A roll call vote may be taken in either house when ordered by the presiding officer or at the desire of one-fifth of the members present or a lesser number if so provided by the house rules.[76] The Senate provides for a roll call if five members so request.[77] Senate rules also provide for a roll call on the final vote of all general bills and resolutions having the effect of law, the adoption of all conference committee reports, and any action that would have the effect of finalizing the Senate's action on any general bill or resolution.[78]

In the Senate, all roll call votes must be taken on the electronic voting system (if inoperative, a voice roll call is used).[79] In the House, the electronic voting system is used for yeas and nays, unless the speaker orders a *viva voce* roll call vote or the machine is not working.[80]

During a roll call vote, members in both houses are prohibited from attempting to explain their votes, although senators may submit a written explanation (not to exceed 250 words), as may representatives (not to exceed 200 words), for inclusion in their respective journals.[81] Additionally, during a roll call vote, no debate is permitted in either house.[82]

Voting in the House. On the desk of each representative is brass voting console. Each member is issued an electronic card to activate the console in order to vote. Only one card is issued to each representative, and House rules prohibit members from leaving the card in their voting console when they are not at their seat or in the immediate vicinity.[83] The votes are flashed on large tally boards placed on both sides of the House chamber, upon which the names of the members are arranged in alphabetical order. A green light signifies a "yes" vote on a particular question; a red light signifies a "no" vote. After allowing at least 60 seconds for members to vote and to change their votes, the speaker orders the voting machine to be locked. Before locking the machine, the speaker will typically ask several times, "Have all members voted?" The vote totals are then displayed on the boards. Additionally, the vote is permanently recorded on a tape, which is pulled at the conclusion of the vote on each question by the clerk.

Voting in the Senate. The electronic voting system used in the Senate for taking roll call votes is similar in operation to that in the House, except no senator's vote is shown on the tally board until all senators have voted and the machine is locked. Furthermore, the Senate system

LEGISLATORS VOTE ON ALL BILLS AND MANY MOTIONS BY PRESSING A BUTTON ON THE VOTING CONSOLE AT THEIR DESKS.

includes a digital countdown clock showing how much of the time allotted by Senate rules (60 seconds) for voting on each question remains before the machine is automatically locked (in contrast to the House, where the presiding officer determines when the machine is to be locked on a given vote).[84] The Senate uses a single voting board, located on the front wall of the chamber.

In both houses, use of the voting machine in effect dispenses with the call for verification, since each legislator's vote is clearly visible, in addition to being automatically recorded and printed.

ENGROSSMENT

When a bill is passed by the House or Senate, it is engrossed by the clerk or secretary before transmittal to the other house. Engrossment is a proofreading and verification of a bill or resolution, as passed by that house, for the purpose of making certain that the copy being certified is identical with the original bill as introduced and incorporates all amendments to the bill that have been adopted. (Fig. 19 shows the cover sheet for an engrossed bill.)

Senate rules allow engrossment to take place during the legislative process as a means of preventing a measure from being amended in committee or on the floor.[85] At the time of first reading, any senator can give oral notice of intent to move that the measure be engrossed. The motion is debatable; supporters and opponents are allowed 10 minutes each. Approval requires a majority of the entire membership. Should notice not have been given at the time of first reading, a motion to engross can be made immediately before commencement of third reading of general bills. The same majority requirements apply. A bill that is engrossed and passed in the Senate can be amended in the House, but any such amendments are considered engrossed when the bill returns to the Senate. House amendments cannot be further amended by the Senate, which can only vote to agree or disagree with the House amendments. House rules make no provision for engrossment of measures introduced in that body (although the Rules Committee can prohibit amendments once a bill is on the floor).

CONSIDERATION BY THE SECOND HOUSE

Transmittal

Following passage of a bill in the house of origin, it is then engrossed (certified) and prepared for transmittal to the other house. The measure,

FIGURE 19. Cover Sheet for an Engrossed Bill

ENGROSSING

_____ 20_____
The Committee of the House on Information and
Audits has examined the within and finds the same
properly engrossed.

H.B. No. _____

A BILL

SENATE SPONSOR (S)

_____
Chairman

_____ 20_____

The Committee of the Senate on

_____
Recommends that this Bill

do _____

_____
Chairman

IN HOUSE

Read 1st time
Read 2nd time
Read 3rd time

And

Yeas   Nays

_____
Clerk of the House

IN SENATE

Read 1st time
Read 2nd time
Read 3rd time

And

Yeas   Nays

_____
Secretary of the Senate

By:

however, cannot be transmitted on the same day that it passes, unless that house votes for immediate transmittal. The vote in the House must be by unanimous consent or by a majority of a quorum voting; Senate rules provide for a two-thirds vote of a quorum. An exception to this rule is that any bill or resolution that requires action by the other house during the last three legislative days of a session is immediately transmitted.[86] Also, all Senate measures requiring House action on the 30th legislative day are to be immediately transferred to the House, and all House measures that require action by the Senate must be immediately transmitted on the last day the Senate will accept House bills.[87] Toward the end of a legislative session, time pressure causes members of both bodies to approve immediate transmittal of measures rather frequently.

Amendments

In the second house, a bill goes through substantially the same procedures as it did in the first. If passed in the second house without change, it is returned to the first house for enrollment and can then be sent to the governor. If, however, the second house makes changes in the bill, as is usually the case, several options are available.

Assuming a House bill has been transmitted to the Senate, where additional amendments are added before passage, the bill is then returned to the House, which can agree to the Senate amendments. In that case, the bill is ready for enrollment and forwarding to the governor. If, however, the House does not agree to the Senate amendments, the Senate is so notified, and it then has the option of yielding on the matter. If the Senate insists on its position, the House is notified and can itself either yield or insist on its position. At this point, the general procedure for resolving the stalemate is the appointment of a conference committee, if both houses so agree, to attempt to reconcile differences.

Conference Committees

In a bicameral legislature, lawmakers (and others) have two chances to get provisions they want into a bill or resolution—and two chances to keep provisions they don't like out. It is rare for important legislation to pass out of the first house and subsequently be accepted without change in the second house. Battles lost in the first house are fought again in the second. As a result, most major legislation is sent to what amounts to a third "house": the conference committee.

The rules of both houses contain similar and detailed provisions regarding the appointment and functions of conference committees. Neither presiding officer has the express power to initiate the appointment of a conference committee. A motion must be made by a member and approved by the membership. The presiding officer of that body then must appoint three members from his or her house to serve on the committee. Each of the three members appointed must have voted with the majority on the position assumed by his or her house on the bill or resolution, if the vote has been taken. (It should be noted that the rules of some state legislatures do not require that all members of a conference committee be on the prevailing side of their house, and some even expressly state that both majority and minority views of each house must be represented on these committees.)

The purpose of the conference committee is to attempt to reach an agreement or compromise on the points of dispute between the two houses. To this end, the rules provide that the committee may consider the entire subject matter of the bill or resolution and recommend recision by either house, new amendments, new bills and resolutions, or other germane changes. The Senate may instruct its conferees as to what actions they are to take. The instruction, in order to be binding, must be approved by the Senate on motion, before the members are appointed to the committee. If a motion to instruct the conferees passes by a majority required for final passage of the bill or resolution in question, House conferees may not recede from or change the subject matter contained in the bill or resolution. The motion itself is debatable and can be made immediately after the conference committee is appointed. It is applicable only to the committee appointed at that time.

The conference committee cannot hold a bill or resolution indefinitely. Rules of both houses provide that if a conference committee has been in existence for five days without reporting out a bill or resolution, the full body may vote to direct the presiding officer to appoint a new committee. In the Senate, the body may instruct its conferees or take other action not contrary to the rules of that house. To be successful, the motion must receive a majority vote of the members elected to that body. During the last five days of the legislative session, this motion may be made and passed at any time (but no more often than every three hours) whether the conference committee has been in existence for five days or not.

Before a conference committee report can be transmitted to either the Senate or the House for action, it must be approved by a majority vote of the entire membership of the committee. Once approved, the report must be printed and distributed to legislators at least one hour before action can be taken in either house. Members of the House may dispense with the written report by a majority vote of the membership, while senators can do so only on the last day of the session, by a two-thirds vote of the membership.

In the Senate, the president is specifically authorized to rule that a conference committee report is not germane to the original bill or resolution. Unless it is overruled by the Senate, this ruling has the same effect as a Senate vote to reject the conference committee report.[88]

The report of the conference committee must be adopted by the Senate or the House only by the vote required to pass the bill, resolution, or matter under consideration.[89] By rule, House members can only accept or reject the report of the conference committee. If the report is amended or substituted for by the Senate, the House must consider it as having been rejected by the Senate. If both houses adopt the conference committee's report or settlement and enact exactly the same amended bill or resolution, it is transmitted to the governor. In case one of the houses fails to adopt the report or recommendations, the conference committee may be directed to meet and report again, or it may be dissolved and a new committee appointed. The majority of compromise reports of conference committees are accepted by the two houses.

ENROLLMENT

Enrollment is the preparation of the final copy of a bill or a resolution intended to have the effect of law, which has passed both houses in identical form (see Fig. 20). Every enrolled bill or resolution must be certified by the presiding officer of each house, the clerk of the House, and the secretary of the Senate before it is sent to the governor for approval and signature. The enrolled copy of a bill or resolution enacted into law is permanently preserved by the Office of the Secretary of State and is the official text of the act. Thereafter, that office deposits the session acts in the archives and has them printed and distributed throughout the state.

FIGURE 20. Cover Sheet for an Enrolled Bill

ENROLLMENT

_____ 20____

The Committee of the House on Information and Audits has examined the within and finds the same properly enrolled.

_____
Chairman

_____
Speaker of the House

_____
Clerk of the House

_____
President of the Senate

_____
Secretary of the Senate

Received_____
Secretary, Executive Department

This _____ day of _____ 20____

Approved

_____
Governor

This _____ day of _____ 20____

H.B. No. _____   Act No. _____

General   **Assembly**

AN ACT

IN HOUSE

Read 1ˢᵗ time
Read 2ⁿᵈ time
Read 3ʳᵈ time

And

Yeas   Nays

_____
Clerk of the House

IN SENATE

Read 1ˢᵗ time
Read 2ⁿᵈ time
Read 3ʳᵈ time

And

Yeas   Nays

Passed Both Houses

_____
Secretary of the Senate

ACTIONS OF THE GOVERNOR

Legislative actions subject to the governor's veto. Any general or local bill passed by the General Assembly must first be sent to the governor for approval or veto before it can become law. Also requiring executive approval is any resolution passed by both houses "intended to have the effect of law."[90] By statute, the legislature has added one other action requiring submission to the governor: a legislative resolution to override agency rules and regulations is subject to the governor's approval if less than two-thirds of each house vote in favor of adopting the resolution.[91]

Legislative actions exempt from the governor's veto. Georgia's governor is prohibited from vetoing any proposed constitutional amendment or new constitution approved by the General Assembly or by a constitutional convention.[92] The chief executive is not specifically restricted from signing proposed constitutional changes—although such approval would be symbolic only—and the practice in recent years has been that governors sign some amendments while leaving others unsigned.

FREQUENTLY, LEGISLATORS AND OTHERS THAT SUPPORTED A PARTICULAR BILL GET TO WITNESS THE GOVERNOR SIGNING IT INTO LAW.

Other legislative actions exempted from gubernatorial veto include self-convening of special sessions by the legislature, veto overrides, impeachments, election of the state auditor, and resolutions (whether simple or concurrent) not intended to have the effect of law.[93] Additionally, in a somewhat controversial procedure, the General Assembly has provided by statute that the governor's veto authority does not extend to joint resolutions overriding agency rules and regulations should two-thirds of each house vote for the resolution (although the governor can reject the resolution if less than two-thirds of each house vote for its passage).[94]

Type of veto. With the exception of appropriations measures, a governor's veto applies to an entire bill or resolution. Unlike some states, Georgia makes no provision for the "amendatory veto" (a conditional veto that is withdrawn if the legislature makes changes in the bill cited as necessary by the governor). Similarly, once a bill has been passed by both houses, no additional legislative action can be taken before the governor acts on that measure.

In appropriations bills only, Georgia's governor can veto specific funding items, while approving the remainder of the bill.[95] Termed an "item veto," this device allows the governor to delete the funding authorization for a specific budget item or program. Georgia's attorney general has held that an item veto not only eliminates funding for the particular item but also reduces by that amount the overall appropriation to the agency in whose budget the activity was included.[96] In turn, this reduces the total state appropriation by the same figure.

Only eight states and the federal government do not allow item veto of appropriations measures.[97]

Finally, Georgia, like most other states, does not have the "pocket veto." In a pocket veto, bills sent to the governor in the closing days of a session are, in effect, vetoed unless specifically signed within a designated time period following adjournment.[98] In Georgia, the governor's failure to approve a bill within the required time period results in the bill automatically becoming a law.

Sending bills to the governor. Once both houses have passed a bill or resolution, it is enrolled and readied for transmittal to the governor's office. However, any time before adjournment *sine die*, a measure is only sent if the governor specifically requests its transmittal or if two-thirds of the members of each house direct that a bill be forwarded prior to the governor's request. The only exception to this rule is that any local bill for which the constitution necessitates a local referendum can be immediately transmitted to the governor by order of the presiding officer of the house where it was introduced or upon approval by two-thirds of the members of that house.[99] Following the session's final adjournment, all measures requiring the governor's approval that have not been previously transmitted are immediately enrolled and forwarded for executive consideration.

A major reason for most bills not being transmitted to the governor during the legislative session is that a decision to sign or veto would have to be made within 6 days. Because time is needed for the governor's legal staff to study the ramifications of each bill to recommend which ones should be approved and the order in which bills should be signed by the governor, most general bills are sent following adjournment *sine die*, thus leaving the governor 40 days to make these decisions.[100]

Signing and vetoing bills. Once a bill or a resolution that will have the effect of law has been sent to the governor's office, the chief executive has three options: (1) to sign the measure, in which event it becomes law; (2) to veto the bill, in which event it is returned to the house in which it was first introduced; and (3) to neither sign nor veto the measure, in which event it automatically becomes a law following a required waiting period.[101]

Georgia's governor has 6 days to take action on bills and resolutions transmitted during the first 34 days of a regular session. Any bills not signed or vetoed by the end of these 6 days become law automatically without the governor's signature.

The governor has 40 days after adjournment *sine die* to sign or veto any bills or resolutions received after the session's 34th day.[102] At the end of these 40 days, any measures that have not been signed or vetoed automatically become law.

Overriding a veto. Any bill vetoed by the governor must be returned to the presiding officer of the house in which it was originally introduced, along with a statement by the governor as to why the bill was rejected (see Fig. 21). If the veto occurs prior to the last 3 days of the session, the governor must return the measure within 3 days of the veto, which gives lawmakers an opportunity to immediately override the veto. If, as is almost always the case, the veto occurs during the last 3 days of the session, or during the 40 days following adjournment *sine die*, the governor has 60 days to return the vetoed measure. At the subsequent session, the legislature may consider a proposal to override the governor's veto.[103]

To override a veto, a two-thirds vote of the total membership of each house is needed. Should the General Assembly fail in its effort,

FIGURE 21. Governor's Veto Message

STATE OF GEORGIA
OFFICE OF THE GOVERNOR
ATLANTA 30334-0900

Sonny Perdue
GOVERNOR

May 9, 2006

The Honorable Glen Richardson
Speaker of the House of Representatives
332 State Capitol
Atlanta, Georgia 30334

Dear Speaker Richardson:

I have vetoed House Bills 491, 809, 1164, 1168, 1182, 1259, 1272, 1350, 1436, 1469, 1544 and 1646, which passed the General Assembly in the 2006 Regular Session.

Article III, Section V, Paragraph XIII of the Georgia Constitution requires that I transmit these bills to you together with the reasons for such vetoes. These bills and corresponding reasons for the vetoes are attached.

Sincerely,

Sonny Perdue
Governor

SP:jht

Enclosure

cc: The Honorable Mark Taylor, Lieutenant Governor
        The Honorable Cathy Cox, Secretary of State
        The Honorable Thurbert E. Baker, Attorney General
        Mr. Robert E. Rivers, Jr., Clerk of the House of Representatives
        Mr. Robert F. Ewing, Secretary of the Senate
        Mr. Sewell R. Brumby, Legislative Counsel

the bill cannot again be brought before the legislature for the purpose of overriding the governor's action.[104]

Use of the veto. The executive veto has been used in varying degrees by different governors in Georgia (see Table 10).[105] Clearly, the veto—or threat of the veto—is a powerful legislative tool for the governor. Although it may be overridden by the legislature, it hardly ever is. In fact, the only instances in recent history occurred in 1974, when legislators overrode seven 1973 vetoes of local bills.[106] These vetoes

TABLE 10. Summary of Legislative Workload, 1999–2006

Session Activity	Biennium Workloads							
	1999	2000	2001	2002	2003	2004	2005	2006
Bills introduced	1,386	920	1,290	1,075	1,437	1,031	1,304	1,045
Bills pending from previous session	—	916	—	887	—	1,007	—	892
Resolutions introduced	1,125	1,200	1,248	1,575	1,498	1,735	1,672	2,110
Resolutions pending from previous session	—	157	—	141	—	175	—	180
Total Measures Considered	2,511	3,193	2,538	3,678	2,935	3,948	2,976	4,227
Bills lost, unfavorably reported, withdrawn	1	—	2	—	4	—	4	—
Resolutions lost, unfavorably reported, withdrawn	0	—	2	—	0	—	2	—
Total Lost	1	—	4	—	4	—	6	—
Bills passed	461	503	396	621	414	394	408	509
Resolutions adopted	968	1,112	1,105	1,422	1,321	1,549	1,492	1,883
Total Passed	1,429	1,615	1,501	2,043	1,735	1,943	1,900	2,392
Bills vetoed by governor	6	10	7	10	21	19	15	19
Resolutions vetoed by governor	0	1	0	0	0	0	0	0
Total Vetoes[a]	6	11	7	10	21	19	15	19
Bills left pending at end of session	916	1,333	887	1,393	1,007	1,644	882	1,428
Resolutions left pending at end of session	157	245	141	294	175	361	175	407
Total Measures Pending	1,073	1,578	1,028	1,687	1,182	2,005	1,057	1,835

Note: Does not include special sessions held in 2001, 2004, or 2005.

[a]Does not include line-item vetoes in appropriation acts.

were based on legal opinions as to the bills' constitutionality, but subsequent events caused the governor to withdraw his objections and signal legislators that he would not oppose an override. The small number of vetoes overridden during the past century attests to the influence of the governor, the difficulty of obtaining a two-thirds vote on controversial matters in the legislature, and the selectivity of governors in using the veto.

Assigning act numbers to approved bills. Bills signed by the governor are given act numbers in the order in which they are approved, which can become an important legislative tool for the governor. Two or more bills dealing with the same subject area may be passed at one legislative session, and they can subsequently be found to have incompatible provisions. The order in which the governor signs these bills determines which bill will take precedence, with the bill signed *last* assuming priority.[107] Working within the time limits for signing bills, the governor is thus placed in the position of determining which bill will represent the "latest expression of legislative intent" (regardless of the order in which the legislature actually enacted the measures) and thus which bill, incompatible with another, will control.

As a final note, in the second session of a biennium (i.e., in even-numbered years), act numbers are assigned consecutively from the number of the last act in the previous session.

EFFECTIVE DATE OF LEGISLATION

In most cases, a bill is passed on different dates in each of the two houses, with approval first occurring in the house of origin. The day of approval in the second house—providing both houses have agreed on the language of the measure—is often thought of as the bill's "date of passage." This date, however, is of no particular legal significance, as the bill is then proofed, certified, and enrolled. Sometimes a month or more may lapse before a bill is ready for forwarding to the governor.

The Georgia Supreme Court has ruled that a bill becomes a law *not* when it is passed by the two houses of the legislature, but when it is approved by the governor or becomes law without his signature after the lapse of time specified in the constitution or when the legislature overrides the governor's veto.[108] Thus, notations in the annual session laws following each act—such as "Approved March 21, 2006"—refer to the date that the bill became law, not the date of passage in the legislature.

The *effective date of an act* is that date on which its provisions assume the force of law, superseding any conflicting provisions of previous acts dealing with the same subject matter. The effective date of an act can differ from the date that the bill was enacted into law, depending on whether the bill provided for an effective date.

Regardless of when the bill was signed, the effective date of a general bill passed at a regular session of the General Assembly is the following July 1, unless a specific date was provided for in the legislation. Often, a general bill will specify that it will become effective upon approval of the governor or upon its becoming law without approval. However, if no date is specified, the bill's effective date is July 1, providing the bill was enacted into law between January 1 and June 30 of that same year. The effective date of a general bill enacted between July 1 and December 30, as in the case of bills passed at special sessions held after July 1, is the first day of January of the immediately succeeding calendar year, provided no effective date was set forth in the bill.[109]

One exception to the preceding rules on the effective date of legislation is that general acts providing for increases in the compensation of county offices provided for in the state constitution do not go into effect until the first day of January following passage of the act.[110]

Different rules apply to the effective date of local legislation. In most cases, a local act immediately becomes effective upon approval by the governor (or upon becoming law without approval or veto), unless a specific date is provided for in the act itself.[111] For the following categories of local acts, however, the effective date is the first day of January following passage of the act:

1. An act requiring that a city or county create any personnel position that would be funded by the city or county.
2. An act requiring an increase in the salary, benefits, or other compensation of any personnel position, the cost of which would come from city or county funds.
3. An act requiring any capital expenditure that would be paid by city or county funds.

The mandatory January 1 effective date, however, does not apply if the governing authority of the affected city or county has requested by resolution or other written document an earlier effective date. In such cases, the written request must be attached to the local bill on introduction and becomes part of that local bill during legislative consideration.[112]

Resolutions that do not have the effect of law become effective on the date of passage. Resolutions that have the effect of law become effective with the governor's signature or after the required lapse of time if it has been neither signed nor vetoed.[113] Resolutions voiding agency rules and regulations become effective on the day after the governor's signing if passed by less than a two-thirds vote or on the day following passage in the second house if approved by more than two-thirds of each house.[114] Finally, resolutions proposing changes in the constitution become effective only if ratified by the voters in a subsequent general election. Unless the resolution provides otherwise, the effective date of the constitutional change is January 1 following its ratification.[115]

NOTES

1. GA. CONST. art. 3, §5, ¶14.
2. OFFICIAL CODE OF GEORGIA ANNOTATED (O.C.G.A.) §47-20-31.
3. O.C.G.A. §50-18-75.
4. O.C.G.A. §28-1-17.
5. House Rule 54.4.
6. Senate Rule 3-1.2.
7. House Rule 48.
8. For a listing of deadlines by state, see *The Book of the States, 2006* Vol. 38 (Lexington, Ky.: Council of State Governments, 2006), Table 3.15, pp. 102–3.
9. Ibid., procedures for suspending bill deadlines.
10. Senate Rule 3-1.2(b).
11. Senate Rule 3-1.3; House Rules 49 and 51.
12. Senate Rule 7-1.1(b) and 3-1.6(c); House Rule 51.
13. Senate Rule 3-1.3; House Rule 51.
14. GA. CONST. art. 3, §5, ¶7.
15. GA. CONST. art. 3, §5, ¶8.
16. House Rule 48.2.
17. Senate Rule 4-2.6.
18. GA. CONST. art. 3, §5, ¶7.
19. O.C.G.A. §§28-5-4, 28-5-82, 47-20-34.
20. Senate Rule 6-6.1; House Rule 90.
21. Senate Rule 2-3.3.
22. Senate Rule 2-1.7(f).
23. Senate Rule 2-1.5(a); House Rule 54.4.
24. House Rule 13.
25. Senate Rule 2-1.7(a).
26. Senate Rule 2-1.7(b).
27. GA. CONST. art. 3, §4, ¶11.
28. Senate Rule 1-5.1; House Rule 14. In Coggin v. Davey, 233 Ga. 407, 211 S.E.2d 708 (1975), Georgia's supreme court ruled that Georgia's so-called "Sunshine Law" (O.C.G.A. §§50-14-1 through 50-14-6), which requires any meeting of a state agency to be open to the public, is not applicable to the General Assembly or its committees.

29. House Rule 15.
30. Senate Rule 2-1.7(d).
31. Senate Rule 2-6.1.
32. House Rule 57.
33. Senate Rules 2-1.6, 187; House Rule 56.
34. House Rule 56.
35. Senate Rule 3-1.6(c); House Rule 55.
36. Senate Rule 3-1.3; House Rule 51.
37. Senate Rule 118; House Rule 57.
38. Senate Rule 4-2.12; House Rule 58.
39. House Rule 57.
40. Senate Rule 2-5.2.
41. House Rule 59.1.
42. Senate Rules 6-6.3 through 6-6.6; House Rules 90-92.
43. Senate Rule 2-1.10(b): House Rule 33.7.
44. Senate Rule 4-2.10.
45. Senate Rule 4-2.10(b); House Rule 33.1.
46. House Rule 33.2.
47. Senate Rule 4-2.10(b).
48. Senate Rule 4-2.10; House Rule 52.
49. House Rule 33.8.
50. Senate Rule 4-2.8.
51. Senate Rule 4-2.9.
52. Ibid.
53. Senate Rules 9-1.5, 9-1.7, 9-1.10, and 9-1.11.
54. Senate Rule 9-1.4.
55. Senate Rule 9-1.8.
56. House Rule 7.
57. House Rule 7.13.
58. House Rule 7.12.
59. Ibid.
60. House Rule 7.9.
61. House Rule 81.
62. Senate Rule 8-1.7.
63. House Rule 81.
64. Senate Rule 8-1.5(b).
65. House Rule 86.
66. Senate Rule 8-1.5(a); House Rule 85.
67. Senate Rule 8-1.7; House Rule 80.
68. Senate Rule 8-1.6; House Rule 89.
69. House Rule 1.3.
70. Senate Rule 6-8.5; House Rule 124.
71. Ga. Const. art. 3, §5, ¶5.
72. Senate Rule 5-1.1.
73. House Rule 128.
74. Ga. Const. art. 3, §5, ¶12.
75. Ga. Const. art. 3, §5, ¶6; art. 10, §1, ¶2.
76. Ga. Const. art. 3, §5, ¶6.

77. Senate Rule 5-1.3.
78. Senate Rule 5-1.4.
79. Senate Rule 5-1.5.
80. House Rule 139.
81. Senate Rule 5-1.9; House Rule 136.
82. Senate Rule 5-1.6; House Rule 137.
83. House Rule 138.
84. Senate Rule 5-1.5; House Rule 139.3.
85. Senate Rule 6-9.1.
86. Senate Rule 4-2.14; House Rule 150.
87. Ibid.
88. Senate Rule 2-8.5.
89. Senate Rule 2-8.6; House Rule 146.6.
90. Ga. Const. art. 3, §5, ¶13.
91. O.C.G.A. §50-13-4.
92. Ga. Const. art. 10, §1, ¶5; art. 3, §5, ¶11.
93. Because resolutions can be used for many purposes, it is sometimes unclear which are not intended to have the effect of law and thus do not need to be sent to the governor. One court ruling held that legislative adoption of a concurrent resolution suspending an executive official—as provided by statute—did not require the governor's approval, since the suspension could have been achieved by a simple resolution in each house. Gray v. McLendon, 134 Ga. 224, 67 S.E. 859 (1910).
94. O.C.G.A. §50-13-4.
95. Ga. Const. art. 3, §5, ¶13(e).
96. 1974 Ops. Att'y Gen. U74-98, U74-36; 1973 Op. Att'y Gen. U73-94.
97. *The Book of the States, 2006*, Table 4.4, pp.156–57.
98. Ibid.
99. Ga. Const. art. 3, §5, ¶13.
100. Ibid.
101. Ga. Const. art. 5, §2, ¶4.
102. This same 40-day limit applies should the legislature take a recess in excess of 40 days during the session and should there be bills in the governor's possession for which final action has not been taken. Ga. Const. art. 3, §5, ¶13.
103. Ga. Const. art. 3, §5, ¶13.
104. Ibid.
105. *See* Jack B. Hood, "History of the Veto Power in Georgia," 8 *Georgia State Bar Journal* 513 (May 1972).
106. *See House Journal 1974*, vol. I, pp. 25–28; vol. II, pp. 4027–33.
107. Keener v. MacDougall, 232 Ga. 273, 206 S.E.2d 519 (1974); County of Butts v. Straham, 151 Ga. 417, 107 S.E. 63 (1921).
108. Floyd County v. Salmon, 151 Ga. 313, 106 S.E. 280 (1921); Walker v. City of Rome, 16 Ga. App. 817, 86 S.E. 628 (1915).
109. O.C.G.A. §1-3-4.
110. O.C.G.A. §1-3-4.1.
111. O.C.G.A. §1-3-4.
112. O.C.G.A. §1-3-4.1.
113. O.C.G.A. §1-3-4.
114. O.C.G.A. §50-13-4.
115. Ga. Const. art. 10, §1, ¶6.

CHAPTER 8

RULES OF PROCEDURE

Effective legislators frequently are noted for their familiarity with the rules of parliamentary procedure in their house. Knowledge of parliamentary tactics can sometimes mean the difference between a successful and an unsuccessful legislative strategy. The rules of each house contain motions that can be used to help pass—or defeat—bills, resolutions, amendments, and other motions.

Georgia's constitution directs each house in the General Assembly to determine its own rules of procedure.[1] These rules (see Fig. 22) serve as an addition to, and in some cases a restatement of, constitutional and statutory provisions that apply to the legislative process. Although many House and Senate rules closely follow the standard parliamentary rules used by civic and social organizations (e.g., *Robert's Rules of Order*), many are unique to the legislature. Moreover, while both houses have adopted many rules that are similar or even identical, significant differences exist in House and Senate rule books.[*]

One of the first actions each house takes on the first day of the first session of a biennium is to adopt rules of procedure for the biennium. Subject to constitutional and statutory requirements, each body is free to adopt new rules, without reference to those of the previous biennium. In practice, however, the rules in effect at the time of adjournment of the preceding session, perhaps with minor changes, are invariably adopted.

---

[*]The House and Senate no longer print rule books as such. Rather, the rules are maintained online and can be accessed from the General Assembly home page (www.legis.state.ga.us).

FIGURE 22. Page from House Rules

RULES, ETHICS AND DECORUM OF THE
HOUSE OF REPRESENTATIVES

DECORUM

Rule 1.

1.1   All members shall conduct themselves at all times with dignity and with respect for others in a manner to ensure appropriate decorum in the deliberations of the House and to reflect the responsibilities incumbent upon a member of the House.

1.2   Members shall observe decency of speech and gentleness of behavior at all times in the House, the gallery and the lobbies, anterooms and halls adjacent to the House.

1.3   No member in speaking shall be disrespectful to any other member and all members shall carefully avoid references to personalities when addressing the House.

1.4   Members shall, at all times, observe appropriate attire on the floor of the House, in the gallery, and in the lobbies, anterooms and halls adjacent to the House. Appropriate attire for members shall be coat and tie for male members and dignified dress for female members.

1.5   Profane, obscene or indecent language is prohibited in the House and during the meeting of any standing or special committee of the House.

1.6   No member rising to debate, to give notice, to make a motion, or to present any paper of any kind shall proceed until the Speaker has recognized the member as entitled to the floor. While a member is speaking, no other member shall pass between the speaking member and the Speaker.

1.7   The reading of newspapers shall not be permitted on the floor of the House while the House is in session.

1.8   There shall be no smoking in the House of Representatives chamber or in the gallery or lobbies, anterooms, halls or restrooms adjacent to the House.

1.9   Placards, stickers or signs not approved by the Speaker are not permitted in the House Chamber.

1.10   When another member has the floor and is speaking, the members of the House shall refrain from private conversations with persons on the floor, or on cell phones, so as to preserve silence.

1

IN THE SENATE, HAND VOTES ARE TAKEN ON SOME MOTIONS AND
AMENDMENTS (RARELY USED IN THE HOUSE BECAUSE OF ITS SIZE).

In the Senate, initial adoption of procedural rules for the biennium requires approval by a majority of the total membership.[2] House rules do not specify the voting requirement for adoption of new rules for the biennium, which means that adoption requires a majority of the membership.[3] Once adopted, any proposal to change or add to these rules must first go to that house's Rules Committee and be reported back to the house. In the Senate, the change must be approved by two-thirds of the membership, while the House requires a majority of the membership.[4] In both houses, rules may be suspended by unanimous consent or by two-thirds of the membership.[5] In the Senate, if the Rules Committee does not report the proposed change or addition back to the full house within two days, the proposal automatically comes before the body for consideration.[6]

House and Senate rules govern most situations that might arise in the conduct of the legislative business, but situations occasionally arise that are not provided for by state constitution, statutes, or internal rules. In Georgia's Senate, any questions not covered are to be controlled by the most current edition of *Mason's Manual of Legislative*

Procedure.[7] Because House rules are silent, rulings are left to the speaker's discretion, subject to appeal to the membership.

This chapter looks at some of the most important rules of procedure of the two houses of the Georgia General Assembly. The complete current rules of each house are available on the House and Senate Web sites.

QUORUM

A quorum is the minimum number of members of a body required to transact business officially in the absence of other members. The constitution of Georgia declares that a majority of the members of each house constitutes a quorum of the General Assembly.

When there is no quorum, a small number can adjourn from day to day and take measures to compel the presence of the absent members.[8] If it is discovered that a quorum is not present, the roll is to be called and the absentees noted, providing a motion to this effect is made and sustained by five members in the Senate or one-fifth of the members present in the House. The doors of the chamber are then supposed to be closed and the names of absentees called again. Those who do not appear at that time, and who are absent without leave, may, by order of a majority of the members present, be sent for and arrested by officers appointed by the messenger. The body may then determine upon what conditions these members are to be discharged.[9]

The rules of both houses provide another alternative when a sufficient number of members are not present to conduct business. In order to keep or secure a quorum, the speaker of the House and president of the Senate can compel the attendance of members and order the doors of their respective chambers closed. Once the doors are closed, no member may leave without the permission of the speaker in the House and the membership in the Senate.[10]

In many cases, no point is ever raised as to the lack of a quorum. In carrying out the opening business of a day's session and in voting on local bills and similar matters, both houses sometimes ignore the lack of a quorum.

ORDER OF BUSINESS IN THE GENERAL ASSEMBLY

Each house of the General Assembly provides in its rules for the order in which it will conduct its business.

The daily order of business in the Senate is as follows:[11]

1. Report of the Committee on the Journal
2. Reading of the journal
3. Motions to reconsider
4. Confirmation of the journal
5. Introduction of bills and resolutions
6. First reading and reference (committee assignment) of Senate bills and resolutions
7. First reading and reference (committee assignment) of House bills and resolutions (also in order at any later time when no other business is pending)
8. Reports of standing committees
9. Second reading of general bills and resolutions
10. Call of the roll
11. Recitation of the Pledge of Allegiance
12. Prayer of the chaplain
13. Unanimous consents
14. Points of personal privilege
15. Adoption of privileged resolutions
16. Motions to withdraw bills or resolutions from one committee and commit to another
17. Passage of uncontested local bills and resolutions
18. Consideration of contested local bills and resolutions
19. General consent calendar for commemorative resolutions
20. Motions to engross
21. Third reading and consideration of general bills and resolutions

Senate rules provide that the report of its Rules Committee and messages from the governor or the other house are in order at any time and may be received under any order of business.[12]

In the Senate, all questions on the priority of business are decided by the president.[13] A motion to change the order of business is not debatable and requires approval of two-thirds of those voting, providing that two-thirds amounts to a majority of the total membership of the Senate.[14]

The rules of the House of Representatives set the following daily order of business:[15]

1. Call of the roll
2. Scripture reading and prayer by the chaplain

REPRESENTATIVE GOVERNMENT AT WORK

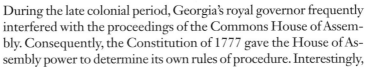

During the late colonial period, Georgia's royal governor frequently interfered with the proceedings of the Commons House of Assembly. Consequently, the Constitution of 1777 gave the House of Assembly power to determine its own rules of procedure. Interestingly, this provision disappeared when a new constitution was adopted in 1789 and was omitted from the next seven state constitutions. It did reappear in the Constitution of 1983, this time with a guarantee that each house determine its own rules of procedure—perhaps to assure a bicameral legislature of two independent houses.

3. Pledge of Allegiance to the U.S. flag
4. Report of the Committee on Information and Audits
5. Confirmation of the journal
6. Unanimous consents
7. Introduction of bills and resolutions
8. First and second readings and reference (committee assignment) of House bills and resolutions
9. Reports of standing committees
10. Third reading and passage of uncontested local bills
11. First and second readings and reference (committee assignment) of Senate bills and resolutions
12. Unfinished business of previous day's session
13. Orders of the day
14. Senate amendments to House bills and resolutions and reports of conference committees
15. Motions to reconsider
16. Morning Orders
17. Third reading of (a) resolutions on the uncontested resolutions calendar or (b) other bills and resolutions
18. Evening Orders

House rules allow members to address the House on points of personal privilege and other matters two times during the daily order of business. There is a 15-minute period immediately preceding third reading of bills and resolutions known as Morning Orders. During this time, members may take the well for not more than 5 minutes. All requests to use this time must be submitted to the messenger or such other person designated by the speaker at least one hour prior to the convening of that day's session, and the speaker allocates the amount of time any member can use within the 15-minute limit. A second chance for members to speak is during Evening Orders, the final order of business each day, which follows third reading of bills and resolutions. Unlike for Morning Orders, House rules specify no time limit on speeches or overall time limit for Evening Orders, nor are members required to notify the speaker in advance of their desire to speak. The order and amount of time a member has is determined by the speaker.[16]

In the House, all questions on the priority of business are decided by the speaker.[17] A motion to change the order of business requires unanimous consent or approval by two-thirds of the total membership of the House.[18]

MOTIONS IN THE GENERAL ASSEMBLY

Although certain actions (e.g., reading of bills) occur automatically in each house and do not require initiation by a member, many of the most important actions require a motion from the floor.

A motion is a formal proposal made by a member to the presiding officer that some action or procedure requiring approval of the membership take place. The presiding officer then submits the motion to the full body for approval or rejection.

Various provisions in the rules of both houses of the Georgia General Assembly relate to motions in general:

1. No member can make more than one motion at a time; after offering a motion, the legislator must resume his or her seat, unless again recognized by the presiding officer.[19]
2. No member may speak on a question and then offer a motion to cut off debate without first relinquishing the floor.[20]
3. When a motion is made on the floor by any member, no second motion is necessary to put the motion before the body for a vote.[21]
4. In either chamber, after a motion has been stated by the presiding officer or read by the secretary or clerk, it is deemed to be in the possession of that body but may be withdrawn by unanimous consent of that body at any time before being decided.[22]

To understand legislative procedure in the General Assembly, it is helpful to know the different types of motions that may be offered on the floor of each house. Many of these same motions can be made in committee meetings, although the Senate has a number of specific rules for committee deliberation.[23]

Precedence of motions in the two houses. Although dozens of motions can be found in the rules of each house, some of the most important apply to the stage between a bill's third reading and its final floor vote. To avoid the confusion that might result when different motions are before the body at the same time, each house has limited the number of motions that can be offered during a measure's floor consideration to nine. Moreover, the rules establish a specific order of precedence for these motions.[24] In order of priority, these motions are

1. motion to adjourn,
2. motion to lay on table,
3. motion for the previous question,
4. motion to adjourn to a time definite,
5. motion to indefinitely postpone,
6. motion to postpone to a day (or time) certain,
7. motion to commit,
8. motion to amend, and
9. motion to print.

The Motion to Adjourn

First in order of precedence is the simple *motion to adjourn*. This is one of two motions (the other being a *motion to adjourn to a time definite*) used during a session by each house to terminate legislative business for the day.

The House is adjourned following approval of the motion until the next legislative day and the Senate until the "next fixed sitting day or time," which unless a different time has been specified, is 10 a.m. on the next legislative day.[25] Adjournment of this type occurs independently in each house (meaning that each house concludes its daily business at different times) and does not suspend the count of legislative days for the session (as does adjournment through concurrent resolution).

The simple motion to adjourn is not debatable and cannot be amended.[26] Moreover, it can be made at any time by any member who can legitimately obtain the floor to offer the motion.[27]

There are, however, certain times when adjournment cannot take place. Once the call for the main question (i.e., a final vote on a measure) has been approved, a motion to adjourn is out of order if (1) the presiding officer has ordered that the voting machines be unlocked, (2) one vote in a voice roll call vote has been taken, or (3) a vote by division has been ordered and the hand count has begun.[28] In these situations, the motion to adjourn must await announcement of the final vote.

Two other restrictions limit the use of the motion to adjourn. In the House, once the call for the previous question has been approved, a motion to adjourn can only be made once.[29] In both houses, the motion cannot be made a second time "until further progress has been made in the business before the House (Senate)."[30]

Since the rules of each house are silent on the specific vote required for a motion to adjourn, the general requirements of each house control are, respectively, a majority of a quorum voting in the Senate and a majority of the membership in the House.[31]

The Motion to Lay on the Table

Ranking second in order of precedence in both houses is the *motion to lay on the table*. The rules of both houses state that, when this motion prevails, it removes the measure from consideration of the House or Senate, together with all the motions attached to it at the time.[32]

The motion to lay on the table is usually made by a member who is opposed to the measure being considered. Sometimes, however, a member favoring a measure will deem it expedient move to table, lest the measure be defeated.

In neither house of the General Assembly is the motion to lay on the table or the motion to take from the table debatable or amendable.[33] That is, once the motion is made, an immediate vote on it ensues. Should it fail to carry, the motion can be renewed when new business has intervened between the votes.[34]

The rules of both houses prohibit the tabling of an amendment,[35] and Senate rules state that nothing can be legitimately laid upon the table that cannot be taken up again.[36] As an example, if a matter can be decided at a particular time but will be past deciding subsequently, it probably could not be legitimately tabled.

The motion to table is apparently in order at any time in both houses, except when the body has voted affirmatively that "the main question shall now be put."[37] In the House of Representatives, after the call for the previous question, a motion to lay on the table or a motion to adjourn may be made only once.[38]

To table a measure, a majority of a quorum voting is necessary.[39] However, the motion to table is not a final action. In both houses, a majority of a quorum can order that the measure be taken from the table if the body is not engaged on any other measure.[40] When removed from the table, the proposition is placed at the bottom of the calendar of bills then in order for a third reading in the Senate.[41] In the House, if a measure is tabled and then taken from the table on the same day, it remains on that day's rules calendar.[42] The rules of the two houses provide that this measure then stand before the body in the exact form, with all the motions pertaining to it, as it did when it was tabled.[43]

The Motion for the Previous Question

The *motion for the previous question* is designed to cut short the debate on a measure and to bring that measure, the "main question," to a vote. It has precedence over all other motions except those to adjourn and to lay on the table.[44]

The motion for the previous question may be stated by a member so that it applies only to a single motion or amendment; or it may be made to embrace all authorized motions, amendments, and the entire bill.[45]

Once the motion for the previous question is made, it is decided without debate.[46] The presiding officer states the motion to the body as two questions. The first is, "Shall the motion for the previous question be sustained?" The rules of both houses provide that the question be decided by a majority of a quorum voting. The presiding officer then asks, "Shall the main question be now put?" If this question receives the required affirmative vote, then the bill under consideration is voted on by the body.[47]

The rules of both Senate and House provide that once the body has decided that the main question is to be put, no other motion is in order except one to reconsider the body's action. Even a motion to reconsider, however, is not in order when one vote has been given on a yea and nay vote, a hand vote has been taken, or the presiding officer has unlocked the electronic voting machine for a roll call vote.[48]

A motion to reconsider the ordering of the main question can be made only once, and its passage, in effect, repeals the ordering of both the previous and the main questions, leaving the bill under consideration open again to debate and amendment.[49]

If incidental questions of order arise after a motion for the previous question is made, they are decided without debate.[50]

VOTING BOARDS IN EACH CHAMBER
SHOW THE RESULTS OF EVERY RECORDED VOTE.

The Motion to Adjourn to a Time Definite

The *motion to adjourn to a time definite* allows either house to terminate its business for a specified period of time, after which proceedings reconvene. The period of adjournment can be for less than an hour or up to three days. The constitution, however, prohibits either house from adjourning for more than three days without the consent of the other house.[51] Thus, an adjournment for longer than three days can only be authorized through concurrent resolution.

The motion to adjourn to a time definite is a qualified version of the simple motion to adjourn and ranks fourth in the priority of motions. It differs from the simple motion in that it may be debated if it is made when the Senate and House are not actually engaged in other business. In both houses, it may be amended by substituting a day or time other than the one originally proposed.[52]

Because House and Senate rules are silent on the vote required for this motion, the general voting requirements of each apply: a majority of a quorum voting in the Senate and a majority of the membership in the House.[53]

The most frequent use of the motion to adjourn to a time definite is for daily adjournment of each house. Customarily, the majority leader in each house will offer the motion specifying the time for reconvening the next day. Unless another time is specified, a motion to adjourn ends floor activities until 10 a.m. the next legislative day. Toward the end of a session, an earlier time for reconvening may be specified as the amount of business facing the house increases.

Neither House nor Senate rules provide for a motion to recess, nor is the presiding officer of either house given an express rule to declare a recess. Presumably, the proper procedure for taking a recess (e.g., for lunch) would be a motion to adjourn to a time definite. In practice, however, the presiding officer simply announces to the body that a recess will be taken and indicates the time for reconvening.

The Motion to Indefinitely Postpone

Next in order of precedence in both houses is the *motion to indefinitely postpone*. A motion to postpone without setting a date or time for the measure to be brought up has the same effect as a motion to indefinitely postpone.

This motion offers an effective method of killing a bill being considered on the floor without allowing a vote on the bill's merits, since approval of the motion removes the measure from the floor for the remainder of the session.[54]

The motion to indefinitely postpone "lays open the whole question for debate" but is itself not amendable.[55] This means that not only the motion itself, but also any related matter that the measure is intended to indefinitely postpone can be debated. Approval of a majority of a quorum present and voting is necessary for the motion to carry.[56] If the motion fails, however, it cannot be made again with regard to the same measure.[57]

Rules in both houses specify that the motion to indefinitely postpone takes precedence over, but cannot be applied to, a motion to postpone to a day certain, commit, or amend. Further, the motion cannot be applied to incidental matters such as points of order, reading reports or papers, withdrawal of a motion, or suspension of a rule.[58]

The Motion to Postpone to a Day Certain

When a motion to postpone a measure to a day certain is carried, the body reconsiders the measure at the time designated in the motion.

Unlike the motion to indefinitely postpone, the *motion to postpone to a day certain* does not lay open to debate the merits of the bill, resolution, or other measure being referred to. Debate is allowed on the motion itself, but both houses require that the debate be confined strictly to the proposition of postponement and to showing why one day is preferred over another.[59] Accordingly, the motion may be amended by substituting one day or time for another.[60]

The rules of the House require an affirmative vote by a majority of a quorum voting in order to carry the motion to postpone to a day certain.[61] Because the Senate rules do not otherwise specify, the general voting requirement of a majority of a quorum voting applies.[62]

Should a senator make a motion to postpone to a day certain but name a time beyond the session, the presiding officer is required to treat the motion as one to indefinitely postpone, and the rules on that type of motion would then apply. House rules declare a motion under such circumstances out of order.[63]

As is the case with the motion to indefinitely postpone, the motion to postpone to a day certain cannot be applied to subordinate or incidental questions but only to the entire measure before the body.[64] House rules further declare that when the motion prevails, it also carries forward all amendments to the measure.[65]

If the motion to postpone a measure to a future day fails to carry when put to a vote, it cannot be renewed or made a second time on the same day.[66]

The motion to postpone consideration of a particular measure to a future day or time is used for a variety of reasons. Supporters of a bill about to be voted upon may feel that sufficient support is not present for the bill's passage. Rather than risk its defeat, they will seek postponement to gain time to build support. Opponents may seek the delay to give themselves time to build support for their side. The motion is also used to extend legislative courtesy among members. Should a measure come up before the body when its sponsor or a member who is known to be particularly interested in it is out of the chamber, a member may move that consideration of the measure be postponed until a time when the absent legislator can be present.

In the Senate, a bill or resolution that is postponed moves to the bottom of the calendar on the day it will be considered. After the fifth day of the session, if a measure is postponed for a second time, it is placed on the general calendar on the day to which it was postponed, which leaves the rules committee free to decide whether it will come before the full body.[67] House rules are silent on replacement of a postponed bill on the calendar of that body.

The Motion to Commit (or to Recommit)

The *motion to commit* (sometimes referred to as a *motion to recommit* if its purpose is to reassign a bill that has already been in one committee to the same or a different committee) is used to refer a bill or resolution to a particular standing or special committee or to the Committee of the Whole of that house.[68]

On the day of introduction, all bills (and many resolutions) are assigned to committee for study and recommendation. The assignment is at the discretion of the president pro tempore in the Senate and speaker in the House and is not debatable.[69] The author may disagree with the presiding officer's choice and wish to name the committee that would have jurisdiction of the bill. In such instance, a motion to commit to a particular committee would be the proper procedure to overrule the initial assignment. It should be emphasized, however, that seldom if ever do members challenge the presiding officer's initial committee assignment on the day of a bill's introduction. Almost always, a motion to commit or recommit is offered only after the first committee has had an opportunity to study the bill.

In both houses, a bill that has been referred to one committee may be recommitted to the same or to another committee upon approval of a majority of a quorum voting.[70] The House allows no debate on a motion to commit the bill, but Senate rules allow one senator three minutes to support the motion and one senator the same time to oppose it.[71] The Senate, however, allows instructions to be added to the motion to guide the committee that will receive the bill, and these instructions can be debated.[72] In the House only, the Rules Committee may also recommit a bill that has been reported from committee back to that committee on its own motion.[73]

A motion to commit or recommit may be amended in the Senate by adding instructions or substituting another committee for the one originally named in the motion; in the House, only the latter is permissible.[74] However, in both houses a motion to commit to a Committee of the Whole takes precedence over a motion to commit to a standing committee.[75] Moreover, when either body is meeting as a Committee of the Whole, it is not in order to commit a matter to any other committee.[76]

To illustrate how a measure might be recommitted, assume that a bill that was referred to a standing committee has been favorably reported back to the body and is now ready for third reading. If during the debate and discussion of the bill the body suggests a large number of amendments to it, it might seem desirable to send the bill, with its amendments, back to the same or to another committee for reconsideration. A motion to commit, carried by a majority of those voting (provided the total vote constitutes a quorum), is an option. The motion could include specific instructions to guide the committee in its consideration of the bill.

Because the motion to recommit in effect postpones the vote on a measure, it is sometimes used to prevent a measure's passage. For example, a member who is unfriendly to a particular bill may offer a motion to send the bill back to a committee, realizing that it will not be possible for the bill to get through committee and be reconsidered by the body and passed before the end of the legislative session.

The Motion to Amend

An important part of the legislative process occurs during both committee and floor consideration, as bills and resolutions are "perfected" through use of the *motion to amend*. Few general bills emerge from the General Assembly without having been amended in one or both houses.

The rules of both the Senate and House specify three ways in which a measure may be amended. First, words, numbers, punctuation, or letters may be inserted or added; second, they may be stricken; and third, they may be both stricken from and inserted in the measure.[77] An amendment itself may also be amended in these three ways, but the rules forbid amending an amendment to an amendment (except by unanimous consent only in the House).[78]

Limitations on Amendments

Both houses have procedures for limiting or prohibiting amendments. In the Senate, adoption of a motion to engross a bill at the time of third reading precludes any amendments during floor consideration. If an engrossed Senate bill is later amended in the House, the Senate cannot amend those House amendments but may only agree or disagree with those amendments.[79]

House rules do not provide for a similar engrossment procedure to prevent amendments of House bills. However, the Rules Committee is empowered to place a special rule on each measure called up from the rules calendar for floor consideration. The four rules that govern floor amendments are open rule, modified open rule, modified structured rule, and structured rule.

According to House rules, a floor substitute is treated as an amendment and is permitted only in accordance with the special rule applied to the measure by the Rules Committee.[80]

Germaneness of Amendments

Amendments are expected to relate directly to the matter under consideration, and both houses prohibit use of the motion to amend to introduce subject matter different from that under consideration.[81] The House specifically directs the speaker to rule out of order any amendment not germane to the measure before the House, while Senate rules direct the president to rule out of order any amendment obviously offered for the purpose of delay.[82] A similar fate awaits "irrelevant amendments" in either body.[83]

Legislators should note that adoption of nongermane amendments to a bill can later serve as grounds for the bill being declared unconstitutional because of multiple subject matter within a single act.

Floor Substitutes

In some cases, a member may wish to offer an entire bill in the place of the one originally introduced and reported by committee. The new bill, known as a *floor substitute*, does not have to be introduced, read, or referred to committee but may be offered from the floor. The rules of both houses expressly classify a substitute as an amendment; however, the prohibition against amending an amendment to an amendment does not apply to amending substitutes.[84] In the Senate, no substitute can be offered to another substitute.[85]

An illustration explains the priority of voting on amendments and substitutes. Suppose that one member of the legislature has proposed an amendment to a bill and that another member has proposed a substitute for that same bill. Suppose that an amendment to the substitute is then proposed. The rules of both houses provide that, in this situation, the body first vote on the amendment to the original bill; second, on the amendment to the substitute; and finally, on the substitute as amended, if the amendment was adopted. If the substitute fails to carry, a vote on the original bill follows. In the House only, if both a committee and floor substitute are offered on the same bill, a vote is taken first on the committee substitute.[86]

Legislative authorities often criticize the floor substitute because it provides a procedure for bypassing the committee system and because it bypasses the various safeguards that ensure that legislators—and the public—know the language and effect of measures before the leg-

FLOOR ACTION ON A BILL MAY BE TEMPORARILY SUSPENDED SO THAT
PRINTED AMENDMENTS CAN BE DISTRIBUTED BEFORE VOTING.

islature. In some cases, "skeleton" bills with innocuous provisions have been introduced and referred to committee, and only after a bill is before the body for final voting are the substantive provisions added by substitute. Interestingly, with a substitute, the original bill number and author are retained, but the act may be changed so that there is little resemblance to the original bill. Sometimes, when this has happened, the bill's original author will take the floor to ask for the defeat of the bill, which has changed through substitute.

Consideration of Floor Amendments

All motions to amend any matter before either house must be in writing and must plainly and distinctly state the language of the amendment and the part of the bill or resolution where the amendment is to be inserted or added.[87] In addition to having printed amendments on paper, both houses have large screens that are suspended at the front of House and Sentate chambers for projecting amendments proposed during the floor debate on a measure. Handwritten or typed amendments can be projected onto the screens, enabling all members to read the proposed amendment and permitting the House to proceed immediately with floor debate and voting.

House and Senate rules provide that a member cannot offer an amendment to a measure after his or her house has agreed to the committee report on that measure, unless the body's agreement is reconsidered.[88] When a measure under consideration in the Senate contains blanks, these blanks must be filled in before a motion can be made to amend the measure.[89] Thus, once the blanks are filled in, the need for the amendment may not exist. Should several amendments be offered to the same measure, the last ones offered are voted on first in the House; the process is reversed in the Senate. Actually, the rule as to priority of voting is quite broad. House rules provide that on all questions, whether in the House or in committee, "the last amendment, the most distant day, and the largest sum" will be put first. Senate rules state that on all questions, whether in committee or in the Senate, "the first amendment, the most distant day, and the largest sum" will be voted on first.[90]

A bill or resolution being amended is considered in two parts: first, the body of the bill, and second, its title. Senate rules provide that the title cannot be considered or amended until the body of a bill or resolution has been perfected.[91]

When a bill or resolution is in its final reading and a motion for division of a question has been made, the body may agree to consider it by sections or paragraphs. The secretary who then reads the bill is required to pause at the end of each section or paragraph, and the amendments to that section or paragraph must be offered at that time. In the Senate, once a section or paragraph has been considered, it is not in order to go back and amend it unless a motion to reconsider is adopted. Further, the amendments to the bill or resolution that were offered by the committee to which it was referred are read by the secretary as a matter of course and without any motion being made.[92]

In the event that a motion is made to amend a measure by striking out a portion of it and another motion is made to amend that portion of the bill proposed to be stricken for the purpose of perfecting it, the perfecting amendment is voted on first.[93]

House and Senate rules do not make reference to the voting requirement for approval of amendments in the house in which a measure is introduced. Thus, the general voting requirements for each house apply: a majority of a quorum voting in the Senate and a majority of the membership in the House.[94]

Amendments Made by the Other House

An important aspect of the amendment process concerns measures that are returned by the other house with amendments. A house may, of course, amend a measure sent to it by the other house. The amended measure is then returned to the house in which it originated. The originating house may amend the other house's amendments. However, House rules prohibit further amending a House amendment to a Senate amendment. A House amendment to a Senate amendment must be agreed to or voted down before the Senate amendment, as amended by the House amendment, can be accepted or rejected. In the Senate, unless the bill was engrossed earlier, a proposed Senate amendment to a House amendment can be further amended.[95] If agreement cannot be obtained, a conference committee may be appointed to attempt to work out a compromise measure acceptable to both houses.

Assume that a bill originates in the House of Representatives and is passed by that body. It will then go to the Senate. If the Senate passes the bill with amendments, it will then be returned to the House of Representatives, which will then consider the amendments to the measure that have been made by the Senate. The House may accept these amendments, and the amended measure will then be transmitted to the governor. If the House amends the amendments made by the Senate, the bill is returned to the Senate, after which point the House may not further amend the Senate amendments.

Rules of both the Senate and House list the following motions as those that can be used regarding amendments made by the other house to its bills or resolutions. In the Senate, the motion with highest precedence is to agree to a House amendment as amended by the Senate. (The House does not have a similar motion.) Next in order of precedence for both houses are

1. motion to agree to the amendments of the other house;
2. motion to disagree to the amendments of the other house;
3. motion to recede from its disagreement or amendment; and
4. motion to insist on its disagreement or amendment.[96]

The Senate has one additional motion: to adhere to its disagreement or amendment, which ranks fifth in priority.[97]

The rules of the House of Representatives further provide that when any question of disagreement with the Senate arises, the motions that are in order are (1) a motion to insist upon the House position, and (2) a motion to recede from the House position. A member can make either of these motions at any time that he or she can legally obtain the floor.[98]

The question of germaneness of subject matter of one house's amendments to a bill passed by the other house is decided by the speaker in the House and president in the Senate. House rules allow the speaker to rule on germaneness with or without a point of order being made, while Senate rules provide that the president make a ruling upon a point of order. If the ruling is that an amendment from the other house is not germane, that amendment is ruled out of order. Unless overruled by an appeal from the floor, the action is considered the same as a vote by the house to disagree to the amendment.[99]

The rules of the Senate and the House of Representatives provide that the vote for the adoption of a House amendment to a Senate measure or a Senate amendment to a House measure must be by a majority of the membership.[100] The same vote requirement applies to the adoption of a conference committee report.[101]

Often, the author of a measure will announce to the body his or her acceptance of particular amendments in order to forestall or end debate on the amendment.

The Motion to Print

Last in the order of precedence of motions applicable during floor consideration of bills and resolutions is the *motion to print*. This action allows a majority of a quorum in a house to suspend action while amendments are being offered on the floor so that amendments and substitutes to a pending measure can be printed and distributed to each member.[102] Although amendments must be submitted in written form to the clerk or secretary to be read before voting takes place, a member may feel that because of the length or number of amendments, it is important to see the text of the amendment or substitute. Seeing the text can be especially important in the Senate, which unlike the House, does not have the large screens within the chamber that allow the language of each amendment to be seen.

Other Motions

Although the rules of each house provide that when any subject is before the body for consideration or under debate, no motion can be received except for the nine motions discussed previously, other motions are in fact also used. They are discussed in this section.

The Motion to Reconsider

Potentially, one of the most important motions to affect the legislative process is the *motion to reconsider*. This motion allows a legislative body to rescind its "final" action on a measure and, in effect, take a new vote. For example, a bill may be passed on the floor of a house one day only to be defeated the next day (usually following late-hour politicking) after a motion to reconsider.

According to traditional parliamentary practice, the motion to reconsider was used as a device to perfect a bill that had passed, as when a defect was discovered after a bill's approval. Reconsideration was not intended to give bills that were defeated on the floor a second chance.

Athough many states still maintain this restriction on the use of reconsideration, in Georgia, both approved and defeated bills can be reconsidered. Moreover, Senate rules provide that any member can move to reconsider action on a measure; however, House rules are silent on who can make the motion.[103]

The reconsideration process is sometimes confusing because it involves three steps: (1) giving notice that a motion for reconsideration will be made at a later time; (2) raising the motion for reconsideration, at which time a vote is taken on the motion; and (3) if the motion passes, placing the measure back on the calendar and taking a new vote.

Both houses have strict rules that any member desiring reconsideration must first give the body notice of intention to move for reconsideration. Such notice must be given during the legislative day on which a vote is taken on a measure to be reconsidered.[104] In actual practice, this notice is usually given immediately following a vote. For example, following the defeat of a bill, a member will say, "Mr. President, I give notice that at the proper time, I will move to reconsider the action of the Senate in defeating Senate Bill 412." The body then passes on to other business with the knowledge that a motion for reconsideration will later be made. Once this notice has been given, it can be withdrawn only on the same day it is given in the House. It cannot be withdrawn in the Senate.[105]

Although many members may desire reconsideration of a bill or resolution, it is only necessary that one legislator give notice to seek it. However, when it is time for the motion to be raised, any member—not just the person who gave notice—may raise the motion.

When notice has been given, the time for making the motion to reconsider occurs during the morning order of business on the following legislative day (with certain exceptions). Senate rules provide that the motion be made immediately following the reading of the journal of the preceding day's happenings. At this time, a motion can be made to reconsider any matter that the journal contains, except those that have been previously reconsidered or transmitted to the House.[106] In the House, motions to reconsider are to be made immediately before Morning Orders.[107]

In both houses, the motion to reconsider requires approval of a majority of a quorum voting. If the motion is adopted, the bill is placed back on the calendar for a new vote. In the House, the bill is placed in numerical order on the general calendar, along with any substitute and all amendments that were a part of such bill when the motion to reconsider was passed.[108] In the Senate, during the first 5 days of the session, all bills and resolutions that are being reconsidered are placed at the bottom of the general calendar. During the last 35 days, however, bills for reconsideration that had previously passed on the Senate floor appear at the bottom of the *rules calendar*, while bills that had previously been defeated are placed on the *general calendar*.[109]

There are exceptions to these general rules. In the House, if the action to be reconsidered occurs on the last three days of a session, reconsideration must occur before the transaction of other business. When the action to be reconsidered occurs on the last legislative day of the week, the motion to reconsider should be made on the following Monday or, if the House will not be in session, on the next legislative day.[110]

In the Senate, during the last three days of the session and on the 30th day, notice of intention to move to reconsider must be given immediately following a vote. The president must then set a time during that day when the motion will be voted upon. Such time can be at the presiding officer's discretion, but at least 10 minutes must be allowed following notice.[111] On a motion to reconsider, debate is limited to 3 minutes for each side.[112]

In either house, reconsideration of the vote on an amendment to a measure may take place at any time before final action is taken upon the section, bill, or resolution to which the amendment relates.[113] Additionally, in the House, reconsideration of House actions on Senate amendments must take place immediately.

The presiding officer's ordering of the main question in preparation for a final vote can also be reconsidered. However, in the House, the motion must be made prior to the unlocking of the voting machines, the first vote cast in a voice roll call vote, or a hand count begun of a vote by division.[114] Adoption of the motion to reconsider effectively repeals the ordering of both the main and previous questions, thus reopening the floor for debate and amendment on the pending measure. If the motion is defeated, the presiding officer can again order the main question.[115]

So that motions to reconsider do not indefinitely postpone the legislative process, both houses limit reconsideration to one for each "matter" in the Senate and "bill, resolution, or amendment" in the House. Also, Senate rules provide that a motion to reconsider is not subject to reconsideration.[116]

The Motion for Division of a Question

When an involved question or one that contains parts that may readily be separated is before either house for consideration, legislators sometimes want to discuss and consider the question by part rather than as a whole. To make this possible, the rules of both houses provide that any member may make a *motion for division of a question* on a subject that may be divided into separate propositions.[117]

The member calling for this division must state exactly into which parts the question should be divided. Each part of the divided proposition must be so distinct that if it was taken away, the remainder of the question could stand by itself and be consistent and entire.[118] For example, according to the rules of the House of Representatives, a qualifying paragraph, an exception, and a proviso are not distinct or entire parts that could be divided from the remainder of a measure. House rules also state that, when amending a measure on the floor, no member may call for a division of the question on a motion "to strike out and insert."[119]

The speaker of the House determines whether the requirements for the division of a particular question are met. Senate rules provide that any senator can demand a division of the question.[120]

COMMITTEE OF THE WHOLE

The entire House of Representatives or Senate can make up what is known as the Committee of the Whole House or the Committee of the Whole Senate. These committees are devices used by the two bodies to relax some of the formal rules, thereby allowing more informal discussion and prompt action on important bills.

In actuality, the Committee of the Whole is the entire membership of either the House or Senate sitting as a single, large committee.

The rules of both houses contain separate provisions that apply to the actions of each body when meeting as a Committee of the Whole.

When used. House rules provide that all appropriation bills be considered in the Committee of the Whole House.[121] The rules of the Senate do not explicitly state conditions under which the Senate must meet as a Committee of the Whole Senate. Generally, the Senate considers appropriation acts as a Committee of the Whole.

The speaker may resolve the House into a Committee of the Whole without the necessity for a motion from the floor to that effect.[122] The rules of the Senate do not grant this same power to the president of the Senate.

The House or Senate may resolve itself into a Committee of the Whole if a motion is made to that effect and passed by a vote of a majority of a quorum and when one day's notice of the intention to make the motion has been given. If the member making the motion has not given one day's notice of his or her intention to do so, an affirmative vote of two-thirds of those voting is required to pass the motion. The two-thirds must equal a majority of the total membership of the House or Senate.[123] For considering the general appropriations bill in the House, however, no previous notice is necessary; the House may resolve itself into a Committee of the Whole by the vote of a majority of a quorum if a motion to that effect is made.[124]

Both houses limit individual speeches on the motion for the Committee of the Whole to three minutes.[125]

In the event that the House or Senate refers a measure to the Committee of the Whole and then a motion to resolve the body into the committee fails, the motion cannot be renewed. On the day following the failure of a motion, the speaker or the president is required to have the measure reintroduced and to refer it to the appropriate committee, unless otherwise ordered by the House or Senate.[126]

Procedures when in operation. When a Committee of the Whole House is formed, the speaker leaves the chair and appoints another legislator to preside. The speaker is then free to take part in the proceedings and must vote on all questions that come before the committee, unless he or she is excused from doing so.[127] When the Senate resolves itself into a Committee of the Whole, the president pro tempore presides.[128] The president of the Senate (lieutenant governor) does not take part in the proceedings of the Committee of the Whole or vote on matters that arise during the session.

The Committee of the Whole is prohibited from punishing its members for disorderly conduct but must report the behavior for action by the House or the Senate in regular session.[129] The chair of the Committee of the Whole in both houses has the power to clear the galleries or lobbies in case of disorderly conduct.[130]

The rules of the House of Representatives and Senate apply to procedure in their respective Committees of the Whole, with certain exceptions. The Committee of the Whole cannot

1. refer a matter to any other committee,
2. adjourn,
3. enforce the previous question,
4. entertain a motion to lay on the table or indefinitely postpone,
5. limit the number of times a member may speak,
6. allow a call of the House or Senate, or
7. take a roll call vote.[131]

Senate rules provide that in the Committee of the Whole, the secretary must first read the bill under consideration in its entirety, after which it is then read or debated by clauses or sections; the title is the last portion to be considered. This procedure may be otherwise ordered by the body.[132] The House does not have a similar rule.

During a meeting of the committee, when a vote on a question discloses that a quorum of the House or the Senate is not present, the committee cannot proceed with its business.[133] Further, upon the suggestion that a quorum is lacking, the chairperson must make an actual count. If he or she finds that a quorum is lacking, he or she must order that the committee immediately rise and report absence of a quorum to the House or the Senate in regular session.[134]

If at some stage in the proceedings in the Senate or House a committee desires to close the debate on a question or to limit a member's speaking time, the committee may rise and report its intention to the Senate or House in regular session (the chairperson makes the report to the president or speaker). The Senate acts on a motion or resolution to close or limit the debate, after which it may resolve itself again into a Committee of the Whole. If the motion or resolution is passed, debate is limited to the subject matter then before the committee.[135] House rules only provide for the body to take action as it sees fit.[136]

The rules of the House provide that the motion to reconsider may be used in the Committee of the Whole.[137]

When the body is meeting as a Committee of the Whole, a member may call for any papers that are in possession of his or her house and have them read for the information of the committee, unless the committee orders otherwise.[138]

A motion to adjourn cannot be made in the Committee of the Whole. In the event that the Committee of the Whole does not have enough time at one sitting to finish its business, a motion may be made "that the committee rise, report progress (to the House or Senate in formal session), and ask leave to sit again." As is true in a formal session of the House or the Senate, a motion to adjourn may be made at any time the member who makes the motion can legitimately obtain the floor. It takes precedence over all other motions and is decided without debate.[139]

Should a predetermined hour of adjournment of the House or Senate arrive while its members are sitting as a Committee of the Whole, the committee then, without motion, automatically rises, and the speaker or the president assumes the chair.[140]

The proceedings of the Committee of the Whole are not recorded in the *House Journal* or the *Senate Journal*, except as reported to the House or the Senate by the chairperson.[141] The report contains only the result of the committee's action on the measure under consideration.[142] This limited recording of transactions in the Committee of the Whole is designed to promote greater freedom of discussion than occurs when the House or the Senate is officially in session.

After business is completed. When the committee completes the business before it, it rises, and the chairperson is instructed to report the committee's action to the House or to the Senate in formal session while the speaker or the president is in the chair. The chairperson states to the speaker or president that the committee has had a certain measure under consideration and reports it back with the recommendation that it (1) pass, (2) pass as amended, (3) pass by substitute, or (4) not pass.[143] The report of the Committee of the Whole has precedence over all other committee reports in both the House of Representatives and the Senate.[144] The speaker or the president repeats this report, and the matter is then before the House or the Senate for action "just as though reported by any other committee."[145]

It should be emphasized that a measure cannot be passed in the Committee of the Whole. Like any other committee, it can only report recommendations to the House or the Senate. Obviously, the action taken on a measure by all members sitting as a Committee of the Whole is likely to be the action taken by these same members sitting in formal session. But only in formal session can a measure be passed by the House of Representatives or by the Senate.

As is true in the case of a measure reported by other committees, amendments to a measure that are offered by the Committee of the Whole may be further amended or rejected by the House or Senate. Likewise, the House or the Senate may restore amendments to a measure that were stricken by the committee.[146]

JOINT SESSIONS

Joint sessions are convened for presentations by the governor of the annual "State of the State" address and budget message, guest speakers who have been invited to address the General Assembly, and the election of state officers whom the legislature is required by law to elect.[147] Additionally, the two houses may meet in joint session from time to time for other purposes as deemed necessary.

Until 2003, the House and Senate had specific sets of parallel rules that governed joint sessions. Those rules provided that joint session rules could be amended by concurrent resolution or terminated when either house notified the other of the withdrawal of its consent. It may be inferred that such consent was withdrawn, as neither House nor Senate rule books since 2003 contain joint session rules.

To convene a joint session, a concurrent resolution is adopted designating the purpose, day, and hour of the session. Joint sessions are always held in the House chamber because it can accommodate more people. In the absence of specific rules, procedures are based on tradition, except that decisions as to who presides and who is seated on the main podium are decided by informal agreement between the House and Senate leadership.

NOTES

1. Ga. Const. art. 3, §4, ¶4.
2. Senate Rule 10-1.3(b).
3. House Rule 128.
4. Senate Rule 10-1.3; House Rule 37.
5. Senate Rule 10-1.2; House Rule 36.
6. Senate Rule 10-1.3.
7. Senate Rule 10-1.4.
8. Ga. Const. art. 3, §4, ¶3.
9. Senate Rule 5-1.10; House Rule 46.
10. Senate Rule 5-1.2; House Rule 45.
11. Senate Rule 4-2.1.
12. Senate Rule 4-2.2.
13. Senate Rule 8-1.8.
14. Senate Rules 6-9.2, 6-9.3.

15. House Rule 31.
16. House Rule 40.
17. House Rule 23.
18. House Rule 36.
19. Senate Rule 6-1.1(c); House Rule 88.
20. Senate Rule 8-1.6; House Rule 89.
21. Senate Rule 6-1.1(b); House Rule 87. In the Senate, however, there is a specific rule that all motions in standing committees must have a second motion (Senate Rule 2-5.1).
22. Senate Rule 6-1.1(a); House Rule 87.
23. Senate Rules 2-1.5 through 2-6.2.
24. Senate Rule 6-1.2; House Rule 87.
25. Senate Rules 6-2.4, 4-1.1; House Rules 156, 41.
26. Senate Rule 6-2.2; House Rule 154.
27. Senate Rule 6-2.1; House Rule 152.
28. Senate Rule 6-2.1; House Rule 153.
29. House Rule 123.1.
30. Senate Rule 6-2.2; House Rule 154.
31. Senate Rule 5-1.1(b); House Rule 128.
32. Senate Rule 6-3.1; House Rule 97.1.
33. Senate Rule 6-3.4; House Rule 95.
34. Senate Rule 6-3.2; House Rule 96.
35. Senate Rule 6-3.3(c); House Rule 94.
36. Senate Rule 6-3.3(a).
37. Senate Rule 6-3.2; House Rule 93.
38. House Rule 123.1.
39. Senate Rule 5-1.1(b); House Rule 98.
40. Senate Rule 6-3.5(c); House Rule 98.
41. Senate Rule 6-3.5(b).
42. House Rule 97.2.
43. Senate Rule 6-3.5; House Rule 97.2.
44. Senate Rule 6-8.1; House Rule 123.1.
45. Senate Rule 6-8.3; House Rule 121.
46. Senate Rule 6-8.1; House Rule 123.1.
47. Senate Rule 6-8.6; House Rule 126.
48. Senate Rule 6-8.2; House Rule 123.2.
49. Senate Rule 6-8.7; House Rule 127.
50. Senate Rule 6-8.6; House Rule 125.
51. Ga. Const. art. 3, §4, ¶1(b).
52. Senate Rule 6-2.3; House Rule 155.
53. Senate Rule 5-1.1(b); House Rule 128.
54. Senate Rule 6-4.1; House Rule 99.
55. Senate Rule 6-4.3; House Rule 101.
56. Senate Rule 6-4.1; House Rule 99.
57. Senate Rule 6-4.4; House Rule 99.
58. Senate Rule 6-4.2; House Rule 100.
59. Senate Rule 6-5.2; House Rule 103.

60. Senate Rule 6-5.1; House Rule 104.
61. House Rule 107.
62. Senate Rule 5-1.1(b).
63. Senate Rule 6-5.1; House Rule 105.
64. Senate Rule 6-5.1; House Rule 102.
65. House Rule 102.
66. Senate Rule 6-5.2; House Rule 106.
67. Senate Rule 6-5.4.
68. Senate Rule 6-6.1; House Rule 90. Rules of both houses note that a bill or resolution can be recommitted to a standing or special committee or to the Committee of the Whole. In practice, only the House assigns bills to special committees.
69. Senate Rule 4-2.5; House Rule 54.1.
70. Senate Rule 6-6.6; House Rule 92.
71. Senate Rule 6-6.3; House Rule 90.
72. Senate Rule 6-6.3.
73. House Rule 33.7.
74. Senate Rule 6-6.5; House Rule 90.
75. Senate Rule 6-6.2; House Rule 91.
76. Senate Rule 2-7.5; House Rule 65.
77. Senate Rule 7-1.1; House Rule 108.1.
78. Senate Rule 7-1.5; House Rule 108.2.
79. Senate Rule 6-9.1.
80. House Rule 33.2.
81. Senate Rule 7-1.2(a); House Rule 111.
82. Senate Rule 7-1.2(b); House Rule 111.
83. Ibid.
84. Senate Rule 7-1.6(c); House Rule 109.
85. Senate Rule 7-1.3(b).
86. Senate Rule 7-1.6; House Rule 112.
87. Senate Rule 7-1.1(b); House Rule 110.
88. Senate Rule 7-1.3(c); House Rule 116.
89. Senate Rule 7-1.1(c).
90. Senate Rule 7-1.4; House Rule 114.
91. Senate Rule 7-1.7.
92. Senate Rule 7-1.8(c); House Rule 122.1.
93. Senate Rule 7-1.8; House Rule 113.
94. Senate Rule 5-1.1(b); House Rule 128.
95. Senate Rule 7-1.10(c); House Rule 119.
96. Senate Rule 7-1.10(a); House Rule 117.1.
97. Senate Rule 7-1.10(a).
98. House Rule 117.3.
99. Senate Rule 7-1.10(b); House Rule 117.2.
100. Senate Rule 7-1.10(d); House Rule 120.1.
101. Senate Rule 2-8.6; House Rule 146.7.
102. Senate Rule 3-1.3; House Rule 51.
103. Senate Rule 6-7.1(a); House Rule 143.
104. Ibid.

105. Ibid.
106. Senate Rule 6-7.1(b).
107. House Rule 143(1).
108. House Rule 145.
109. Senate Rule 6-7.5.
110. House Rule 143(2).
111. Senate Rule 6-7.1(c).
112. Senate Rule 6-7.2.
113. Senate Rule 6-7.3; House Rule 143(3).
114. House Rule 123.2.
115. Senate Rule 6-8.7; House Rule 123.2.
116. Senate Rule 6-7.4; House Rule 144.
117. Senate Rules 6-8.4, 7-1.8(c); House Rule 122.1.
118. Senate Rule 6-8.4; House Rule 122.1.
119. House Rules 122.1 through 122.3.
120. Senate Rule 6-8.4(a); House Rule 122.1.
121. House Rule 60.
122. House Rule 61.
123. Senate Rule 2-7.1; House Rule 62.
124. House Rule 62.
125. Senate Rule 2-7.1; House Rule 62.
126. Ibid.
127. House Rules 63, 67.
128. Senate Rule 2-7.2.
129. Senate Rule 2-7.5(d); House Rule 70.
130. Senate Rule 2-7.5(c); House Rule 69.
131. Senate Rule 2-7.5(a); House Rule 65.
132. Senate Rule 2-7.4.
133. Senate Rule 2-7.3; House Rule 64.
134. Ibid.
135. Senate Rule 2-7.7.
136. House Rule 71.
137. House Rule 66.
138. Senate Rule 2-7.5(b); House Rule 68.
139. Senate Rule 2-7.8; House Rules 72, 73.
140. Senate Rule 2-7.8; House Rule 74.
141. Senate Rule 2-7.11; House Rule 76.
142. Senate Rule 2-7.9; House Rule 75.1.
143. Ibid.
144. Senate Rule 4-2.12; House Rule 58.
145. Senate Rule 2-7.9(b); House Rule 75.2.
146. Senate Rule 2-7.10(b); House Rule 77.
147. Joint Session Rule 1.

CHAPTER 9

LEGISLATIVE STAFF AND RESOURCES

This chapter describes briefly the major kinds of resources and staff services available to the Georgia General Assembly, in addition to those noted in chapters 2 and 4.

LEGISLATIVE RESOURCES

Legislative Services Committee

The Legislative Services Committee is a special joint statutory committee that oversees the administration and management of the General Assembly. Because it is not a standing committee of the legislature, no bills are referred to it.

The committee may study and adopt methods and procedures for more efficient and uniform operation of both houses of the General Assembly, as well as provide for necessary services to the legislative branch. Additionally, it has complete authority over the assignment of rooms, chambers, offices, and other areas on the third and fourth floors of the state capitol and on the mezzanine between these floors.[1]

The Legislative Services Committee is composed of 16 members: the speaker of the House (chair); president of the Senate; chairs of the House and Senate appropriations committees; chairs of the House and Senate judiciary committees; chair of the Senate Banking and Financial Institutions Committee; chair of the House Ways and Means Committee; president pro tempore of the Senate; speaker pro tempore of the House; the majority and minority leaders of the House and Senate; clerk of the House; and secretary of the Senate (secretary for the committee). Members receive no compensation for service on the committee during legislative sessions, but for interim meetings, they are entitled to the standard allowances authorized for other interim legislative committees.[2]

Office of Legislative Counsel

Under direction of the Legislative Services Committee, the Office of Legislative Counsel provides a variety of reference, counseling, and legislative drafting services to members of the General Assembly.

Upon request, this office will advise legislators on proposed legislation, prepare a draft bill, or review legislation prepared by a legislator. Communications between this office and legislators are privileged and confidential and not subject to the state's open records requirements.[3] Both during and between sessions, the counsel's professional staff (which includes attorneys and nonlegal specialists) advises committees and officers of the General Assembly, assisting in the preparation of their reports and recommendations. The staff researches a variety of legislative matters, upcoming policy issues, and related subjects for members, officers, and committees of the legislature. At the conclusion of each legislative session, the counsel's office publishes a summary of the general statutes enacted that year. More importantly, the office is responsible for compiling, indexing, editing, and publishing the text of the acts and general resolutions passed at that session.

The legislative counsel's office serves as staff for the Code Revision Commission, which has broad authority over revising, updating, correcting errors in, and publishing the Official Code of Georgia Annotated.[4] Additionally, the office renders opinions and provides other legal services for the legislative branch and, with approval of the Legislative Services Committee or the speaker of the House, represents the legislative branch and its interests in court litigation. It also has the power to engage the services of others, including private counsel, to assist in these duties.[5]

Georgia law directs the attorney general to act as advisor to this office, and, on occasion, attorneys from both offices will work together.[6] While the attorney general can issue official opinions on matters of law only to the governor, lieutenant governor, and heads of departments in the executive branch, unofficial opinions are issued to legislators on request.

Finally, the counsel's office serves as a major contact point with the Council of State Governments, National Conference of State Leg-

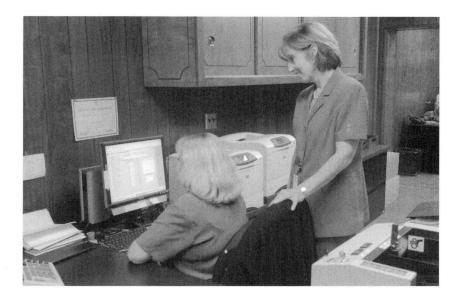

THE LEGISLATIVE FISCAL OFFICE HANDLES ALL FINANCIAL MATTERS,
INCLUDING SALARIES, EXPENSE REIMBURSEMENT, AND PURCHASES.

islatures, and other states for the exchange of information, data, and
other materials relating to Georgia law and the General Assembly.

The legislative counsel is elected by a majority vote of the total
membership of the Legislative Services Committee. He or she must
be an attorney experienced in legislative matters and bill drafting.[7]

Legislative Fiscal Officer

The Office of Legislative Fiscal Officer was established to oversee
and centralize expenditures and fiscal accounting within the legislative branch.

Acting as bookkeeper and comptroller for the General Assembly,
the fiscal officer maintains accounts of legislative expenditures and
commitments. This office oversees the payment of legislative salaries,
allowances, and travel expenses and issues all purchase orders for
supplies and other materials for the General Assembly. He or she
maintains an inventory of the equipment, furnishings, and nonexpend-
able items belonging to the legislative branch. The fiscal officer and
staff are employed by the Legislative Services Committee and may
be entrusted with other duties by that committee.[8]

REPRESENTATIVE GOVERNMENT AT WORK

Prior to 1959, the General Assembly functioned with few staff resources other than the clerk of the House and secretary of the Senate. In 1951, the legislature directed Georgia's attorney general to provide lawyers to help members draft bills. However, this arrangement was not conducive to an independent legislative branch. Consequently, the General Assembly in 1959 created the Office of Legislative Counsel—the legislature's first staff resource to serve both houses.

Legislative Budget Analyst

The Office of Legislative Budget Analyst was created to give the legislature fiscal expertise of its own so that it would not have to rely on the executive branch for revenue estimates, spending projections, and information on departmental budgetary needs. (It should be noted, however, that the governor's revenue estimate is the official estimate used for development of the budget.)

For many years, the legislative budget analyst was employed by the Legislative Services Committee and operated as the Legislative Budget Office (LBO). The LBO worked with both the House and Senate appropriations committees and the leadership of both chambers to produce the House and Senate versions of appropriations measures and to coordinate the work of the conference committees on both the Amended General Appropriations Act and the General Appropriations Act each year. In addition, the LBO coordinated the interaction of the Governor's Office of Planning and Budget and the General Assembly.

In 2005, the House continued to use the services of the LBO. The Senate created the Senate Budget Office (SBO), largely in response to the perception that the LBO worked more closely with the House since, by tradition, appropriations measures originate in the larger chamber. The Legislative Services Committee in 2006 changed the name of the LBO to the House Budget Office (HBO) to reflect the fact that each chamber has its own budget staff office. In 2007, the Senate renamed its counterpart the Senate Budget and Evaluation Office (SBEO). Both the HBO and SBEO have directors to coordinate the work of those offices. The Office of Legislative Budget Analyst still exists technically because the changes sanctioned by the Legislative Services Committee are not statutory, but the position is not active.

Current trends suggest that these two staff offices are becoming more involved in evaluation of agency programs, a function largely performed by the Budget Responsibility Oversight Committee and the Office of State Auditor. The roles will evolve over the next few sessions of the General Assembly.

Budgetary Responsibility Oversight Committee

In an effort to strengthen its capacity to oversee the budgetary process, the General Assembly enacted the Budget Accountability and Planning Act of 1993. One of the most significant changes in the law was creation of a special legislative committee known as the Budgetary Responsibility Oversight Committee. The committee consists of six members from each house appointed by the respective presiding officers who serve until their successors are appointed. Members are appointed within 10 days of the convening of the session in each odd-numbered year.[9] To assist in its responsibilities, the committee has a full-time director and staff.

The committee is required to consult with the governor and the Office of Planning and Budget (OPB) with respect to the state's strategic planning process, which involves a long-range state plan (updated at least annually) and individual agency plans that contribute to the state plan. Once the OPB approves state and agency plans, state law requires the plans to be sent to the Budgetary Responsibility Oversight Committee for review and evaluation. Additionally, the committee can request a performance audit it deems necessary of any agency.[10]

In 1993, the General Assembly established a process for an ongoing review and evaluation of all state programs and functions, with the intent that every state program be evaluated at least once every 10 years. The chairperson maintains a list of programs for which the committee requests evaluations. That list, along with any subsequent revisions, is given to the director of the OPB and the state auditor. The OPB, the Department of Audits and Accounts, and the Research Office of the Budgetary Responsibility Oversight Committee work together to complete as many audits as resources permit. The Office of the Legislative Budget Analyst, the Board of Regents, and all other state agencies are directed to provide assistance as requested. Additionally, the law authorizes contracts with private contractors to perform or assist in evaluations. The results are reported to the Budgetary Responsibility Oversight Committee as they are completed.[11]

When any state agency plans to initiate any new program that will require a state appropriation, that agency must report to the committee by September 1 prior to the session at which funds will be requested. A report must be prepared that contains a description, rationale, and plan for operating the program, plus an explanation of how the program conforms to the state and agency's strategic plan and the extent to which the program's facilities and staff will be decentralized. Committee members must also be provided with information regarding the projected cost of fully implementing the proposed program.[12] The committee then decides whether to recommend funding of the proposed program.

One of the budgetary changes enacted in 1993 requires the OPB to produce a "continuation budget report" covering at least 20 percent of state agencies. By May 1 of each year, the OPB must consult with the chair of the Budgetary Responsibility Oversight Committee to determine which agencies will undergo the OPB's detailed analysis of their purposes, programs, and accomplishments in relation to the funding approved for the fiscal year in which the examination takes place. The committee is responsible for taking the OPB's continuation budget report and the audit report for the fiscal year just ended and determining what, if any, recommendations should be made to the full membership of the General Assembly. This report must be submitted within the first week of the next legislative session.[13]

Georgia's constitution prohibits expenditure of state funds unless authorized by an appropriation act.[14] However, state agencies are involved in numerous programs funded by federal grants or contracts, and it is not uncommon for new sources of funding to become available after an appropriation act has been enacted. State law therefore directs that all federal funds received by the state be "continually appropriated in the exact amounts and for the purposes authorized and directed by the federal government in making the grant."[15] Each year, however, the OPB must report to the Budgetary Responsibility Oversight Committee on any funds received and spent by state agencies that were not contemplated when the appropriation act was approved.[16]

In performing its duties, the committee can request information or reports from the OPB or any agency receiving a state appropriation, and such agencies are directed by law to cooperate.[17] Each year, the committee is directed to make a report to the General Assembly and governor on its activities and findings. The committee's chair is also directed to prepare a written executive summary of the annual report prior to the adoption of the general appropriations act. The committee is not required to distribute the annual report or summaries but must notify General Assembly members of its availability.[18]

Fiscal Affairs Subcommittee

Although a fiscal affairs subcommittee is provided for each house, the primary functions of each are performed through joint meetings as the Fiscal Affairs Subcommittee, which meets at least once each quarter (or more often at the governor's call) to review and approve budget object transfers recommended by the governor. Such transfers require the approval of at least 11 of the 20 members on the subcommittee. The two subcommittees may also meet as one at the call of the lieutenant governor, speaker of the House, or their own subcommittee chairs.[19]

In each house, the fiscal affairs subcommittee consists of four reelected members of the Appropriations Committee appointed by the presiding officer, the presiding officer, and five reelected members of that house selected by the governor. These subcommittees are authorized to review budget requests of the various departments and agencies at any time, with the Office of Planning and Budget, state auditor, and each department or agency directed to promptly furnish them with any requested information. The joint subcommittee must report annually to the legislature on matters coming to its attention and make recommendations for improving the efficiency of the operation and management of various state agencies.[20]

Georgia General Assembly Information Technology Department

An office of technical support was created in 1999 to support the computer hardware, software, and network resources of the General Assembly. The director of the office is hired by and reports to the Legislative Services Committee. Specifically, staff assign all legislative e-mail addresses, provide support for all computers and approved software used by legislators and staff, and maintain the legislative local area network and official Web sites for each house. A help desk can be reached any hour of the day, seven days a week throughout the year at 404-657-4580.

Senate Administrative Affairs Committee

This committee is responsible for (1) employing, supervising, disciplining, and setting the compensation for all Senate aides, secretaries, and other personnel, including those of the Senate Budget, Senate Research, and Senate Information offices; (2) supervising the purchase and allotment of Senate supplies; and (3) supervising and approving all out-of-state travel of Senate members and staff. The committee is composed of the president, president pro tempore, majority and minority leaders, chair of the Rules Committee, secretary of the Senate, and three members appointed by the president.[21]

Senate Research Office

The Senate Research Office, located in the Coverdell Legislative Office Building, serves as an information research and resource center for all senators and the lieutenant governor. The office has a full-time managing director for a staff of full-time policy analysts who provide assistance to standing and interim study committees as well as to senators on an individual basis. The office maintains resource files and a library of current periodicals and publications on legislative issues.

Research Services in the House

Research is provided to House members through a system of committee aides and interns under the direction of the House Committee Services office. Aides are assigned to staff up to four standing committees to help track bills and resolutions referred to the committees and assist the committee chair in presiding over the flow of committee work. Aides provide research and analysis on issues at the request of a House member. They also assist study committees during the interim.

Georgia Reapportionment Services Office

The reapportionment office, a nonpartisan service contracted through the University of Georgia's Office of Information Technology and Outreach Services at the Carl Vinson Institute of Government, is located in the Coverdell Legislative Office Building. The office provides services and assistance to members of the General Assembly relative to redistricting following each decennial census and throughout the year. The services include assistance for congressional, state legislative, county commission, local school board, and city council redistricting. The office works with legislators and the redistricting committees to develop plans and maps, maintains an archive of all plans, and generates legal descriptions for the Office of Legislative Counsel. At the request of a legislator representing an affected jurisdiction, the office provides assistance to local governments with their redistricting needs.

Legislative Interns

Under the Legislative Intern Program, graduate and upper-division students selected on a competitive basis from colleges and universities in Georgia live in Atlanta and work as staff to the General Assembly during the session. Selection and academic requirements for the interns are handled by participating schools. Work assignment and direction of interns during the session are managed by the House and Senate. For their work as interns, the students receive academic credit and are paid a stipend. Approximately 30 interns take part in the program each session and are assigned to both the Senate and the House. Most interns are assigned to work with committees, although some may be assigned to various legislative support staff.

OTHER SOURCES OF ASSISTANCE

Office of Planning and Budget

The General Assembly receives assistance on budgetary and fiscal matters from a number of other sources within state government. A major source of expertise and assistance is located within the Office of the Governor: the Office of Planning and Budget. This office, and in particular its budget division, is responsible for

1. helping the governor draft a general appropriations bill each year,
2. developing and implementing a process of strategic planning to establish and periodically update an overall plan for state government and requiring state agencies to develop strategic plans consistent with the state plan,
3. conducting evaluations of state agencies and programs requested by the presiding officers of both houses,
4. developing plans for improving the economy and efficiency of state agencies,
5. carrying out the fiscal plans and policies as approved by the General Assembly,
6. preparing fiscal notes that give the expected financial consequences of certain types of legislation, and
7. in general, providing the legislature, House and Senate appropriations committees, the legislative budget analyst, and the Budgetary Responsibility Oversight Committee with assistance.[22]

The Office of Planning and Budget is required to develop and maintain (updating at least once each year) a strategic plan for the state as a whole. By law, the plan must cover a period of at least five years. This plan must have as its primary goal (1) improved fiscal responsibility and responsiveness of state government and (2) effective and efficient delivery of services throughout the state, with an emphasis on decentralizing state government.[23]

Department of Audits and Accounts

At least once a year, the Department of Audits and Accounts (headed by the state auditor) reviews the books and accounts of every state officer, department, agency, authority, board, commission, institution, local school system, and official receiving state aid to ensure that funds are expended and administered according to law.[24] A detailed and comprehensive report of the salaries paid to and expenses incurred by every person on the payroll of the state is available to legislators on request.[25]

The auditor is directed to prepare annual and, whenever required, special reports to the governor and General Assembly showing the general financial operation and management of each state agency and whether it is being handled in an efficient and economical manner, calling special attention to any excessive cost of operation or maintenance, expense, or price paid for goods, supplies, or labor by any agency.[26] The House or Senate Appropriations Committee or the governor may direct the auditor to make a special examination and audit of all the books, records, accounts, vouchers, warrants, bills, and other papers and records and the financial transactions and management of any agency at any time.[27] Additionally, the auditor is directed to cooperate with both appropriations committees and to furnish any information they request.[28] The department works with the Office of Planning and Budget to prepare fiscal notes for various types of bills before their introduction in the General Assembly.[29]

Commission on Compensation

The State Commission on Compensation assists the General Assembly in setting the compensation of not only members of the General Assembly but also "constitutional state officers" and full-time heads of state agencies, authorities, boards, commissions, committees, and departments. Of the commission's 12 members, 4 are appointed by the governor, 4 by the justices of the state supreme court, 2 by the lieutenant governor, and 2 by the speaker of the House.[30] The com-

Since 1958, lawmakers have attended the Biennial Institute for Georgia Legislators held at the University of Georgia.

pensation commission is responsible for reviewing the salaries of paid state officials in Georgia and comparing them with salaries received in comparable positions within the federal government, other states, businesses, industries, and the professions. The commission is further instructed to file a written report of its findings and recommendations to the General Assembly in odd-numbered years at least 30 days prior to the beginning of the session.

Universities

The Georgia General Assembly sometimes turns to educational and research institutions of the state for counsel and research assistance. The law schools, both public and private, are called upon from time to time for research and drafting assistance. Law professors, political scientists, public administration teachers and researchers, and other specialists also provide counsel and research assistance to committees on occasion.

The Legislative Intern Program, discussed earlier, is another example of the assistance provided to the General Assembly by educational institutions. The program provides a service to legislators and an educational and work experience for the student interns.

One special resource is the Carl Vinson Institute of Government at the University of Georgia. In addition to producing this handbook, the institute has conducted a number of policy studies for committees of the General Assembly, as well as for the body as a whole. Since 1958, it has cooperated with legislative leaders in conducting the presession "Biennial Institute for Georgia Legislators" to provide information on issues and problems facing the state and to acquaint new members with the organization and procedures of the General Assembly.

In conjunction with the Carl Vinson Institute of Government, the General Assembly in 1998 created the Georgia General Assembly Training Institute. It is headed by a seven-member board consisting of three members from each house appointed by the Legislative Services Committee, plus the director of the Vinson Institute as a nonvoting ex officio member. The training institute is responsible for offering members of the General Assembly a series of instructional classes on the organization and operation of Georgia state government in general and the role and powers of the General Assembly in particular. Additionally, the Training Institute can authorize instruction in such courses as the Georgia Constitution, the role of each branch of state government, the role of state government in the federal system, the relationship of state and local government, sources of state and local revenue, the state budget process, legislative use of computers, and such other matters deemed appropriate by the board. The first course offered each biennium by the Training Institute is the Biennial Institute.[31]

National Organizations

American Legislative Exchange Council (ALEC)

Individual state legislators along with corporate and private foundation members make up this bipartisan organization, which is guided by concepts such as limited government and free markets. ALEC provides an opportunity for public- and private-sector representatives to work together. Created in 1973, the organization has a membership that includes one-third of all state legislators. The national headquarters for ALEC is in Washington, D.C.

Within ALEC are task forces that research and create model policies for national application. The task forces include civil justice; commerce, insurance, and economic development; criminal justice; education; federal affairs; health and human services; homeland security; international initiative; natural resources; tax and fiscal policy; telecommunications and information technology; and trade and transportation.

ALEC's staff assists legislative members with research, policy analysis, bill tracking, and expert testimony on issues. The organization maintains a Web site with current news, a calendar of events, and information about publications and the work of task forces. Also available on the site are more than 400 pieces of model legislation that can be accessed by members. In addition to *ALEC Policy Forum*, a journal published three times a year for members, ALEC produces a monthly newsletter, report cards, white papers, and issue analyses.

A meeting is held annually to bring together legislators, business executives, and policy analysts to discuss issues and policies. ALEC also holds the States and National Policy Summit to educate freshman state legislators on issues they will be facing in their new roles.

The Council of State Governments

Another valuable source of information is the Council of State Governments, headquartered in Lexington, Kentucky. Its southern regional office is in Atlanta and the largest of four regional legislative groups that function under the Council of State Governments. Georgia is part of the Southern Legislative Conference, a 16-state region. On request, the council provides the legislature and its committees with information on various subjects gathered from studies and legislation considered by other states. The council's Suggested State Legislation program publishes model legislation in a variety of areas. The Innovations Awards Program identifies programs that have been implemented successfully by state governments and facilitates similar programs in other states.

Other council publications include *State News*, which highlights information relevant to state legislatures, new laws, issues facing the states, and state government in general. Published annually, *The Book of the States* provides comparative information on constitutions, legislatures, governors, courts, and other areas of state government. The council publishes many studies in specialized areas such as elections, emergency management, intergovernmental relations, transportation, and campaign finance reform.

National Conference of State Legislatures (NCSL)

This bipartisan organization serves all legislators and staff of the states, commonwealths, and territories. NCSL maintains offices in

Denver, Colorado, as well as in Washington, D.C. It provides research, information, and technical assistance to state legislatures and is an advocate for state interests before the federal government.

The NCSL responds to requests for in-depth research on matters of importance to state legislatures as well as requests for immediate information. Its Web site contains more than 500,000 documents, including research reports, legislation, statutes, and state surveys. Legislators can join listservs and discussion groups, receive personalized information, access NCSL books and newsletters, and identify and contact colleagues in other states.

Seminars, conferences, and other programs in areas such as health care, welfare, criminal justice, economic development, energy, the environment, and education are conducted nationwide each year by the NCSL. An annual meeting brings together legislators and staff for a variety of workshops and panels.

The NCSL publishes *State Legislatures* magazine 10 times a year; *LegisBriefs*, in which state data are compared and analyzed; and other specialized reports, books, and materials on federal and state issues and topics of particular concern to legislators.

PUBLICATIONS

Annually, each member of the General Assembly receives copies of the session laws enacted that year, the journal of that member's house, the state budget, the report of the state auditor, some agency regulations and annual reports, and several other publications. Some of these are distributed automatically, while others are available upon request. Many of these publications are also available online.

Georgia Laws

Following each session, the Office of Legislative Counsel publishes the text of all bills and resolutions approved at that session in an annual series titled *Georgia Laws*. Currently, Vol. I, Book I contains the general acts and resolutions; Vol. I, Book II contains the general and supplemental appropriation acts; Vol. II, Book I contains the local acts; and Vol. III contains the index, list of members at the session, results of local referendums authorized by the legislature, list of vetoed measures, governor's reasons for vetoes, and other information.

Rules and Regulations of the State of Georgia

This compilation officially details all rules and regulations adopted by executive agencies, pursuant to law, that are covered under the Administrative Procedures Act. By law, these are to be made available upon request free of charge to any member of the General Assembly. The secretary of state is authorized by law to make them available electronically.[32]

Annual Reports of State Agencies

Although not every executive agency is required by law to file an annual report with the General Assembly, many are. Under state law, an agency that is required to report only needs to notify each legislator that its annual report has been filed and is available upon request.[33]

House and Senate Journals

The journal of each house is the official compendium of daily records reflecting the order of business and action taken on all legislative measures and procedural questions during the session (see Fig. 23). Listed within the journal are the authors of every measure considered by a house, the date of first and second readings of the measure, the name and date of committee assignment, and the committee recommendation on each bill or resolution reported out of committee. The journal does not record the text of bills and resolutions (except for committee or floor amendments and substitutes to a measure) but does reflect all actions taken on them by the full house.

The votes on all motions and questions coming before a house and on the final passage of bills or resolutions are reported. When there is a roll call vote, the names of all members and how they voted (or if they did not vote) is recorded. If the vote is by division (show of hands), the total numbers for and against the question or bill are noted. If the vote was by voice vote or unanimous consent, recorded in the journal is only whether the question or measure passed or failed.

Other journal entries are rules changes adopted by a house, results of elections for officers of that house, "housekeeping" resolutions for the biennium, copies of privileged resolutions adopted by a house, final reports of special interim study committees, messages received from the other house, copies of the governor's annual "State of the State" and budget messages, a list of the bills vetoed by the governor and the reasons for vetoing them, and the names of all lobbyists formally registered with the secretary of state.

Except for the *Congressional Record*—which is not an official journal of Congress—individual floor remarks and debate are not recorded or published by either house, nor is "extension of remarks" permitted. However, any senator may enter a written protest against an action taken by the Senate concerning any matter. The protest must clearly

282

Figure 23. Legislative Journal

SB 525. By Senator Williams of the 19th:

> A BILL to be entitled an Act to amend Chapter 3 of Title 48 of the Official Code of Georgia Annotated, relating to tax executions, so as to change certain provisions regarding the issuance of tax executions by tax collectors and tax commissioners; to provide for a definition; to provide for procedures; to provide an effective date; to repeal conflicting laws; and for other purposes.

The report of the committee, which was favorable to the passage of the bill, was agreed to.

On the passage of the bill, a roll call was taken, and the vote was as follows:

Y Adelman	Y Hill,Jack	Y Smith
Y Balfour	Y Hill,Judson	Starr
E Brown	Y Hooks	Y Staton
Y Bulloch	Y Hudgens	Y Stephens
E Butler	Johnson (PRS)	E Stoner
E Cagle	E Jones	Y Tarver
Y Carter	Y Kemp	Tate
Y Chance	E Me V Bremen	Y Thomas,D
Y Chapman	Y Miles	Thomas,R
Y Douglas	Y Moody	Y Thompson,C
Y Fort	Y Mullis	Y Thompson,S
Y Goggans	Y Pearson	Y Tolleson
E Golden	E Powell	E Unterman
Y Grant	Y Reed	Y Weber
Y Hamrick	Y Rogers	Y Whitehead
Y Harbison	Schaefer	Y Wiles
E Harp	Y Seabaugh	Y Williams
Y Heath	Y Seay	Y Zamarripa
Henson	Y Shafer,D	

On the passage of the bill, the yeas were 40, nays 0.

SB 525, having received the requisite constitutional majority, was passed.

SB 545. By Senators Mullis of the 53rd, Thomas of the 54th, Douglas of the 17th, Balfour of the 9th, Heath of the 31st and others:

> A BILL to be entitled an Act to amend Code Section 16-12-51 of the Official Code of Georgia Annotated, relating to definitions regarding bingo games, so

set forth his or her grounds and may not impugn the motive of that house or of any member.[34] A member may also include statements in the journal, limited to 200 words in the House and 250 in the Senate, explaining why he or she voted in a certain way.[35]

Responsibility for preparation of each day's journal report rests with the clerk of the House and the secretary of the Senate. Both houses provide for examination of this daily report before it is read and adopted on the following day by the whole body. The Committee on Information and Audits in the House and the Committee on Rules in the Senate are responsible for this examination.[36]

The confirmation of the journal each morning by a house officially marks the end of the previous legislative day. The rules of the Senate require the reading of the journal except if waived by either a majority vote or by unanimous consent.[37] In actual practice, this waiver is routinely granted each morning following announcement by a representative of the Senate Committee on Rules that the previous day's record has been examined and found to be correct.

Following a session, these daily reports are chronologically compiled and published by the clerk and secretary for their respective houses on the General Assembly's Web site and in a comprehensive two-volume set, which thereafter serves as the official record of legislative action for that session. Despite the absence of individual floor remarks, debate, statements of intent by a measure's author, and detailed standing committee reports, Georgia courts, in seeking to interpret the intent of the legislature, may review events occurring during the progress of a statute's enactment, as disclosed by the Senate and House journals.[38] However, the journals may not be used to impeach the validity of a bill by showing that the measure was not enacted in accordance with constitutional requirements or the rules of that house. A duly enrolled act authenticated by the presiding officers of both houses, approved by the governor, and deposited with the secretary of state will be conclusively presumed to have been enacted in accordance with necessary requirements, and no evidence to the contrary, even if reflected in the journal, will be considered by the courts.[39]

PUBLIC INFORMATION SERVICES

The Georgia legislature has taken several steps to better convey to the public general information on the operation of the General Assembly and specific information on the status of legislation during a session.

Senate Press Office

The Senate maintains a full-time press office to assist members with official media relations at their request. Office staff write and send out press releases, media advisories, radio feeds, and opinion pieces; set up press conferences; and help senators respond to any media requests. The office provides senators with a clipping service on a weekly basis during the session and on a monthly basis for the remainder of the year. The press office does not participate in any partisan activities or activities that relate to campaigning.

During the session, press office staff monitor the action of Senate standing committees and write summaries of the meetings. If called upon, the staff can take pictures during the meetings and make any media arrangements. The press office maintains the official Senate Web site to serve the public and elected officials.

The Senate Press Office Web page provides daily and weekly reports of the actions of the Senate during the session as well as a final report of Senate action. A list of press releases issued by senators is posted and an audio archive of press conferences and statements is maintained on the Web page. The public also can access broadcasts of Senate action. Photographs of senators in the chamber and at meetings are also posted on the Web page and can be downloaded.

House Communications Office

House Communications is the office responsible for reporting on the day-to-day actions of the House of Representatives as well as providing information and services to representatives and the public. It is a nonpartisan, nonpolitical office and serves all House members. The office has a Web page with links to committee meeting notices, information about each standing House committee (including meeting agendas), and the Georgia Legislative Network, which broadcasts committee meetings. Staff members prepare and post daily and weekly reports of House actions during the session and provide PowerPoint presentations for use by members in their deliberation of specific House bills.

The office is responsible for overseeing the speaker's intern program and assigns interns to serve with committee aides. Reservations for committee and conference rooms are handled by this office. It also issues media credentials to members of the press, which allow them access to the House chamber.

The House Communications Office writes press releases for members and serves as their liaison with the press. Press releases from the

House and Senate Web sites have information on legislators,
committees, bills and resolutions, and status of legislation.

speaker of the House are also posted on the Web site. Members and
the public can link to an online clipping service and access the state's
major daily newspapers. The Web page also contains biographical
information for each representative.

General Assembly Web Site

The Internet has made it easier for the public to obtain information
about the legislature. The General Assembly maintains a Web site
(www.legis.ga.gov) with sections for the Senate and the House. Legislators and the public may access current and archived information
about each session, including the complete text of bills and resolutions, a record of legislative actions on each measure, the text of
amendments, and the committee meeting schedule. By law, this information must be provided on a daily basis in the most current format
available.[40] Consequently, each day following adjournment, staff in
the offices of the clerk of the House and the secretary of the Senate
record the status of every bill and resolution in the General Assembly
and then upload this information to the General Assembly's local area
network for public access.

Citizens can consult the Web site to identify their senator or representative by name or district. There are links to committees in each chamber and other legislative offices such as the clerk of the House and secretary of the Senate, budget offices, House member services, and the Senate press and research offices. The picture book directory of legislative members can be accessed from this site. A series of frequently asked questions helps users to find information on the Web site as well as to understand the legislative process. It also contains information about the operation of the page program in each house. The public may research online specific provisions in the law in the unannotated Georgia Code. A list of links to Georgia's state agencies is also available.

Television and Radio

Since 1971, Georgia Public Broadcasting has provided extensive television coverage of legislative sessions, supplemented by interviews and analyses, enabling state citizens to view taped coverage of highlights of each day's session. The program *Lawmakers* usually airs at 7:00 p.m. on public television stations on weeknights during the legislative session.

In addition to text-based information on the House and Senate Web sites, live video is transmitted from each chamber during the session. This allows anyone in the world connected to the Internet to watch floor debate and voting in either house of the General Assembly. The House of Representatives created the Georgia Legislative Network in 2006 in order to broadcast House standing and study committee meetings and press conferences over the Internet. Archives of these meetings are maintained on the General Assembly Web site.

Finally, the communications and press offices provide a radio service through which stations across the state may get taped excerpts of House or Senate action or receive synopses of major legislative activity without charge.

NOTES

1. OFFICIAL CODE OF GEORGIA ANNOTATED (O.C.G.A.) §28-4-2.
2. O.C.G.A. §28-4-1.
3. O.C.G.A. §50-18-75.
4. O.C.G.A. §§28-9-3, 28-9-4, 28-9-5.
5. O.C.G.A. §28-4-3.
6. O.C.G.A. §28-4-5.
7. O.C.G.A. §§28-4-4, 28-4-3.

8. O.C.G.A. §§28-4-6, 28-4-7.

9. O.C.G.A. §28-5-5.

10. Ibid.

11. O.C.G.A. §45-12-178.

12. O.C.G.A. §45-12-88.

13. O.C.G.A. §45-12-75.1.

14. GA. CONST. art. 3, §9, ¶1.

15. O.C.G.A. §45-12-91.

16. O.C.G.A. §28-5-5 (d)(5).

17. O.C.G.A. §28-5-5 (e).

18. O.C.G.A. §28-5-5 (f).

19. O.C.G.A. §§28-5-20 through 28-5-27.

20. Ibid.

21. Senate Rule 2-1.2.

22. O.C.G.A. §§45-12-71 et seq., 28-4-6(b), 28-5-5(e), 28-5-42.

23. O.C.G.A. §45-12-175.

24. O.C.G.A. §§50-6-6, 50-6-24.

25. O.C.G.A. §50-6-27.

26. O.C.G.A. §50-6-24.

27. O.C.G.A. §50-6-4.

28. O.C.G.A. §50-6-23.

29. O.C.G.A. §§28-5-2, 28-5-42, 28-5-52, 47-20-32 et seq.

30. O.C.G.A. §45-7-90 et seq.

31. O.C.G.A. chap. 28-11.

32. O.C.G.A. §50-13-7.

33. O.C.G.A. §45-6-4.

34. Senate Rule 8-1.12.

35. Senate Rule 5-1.9; House Rule 136.

36. Senate Rule 4-2.3; House Rule 32.

37. Senate Rule 4-2.3.

38. Stanley v. Sims, 185 Ga. 518, 195 S.E. 439 (1938); Sharpe v. Lowe, 214 Ga. 513, 106 S.E.2d 28 (1958).

39. Battalia v. City of Columbus, 199 Ga. App. 897, 406 S.E.2d 290 (1991); Wilson v. Ledbetter, 194 Ga. App. 32, 389 S.E.2d 771 (1989); Collins v. Woodham, 257 Ga. 643, 361 S.E.2d 800 (1987); Atlantic Coast Line Railroad v. State, 135 Ga. 545, 69 S.E. 725 (1910); Capitol Distributing Co. v. Redwine, 206 Ga. 477, 57 S.E.2d 578 (1980). The only exception to the "enrolled bill rule" appears to be the matter of notice of advertisement for local bills (which, incidentally, is not recorded in the journal of either legislative body). Richmond County v. Pierce, 234 Ga. 274, 215 S.E.2d 665 (1975); Smith v. Michael, 203 Ga. 74, 45 S.E.2d 431 (1974).

40. O.C.G.A. §28-3-24.1.

APPENDIX 1
Georgia State Government Complex

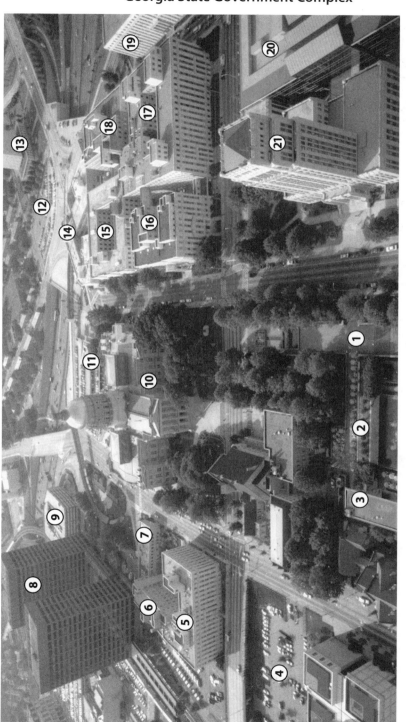

(1) Georgia Plaza Park, (2) Garden Room, (3) Capitol Education Center, (4) Steve Polk Plaza Parking, (5) Agriculture Building, (6) No. 7 Martin Luther King Building, (7) No. 1 Martin Luther King Building, (8) Floyd Building (Twin Towers), (9) Pete Hackney Parking Deck, (10) State Capitol, (11) Parking Lot No. 1, (12) Archives Parking Lot, (13) Former State Archives Building (vacant), (14) Transportation Building, (15) Paul Coverdell Legislative Office Building, (16) Judicial Building, (17) Labor Building, (18) Health Building, and (19) Trinity-Washington Building. Also shown are (20) Atlanta City Hall Annex and (21) Atlanta City Hall.

290

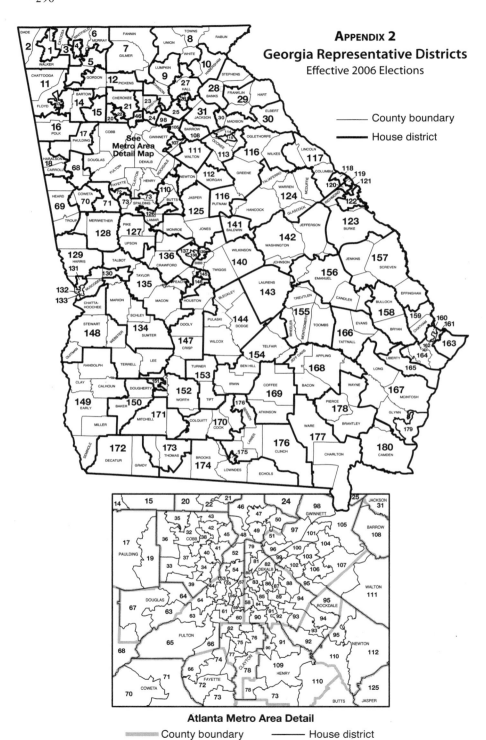

APPENDIX 2
Georgia Representative Districts
Effective 2006 Elections

—— County boundary
—— House district

Atlanta Metro Area Detail
County boundary —— House district

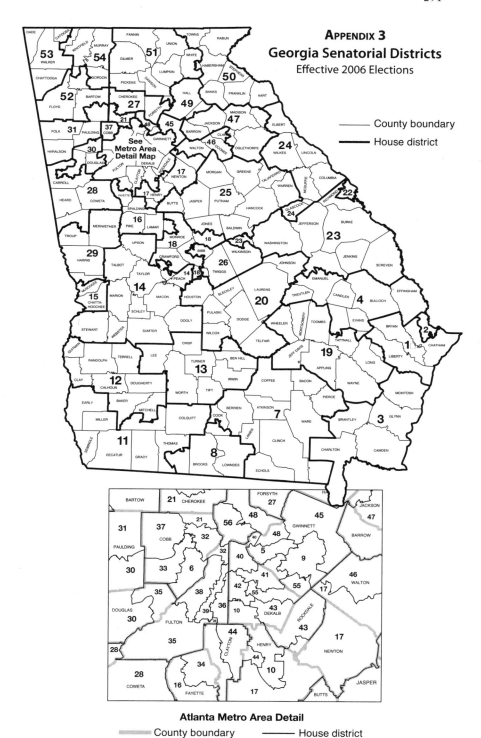

APPENDIX 3
Georgia Senatorial Districts
Effective 2006 Elections

County boundary
House district

Atlanta Metro Area Detail
County boundary   House district

INDEX